P9-DDF-953

DATE DUE			

373.767   Huckaby, Elizabeth.
HUC
Crisis at Central
High, Little Rock,
1957-58.

890327

WINFIELD PUBLIC SCHOOL
WINFIELD, IL. 60190

737272   07494C

CRISIS AT CENTRAL HIGH

CRISIS AT

CENTRAL HIGH

Little Rock, 1957-58

Elizabeth Huckaby
Foreword by Harry S. Ashmore

Louisiana State University Press
Baton Rouge and London

R.I.P.

WINFIELD PUBLIC SCHOOL

Copyright © 1980 by Louisiana State University Press
All rights reserved
Manufactured in the United States of America

Design: Patricia Douglas Crowder
Typeface: VIP Primer
Composition: G& S Typesetters, Inc.

LIBRARY OF CONGRESS CATALOGING IN PUBLICATION DATA

Huckaby, Elizabeth.
  Crisis at Central High: Little Rock, 1957–58.

  1. Central High School, Little Rock, Ark.—history.   2. School
integration—Arkansas—Little Rock.   I. Title.
07501.L6862H82   373.767'73   80-18053
ISBN 0-8071-0779-4

1981 printing

890327

373.767 HUC $17.10

For Emma, Bill, and Glen

Contents

Illustrations
Following pages 64 and 156

Foreword

During the week before Central High School's scheduled opening for the 1957 fall term, only one out-of-town newsman was on the scene in Little Rock. Dr. Benjamin Fine, education editor of the New York *Times*, had arrived early to check out the elaborate plan under which nine black students would be enrolled in the previously segregated school. It would, he thought, provide a model of orderly transition for the thousands of other school districts across the South just beginning to face up to the reality of the mandate the United States Supreme Court had handed down more than three years before.

When Ben Fine first came to call on me at the *Arkansas Gazette*, where I was then executive editor, I still shared the prevailing assumption that there would be no more than verbal protest against this minimal departure from previous patterns of pupil assignment. The school board had provided plenty of notice, announcing just five days after the Supreme Court decision: "It is our responsibility to comply with federal constitutional requirements and we intend to do so when the Supreme Court of the United States outlines the methods to be followed."

Virgil Blossom, the district's energetic superintendent, had begun immediately to lay the groundwork. A year later, when the Court entered implementing orders, he was ready with what came to be called the "Blossom Plan." As two new high schools then under construction became available in the 1957–1958 term, grades ten through twelve would be opened to blacks, but all black schools would be continued. Desegregation would then proceed downward through the grades, year by year, until all schools in the system were open to those who chose to transfer.

Limited and gradual though it was, the Blossom Plan met the test of "deliberate speed" when it was challenged in federal court by the National Association for the Advancement of Colored People. The tireless Blossom peddled his formula in hundreds of speeches before civic clubs, PTAs, and church groups, and defended it before black audiences as the maximum that could be sold to the white majority. The school board, made up of leading members of the Little Rock establishment, gave him full backing. Both the *Gazette* and its afternoon competitor, the *Arkansas Democrat*, endorsed the plan. There was no reason to doubt that it had solid support in the white community, and grudging acceptance among blacks.

What the plan didn't have was the approval of Orval Faubus. The governor had not spoken out against it, although he came under increasing pressure from the segregationist Citizens' Councils. As late as July he had publicly rejected their demand that he interpose his state police power to nullify the federal court order. "Everyone knows no state law supersedes a federal law," he said.

Then, just eleven days before the scheduled opening of Central High, Governor Marvin Griffin of Georgia, accompanied by the firebrand leader of the Southwide resistance movement, Roy V. Harris, appeared at a Little Rock rally to lend his weight to the demand that Faubus adopt the council's interposition strategy. That night a stone crashed through a window at the home of Daisy Bates, the NAACP leader, with a note attached: "Stone this time. Dynamite next time." A calculated campaign of intimidation was under way. There are conflicting views as to whether Faubus covertly encouraged the movement, or simply yielded to it; in any case, he was now fated to emerge publicly as its leader.

On the morning of September 4, 1957, I wrote an editorial that appeared on the front page of the *Gazette*:

> Little Rock arose yesterday to gaze upon the incredible spectacle
> of an empty high school surrounded by National Guard troops called

out by Governor Faubus to protect life and property against a mob that never materialized.

Mr. Faubus says he based this extraordinary action on reports of impending violence. Dozens of local reporters and national correspondents worked through the day yesterday without verifying the few facts the governor offered to explain why his appraisal is so different from that of local officials—who have asked for no such action. . . .

Federal Judge Ronald N. Davies last night accepted the governor's statement at face value, and ordered the School Board to proceed on the assumption that the National Guard would protect the right of the nine enrolled Negro children to enter high school without interference.

Now it remains for Mr. Faubus to decide whether he intends to pose what could be the most serious constitutional questions to face the national government since the Civil War. . . .

Faubus' decision is a matter of history. It robbed Ben Fine of his exclusive story on education; the new dimensions of the assignment were signified by the arrival of John Popham, the *Times*'s expert on southern politics, and Homer Bigart, a veteran war correspondent. As Faubus continued to use armed troops to bar entry of the black children the *Gazette* office swarmed with journalists from this country and abroad, among them brash young reporters who have since become the gray eminences of network television—John Chancellor, Howard K. Smith, Harry Reasoner, Mike Wallace, Sander Vanocur.

Three weeks later, when President Eisenhower finally responded to Faubus' continued defiance by sending a detachment of the 101st Airborne Infantry to reassert the primacy of federal law, the Little Rock Story was established as a headline staple around the world. As it ebbed and flared through that school year, and the next, my office was rarely without a clutch of correspondents drawn by some new development in a running drama usually presented as a black-and-white morality play.

The enduring impression left by the millions of words that found their way into print, and the pictures that lit up television screens around the world, was one of a beleaguered city beset by sustained racial violence. Yet, in a physical sense, that was the least of it. In all the months of military occupation of the school grounds no one was killed, or injured seriously enough to require hospitalization, and outside the immediate vicinity of Central High white and black citizens went about their ordinary business without any visible signs of increased tension.

There was never any chance of a confrontation in terms of brute force. The National Guard at near battalion strength clearly outmatched the nine black teenagers and any escort that could have been assembled locally. The mob that materialized after the guard was withdrawn could bring enough pressure to prompt the Little Rock police to withdraw the children from the school, but most of its active members were from out of town and it had no staying power. The mere presence of the disciplined federal paratroopers ended any further attempts of that kind.

Unable to forcibly bar the black children's attendance at Central High, the segregationists concentrated on creating a situation within the school that would force their withdrawal. Thus began a rhetorical guerrilla campaign orchestrated by Governor Faubus, whose political future now depended upon keeping the race issue alive. The object was to panic the parents of white Central High students and destroy the credibility of the administration, thereby minimizing its capacity to resist a concurrent campaign of harassment waged against the black children within the school.

In the short haul, the maneuver succeeded, or seemed to. No one this side of paranoia could take seriously a propaganda campaign based on the charge that Dwight D. Eisenhower, the United States Supreme Court, the Little Rock School Board, and the leaders of the Chamber of Commerce were united in a Communist-inspired conspiracy to force the wholesale social mixing of blacks and whites. But there were not many who were prepared to say so out loud. Anyone who spoke out in support of compliance with the continuing series of court rulings that attested the illegality, and the ultimate futility, of dead-end resistance could expect a withering blast from the governor's office—and with it came an implied threat of economic penalty against any who did business with the state or needed the sanction of its regulatory agencies.

The *Gazette* soon stood virtually alone in its insistence that the real issue was law and order, and, thus isolated, provided an object lesson for any who doubted the governor's willingness to use his office to support the Citizens' Councils. With his blessing the newspaper was subjected to a boycott that cost its owners a million dollars in lost earnings—and its long standing circulation lead over the *Democrat*. The afternoon newspaper withdrew its support from the school board and opened its columns to sensational, and usually groundless, charges brought by the council and its auxiliary, the Mothers' League of Central High.

This posed an almost insuperable problem for responsible journalists trying to treat inherently sensational developments so as to minimize any further increase in racial tensions. The school administration, quite sensibly, barred all reporters and photographers from Central High, but the manufacture of inflammatory rumors became a cottage industry. Checking out these exaggerated, and often wholly fabricated reports became a major undertaking, and, as always, the truth rarely caught up with the lie.

Crisis at Central High provides the first reliable eyewitness account of what went on in the corridors and classrooms during that critical year at Central High. Here we see close up the nine black children who deservedly became heroic media symbols of their people's determination to demand the rights the Supreme Court had declared to be theirs. We also see the fifty or so white students who were used as surrogates by diehard segregationist adults to disrupt the orderly process of transition that had been so painstakingly planned. And for the first time we are given a clear picture of the nearly two thousand white students who were also victims— the minority who, at considerable penalty to themselves, actively supported their black classmates, and the majority who accepted the new dispensation and simply wanted to get on with their education. These, as it turned out, reflected the submerged views of the community at large.

All this is set forth with rare eloquence by Elizabeth Huckaby, who saw it from the vortex of her office as assistant principal. She never thought of herself as a social crusader, and she emerges here as the dedicated, highly professional English teacher she had set out to be when she graduated from the University of Arkansas thirty years before. As a Presbyterian minister's daughter she had her moral convictions, and she never had any doubt that justice was on the side of the blacks. But she did not allow the depredations of a few of her fellow citizens, and the default of most of the others, to corrode her deep affection for her home country and its people. She sensed then, and time has proved her right, that the segregationist crusade was an aberration that ran counter to the basic good sense, and good feeling, of the majority of Arkansans of both races.

To the rising generation the crisis at Central High is ancient history. The present members of the student body are divided evenly between the two races, kept that way by a busing program that brings whites into the center city from upper-class suburbs. They have never known the walls of segregation that once set the black minority apart. But the Little Rock Story is not yet over. The school district, like most of those in major cities everywhere, is beset by demographic change that has separated the well-to-do from the poor—sending many of the more affluent beyond the district limits, changing the population mix to the point where blacks will soon constitute a majority of the school population. The racial composition of the system has again become an urgent subject of conversation among the leaders of both races.

The Little Rock establishment, once frustrated by Orval Faubus in its effort to achieve orderly desegregation, now sees the possibility of re-segregation as a threat to the city's good name and economic well-being. In the spring of 1980 leading ministers convened a Consultation of Community Cooperation. So-called "white flight," whether induced by natural growth patterns or residual race prejudice, was recognized as a threat to the quality of the public schools. The problem now, the churchmen agreed, is not one of hostile confrontation but, as the Episcopal bishop, Christopher Keller, Jr., put it, the fact that "the two communities seem to be going in different directions and the larger community is suffering."

If Central High is again caught—or perhaps more accurately, left—in the middle, I can only hope that it has on hand an ample supply of the spiritual heirs of Elizabeth Huckaby, teachers and administrators endowed with her remarkable combination of sensitivity, courage, and professional commitment.

Harry S. Ashmore
Santa Barbara, California

Preface

This is not the story *behind* the integration of Little Rock Central High School. It is not the story of *why* things happened as they did. It is the story of *what* happened, September, 1957, to May, 1958, as I saw it, and as it was told to me from day to day by those who were there and by those children, black and white, who were the actors in it.

Few teachers at Central knew all the Nine as I did. Many knew those in their own classes much better than I did. But because they were likeable, admirable young people and perhaps, too, because their precarious situation at school caused me so much concern, I loved each one.

But then, I am inclined to like all young people. And I genuinely enjoyed my thirty-nine years at Central with its hundreds of teenagers, worshipping their current idols and fads, from Lindbergh through Elvis to the Fifth Dimension; wearing the current styles from Empress Eugenie through the sack to the mini-skirt; living in each crisis from the Great Depression through World War II to integration; in many ways remaining the same—noisy, but good-humored; opinionated, but educable; excitable, but reasonable; and altogether wonderful because they are the Future.

Some of these boys and girls whom I knew at school I no longer recognize in their masquerades of middle age and dignity. But this account is for them. It is also for those young people I have mentioned by name: for Barbara and Carlotta and Thelma and Amanda

and Elizabeth and Ernest and Mildred and Minnijean and Betty
and Robin and Billye Jean and Mary Ann and Bruce and Craig and
Ann and Ralph and Jefferson and Melba and Jane and Gloria and
Terrence and Marianne and Robin. And it is just as much for those
hundreds of boys and girls who were at Central during the integration crisis but whose names are not in this story because they were
too busy just getting their lessons and helping at home and working at odd jobs and going to Sunday school and hunting and dating
to pay much attention to their elders' stir and confusion over the
color of their classmates' skin.

Acknowledgments

I am grateful to the Little Rock Public Library for access to microfilm of the *Arkansas Gazette* and the *Arkansas Democrat*. The information from film and from the extensive clippings from 1957 and 1958 in the scrapbooks of Maud Klepper Henderson helped me put my personal observations into a framework of current happenings outside the school.

I also want to thank Bob Douglas of the *Arkansas Gazette* and Bill Husted of the *Arkansas Democrat* for permission to use pictures from their files, and the librarians of those papers, Betty Turner and Betty Seager, for helping me find them. Also I appreciate the help of Charles Lance of the journalism department of Central High School for pictures from his files and for a new picture of the school made by a journalism student, Jeff Bullard.

I am especially appreciative of work by the staff at Louisiana State University Press for guiding my manuscript to publication so expertly—especially Beverly Jarrett, executive editor, for her enthusiastic appreciation of my narrative, and to Martha Hall, managing editor, for working with me so sensitively, curbing my verbosity, and updating my syntax and punctuation.

I thank my friends and members of my family who read versions of this account over the years and urged me not to abandon it. To them I offer not only thanks, but love. Particular, affectionate thanks go to my sister, Clara Doyle, who assumed all my housekeeping chores to give me time for final revision and editing.

CRISIS AT CENTRAL HIGH

The Preparation

Labor Day, 1957, was much like other Labor Days for Glen and me, except that there were no muscadines in the woods that fall. For teachers in Little Rock, as in many cities, Labor Day had a particular significance—"the last day of an expiring vacation," Glen called it. Traditionally Little Rock schools began classes on the Tuesday after Labor Day, after which weekdays were school days. But that Monday was ours, and Glen and I always celebrated.

Since celebrating meant being outdoors on some pretext or other; since muscadines ripen in the central Arkansas woods in early September; and since they make excellent jelly to serve with our wild game—duck, squirrel, and turkey—we picked our share of the fruit, year after year, from the roadsides along unfenced timberlands twenty or thirty miles south of Little Rock. August scouting along these roads had revealed no muscadines this year, so we went to our shack at Smoke Hole Club on Two Prairie Bayou, just to relax for the day.

I had been somewhat more concerned than usual during the past few weeks about the opening of school, for this year Central High School was to begin racial desegregation. It would be a new experience, one that we would have to work out as we went along. Integration, however, wasn't our only problem. Twenty of our most dependable teachers had been assigned as a nucleus faculty for the

I

new Hall High School in the growing northwest section of Little Rock. Our student body, too, would lose its citywide character; except for a hundred of our seniors who had elected to stay at Central for their final year, we would have no more boys and girls from that section of Little Rock where the finest houses were being built, where the families of the most successful businessmen were moving, where the country clubs are—as well as where many less affluent families live.

But this integration had been more on our minds than had our loss of faculty. Glen, having retired four years before, was not so personally involved. Ever since the School Board had announced its plan to begin desegregation at the high school level, and particularly since this plan, challenged by the NAACP because it was not immediate and total, had been approved by the federal court, I had known that I, as vice-principal for girls, would be involved.

And I was glad to be involved. Like many southerners—a larger number than was at first evident—I felt that the decision of the Supreme Court on May 17, 1954, had been eminently fair and just; that no public school system segregated by law on the basis of race was consistent with democracy. The Christian ethic proclaimed by my father, a Presbyterian minister, had its foundation in a belief in the worth of the individual and in our common humanity. Having grown up in the South, I had never known any black well except those in household employ. I had an understanding of its prejudices; but as I grew into the recognition that they were just that, I had set about eradicating them from my thinking. I knew now that I would welcome our black pupils and was eager to play my proper role in the integration of Central High School.

All this was in the back of my mind this Labor Day, September 2, 1957. Glen and I were up at five, off at six, the fog rising and forming clouds over the late summer rice fields as we drove east, then south toward Smoke Hole. Beside the muddy road, as we rounded a bend a few miles south of Carlisle, a young deer bounded along the ditch, then floated over the fence and sailed away across the field, its flag white against the green of the field.

At Smoke Hole, the white oaks on the knoll at the edge of the tupelo gum swamp were tall and lovely, as they are at any season. But peace was not all we had come for. A summer's growth of weeds about the unpainted shack would become a fire hazard as they dried. So we got to work with the weed cutters. After clearing the yard we worked inside the house, Glen rigging some electric extensions and I giving the place a sweep-out. The only inhabitants since our last duck hunt in January seemed to have been wood mice, spiders, and dirt daubers, all of whom had left debris. It's the sort of work that relieves tension—muscle-tiring, but not mentally stimulating. I relaxed.

After our picnic lunch I stretched out in a canvas reclining chair while Glen sighted in his rifles. The squirrel-hunting season would open in a few weeks, and his rifles had to be accurate. The regular explosions of their firing did not disturb me at all. Twenty-four years of being married to a hunter had taken care of that. But as I thought back about what we had done at school in preparation for this unusual school beginning, my thoughts were not altogether happy. We hadn't been able to do exactly what we had planned.

In 1955, the school board having announced its determination to comply with the Supreme Court's ruling, we of the faculty Guidance Committee at Central had discussed our responsibilities and had decided to have a series of assemblies to prepare our students for integration. In our discussion, I described a profound experience—my first introduction to a black woman who was not a servant. It had been at a YWCA convention in Indianapolis, during my college days, and naïve as it sounds today, I had discovered that blacks could be as interesting and attractive as my white acquaintances—and in the same way. Perhaps, if our students could have a similar experience, they might learn as I had. At a recent meeting of social workers I had heard Dr. Hugh Brown of the Arkansas State Tuberculosis Sanatorium for Negroes read an excellent paper, and I expressed a wish to include him at an assembly program. Bob Parson, a member of our committee, agreed, adding that the effect might be better if we had a panel discussion, by students and adults, on how to solve teen-age problems. And so it worked out: Dr. Brown on teen-age health problems; Mrs. W. P. McDermott, executive secretary of the Family Service Agency, on family problems; Mr. James Clemons, a young Methodist minister, on religious problems; three or four students, selected for intelligence and leadership qualities, to ask questions of the adults; and Dr. John Anderson, dean of students at Little Rock Junior College, as moderator. Two teachers on the Guidance Committee were reluctant to invite a black to our stage. But they acquiesced in the majority decision. I asked the students about their possible objections, and they were insulted. Of course they wouldn't mind!

We had a rehearsal a few days before the assembly, and Dr. Brown and his wife came to school for this. Their presence about the school caused no stir or public comment by pupils or teachers. The assembly itself went off well, and at the end of the formal presentations, the students in the audience—two thousand of them— were invited to write questions for the experts. A student committee screened the questions, selecting a few to be answered in the assembly, but after the program all written questions were turned over to the Guidance Committee. Of nearly a hundred questions, only three or four took note of Dr. Brown's color. Only one was insulting: "What is that nigger doing on our stage?" Only one faculty member made open comment about our integrated panel. A picture of the panel appeared in the student newspaper, the *Tiger*, and no comment came back to the school from any parent or the general public. The committee felt pretty good about our start in educating for integration. Jess Matthews, the principal, predicted that the Guidance Committee, of which Orlana Hensley was chairman, and the Community Cooperation Committee, of which I was chairman, would have joint responsibility during 1956–1957 in preparing for the integration of the school in the fall of 1957.

However, at midyear, when Miss Hensley and I asked Jess when he wanted us to begin our preparations, he told us that Virgil Blossom, the superintendent of schools, had decided to use another approach. The school board plan for desegregation, we were told, had been outlined for all principals and teachers at our preschool meetings: a small, carefully screened group of black applicants would be admitted only to Central. Mr. Blossom was appearing before civic groups in the community with this explanation. Our high school faculty committees were not to take any part in this community preparation, even with our own students. So we did nothing. After all, Mr. Blossom had worked out a plan for desegregation, for economic reasons, of Fayetteville High School before he transferred to Little Rock in the summer of 1953.

One spring meeting of the PTA at Central was an evening program to which all ninth graders who were to attend Central the next year were invited to bring their parents. By this time in the school year our guidance counselors already had interviewed the ninth graders in their various junior high schools and helped them plan their high school subject choices; so at Ninth Grade Night at school our scholastic offerings were discussed only generally, in a talk by the principal. Emphasis at this meeting was on the developmental opportunities of the school, the "extras" to be found in service and interest groups, in athletics and publications. Sometimes student speakers discussed the values they had found in these activities. But always, after the program, we asked the ninth graders and their parents to come to the Field House for a display and demonstration and for refreshments.

In March, 1957, however, those of us from the faculty and the PTA who were planning Ninth Grade Night felt that this was the ideal time for Mr. Blossom to explain the plan of desegregation to incoming pupils and their parents. The school board election on March 16 had turned out well. Both candidates running as segregationists had been soundly defeated. The newly elected members of the board were respected community leaders. Their election seemed an endorsement of the law and order stand of the superintendent and the board, and of their plan of gradual (and token) integration. Mr. Matthews asked Mr. Blossom to speak to the Ninth Grade Night audience about the desegregation of Central High School. He agreed to speak. So we cut out the usual student speakers and programed the principal only for some brief remarks to the parents about school costs, rules, and procedures. Invitations were mailed to ninth graders who were due to come to Central (only those from the junior highs that normally promoted their students to us—all white, of course) listing the program as an "Address by the Superintendent." Refreshments in the Field House would follow.

On the evening of March 27, 1957, at 7:30 P.M., there were almost a thousand persons, ninth graders and their parents, gathered in our school auditorium. In the Field House, Helena Quigley, activities director, was making leisurely preparations for the entertainment after the program. Her entertainers and musicians had been asked to report at 8:30, since the program, including Mr. Blossom's explanation of the integration plan, was expected to last past that time. The PTA members who would serve punch would slip out of the program at 8:30 at set up the refreshments. I stayed in the auditorium to hear Mr. Blossom's explanation and to try to assess parent reaction.

Jess Matthews talked first. I didn't need to listen, since I had heard what he was saying many times. But when the student body president introduced Mr. Blossom, I gave my full attention. It was 7:55, I noted, and I looked forward to Mr. Blossom's explanation, which he had been giving to various civic organizations, but which I hoped would give us and these incoming students and patrons a more specific idea of what to expect in 1957–1958. Mr. Blossom greeted the ninth graders and their parents. He told them that they were coming to a high school with great traditions and great opportunities. Then he sat down. It was 8:00. The program was over. I was flabbergasted. But I quickly left the auditorium and took the short way to the Field House to let Helena Quigley know that the crowd was on its way, a half hour early. By 9:00 everyone was back at home, no better informed about integration and how it would affect Central High School than they had been before the meeting.

Later in the spring, Jess Matthews and George Miller, principal of North Little Rock High School (in a different school district), made a trip to Oklahoma City to take a look at one of the recently desegregated high schools there. Before leaving for Oklahoma, Jess had asked me to jot down some questions that he might ask the administrators in Oklahoma City. I had given him quite a list, three pages of them, in which I tried to cover all the fears and uncertainties I had heard discussed among faculty members and acquaintances. They concerned the possible reluctance of individual parents and students, black and white, to be a part of desegregation; the likelihood of organized opposition to desegregation; possible threats to the maintenance of social and scholastic standards in a desegregated school; problems of scheduling in appropriate classes; the effect of desegregation on athletics and social affairs; and problems of discipline arising out of desegregation. But when Jess returned from Oklahoma City, he had no answers to my specific questions. He said that he and Mr. Miller had found integration working so smoothly there that he did not feel it was necessary to ask such questions. That was cheerful news.

Only once during the summer had Jess called me to come to school on any integration problem. Mr. Blossom had been given a list of "scare" questions about what school policy would be in certain activities. We were to answer these questions: "Will the Negro boys and girls be allowed to join the school sponsored clubs that the white children belong to? When out of town trips are taken by these children, will the Negro boys and girls be permitted to go along? Will they stay in the same hotels, motels, or private homes with the white children? Or will discrimination be permitted here?" So, on July 17 Jess and I met with Terrell Powell, principal of the new Hall High School to see how we felt about these matters. Mr. Powell was included because, although there were only a handful of high school age blacks in his district, if one or more of them should apply for admission, Hall High might be integrated, as well as Central. J. O. Powell, boys' vice-principal of Central, missed the discussion because he was out of town.

We found ourselves in complete agreement on the answers to these questions, but they were only one section of a longer list that was designed to inflame racial fears in the parents of high school pupils. Jess summed up our discussion by saying he didn't see how we could exclude any student in our school from any activity for which the student's school record, abilities, and character qualified him. We wrote our report to the superintendent more formally:

Answer:
The policy of Central High School has been to require average scholarship, good character, and acceptable attendance as standards for membership in honor or service clubs. It is planned that these standards will remain in effect.
The School Board authorizes grade level social clubs, formed and supervised by the parents, with the cooperation of the faculty. Such clubs have been organized in the past when sufficient pupil and parent interest was shown, and will continue to be organized under those same conditions.
On school club trips particular care has always been taken for the welfare of each child. The selection of pupils to make the trip, the choice of chaperons, housing arrangements, and the conduct of pupils on the trip have always been subject to the best judgment of

school authorities and in harmony with social customs acceptable in our community and in the community visited. This same policy will continue.

At this midsummer conference I had my first information about the extent of our possible desegregation. About twenty black boys and girls were due to register with us. More—some football players—had wanted to come, but their counselors had discouraged them since their low scholastic achievements in Horace Mann would make it almost inevitable that they would fail in Central. Terrell Powell said, half humorously, that he almost hoped he would get at least one black registrant in Hall High—to take his school out of the position of being a refuge for rabid segregationists.

My contract called for me to report to work on Tuesday, August 20. On that day and the next two days, we principals and vice-principals met with the superintendent on administrative matters. The group was an integrated one. Legal maneuvers about school desegregation were already in the news. On August 16, a Little Rock citizen, W. F. Rector, had asked in Pulaski County chancery court for a declaratory judgment on the validity and effect of the segregation acts passed by the legislature at its last session. On the same day, ten black ministers had filed suit in federal court contesting the validity of these same acts. On August 20, our meeting day, a Mrs. Wilbern, whose daughter was a potential Central High School student, sought a court order permitting pupils who did not want to attend an integrated school to transfer to a segregated one.

With the headlines of both Little Rock papers reporting these legal contests, preregistration of pupils at Central and other schools began on Friday morning, August 23. Preregistration consisted of each student's picking up a copy of his schedule card, a list of books required for each course, and an instruction sheet from the principal, giving first-day directions and school rules. Only if there were an error to be corrected in his schedule was there anything else for the student to do at preregistration. But the occasion is always a sort of teen-age get-together after a summer apart. As usual I had a group of dependable girls to distribute schedules. To their tables, set up in the hall that faces the front entrance, flocked the other youngsters, most of them still in summer shorts, to be given their schedules, compare them with their friends', gripe or gloat over the teachers or lunch periods they had been assigned. It was a typically noisy, unorganized-looking procedure, the kind dear to the hearts of teenagers, with *everyone* there, sooner or later. So, as usual, the crowd grew. We administrators retreated gratefully to our air-conditioned offices to attend to new registrants. After talking the matter over with Jess, I had told the girls at the registration tables that if any black pupils asked for their schedules to send them to the main office as new pupils. But none came.

Monday and Tuesday, August 26–27, were busy days at school. For one thing, Jeanne McDermott, who usually sees new pupils first to help them fill out the preregistration questionnaire, was absent because of her mother's death. I took over her job in the main office, going from time to time past the registration tables in the hall to my own office to help indigent students get books and supplies for school. Besides Jeanne's absence, another complication was the decision of the Pulaski County (rural) superintendent to transport and pay tuition for the sixty high school pupils (white) from Scott High School, since a school of that size would be so limited in its high school offerings. Each of these sixty now had to be registered as a new pupil. As I worked at the unfamiliar task, I wondered whether these students and their parents were expecting the whole matter of our integration to be resolved and segregation to be established before classes began. These were farm children, mostly from large cotton-producing farms on which many blacks lived and worked.

I moved my registration operations down the hall to my office on Tuesday to reduce the growing congestion in the main office. On one of my trips back to that office for supplies or instructions, I nodded to Dr. Leroy M. Christophe and Mr. Edwin L. Hawkins, the principals of the black high school and junior high school. I assumed they were waiting to see Jess Matthews in order to transfer records of their pupils to Central.

At midmorning I needed more supplies. As I picked my way between the crowds of pupils, I met a small group of black students coming from the direction of the office; they turned and went out through the lobby. I got my supplies, making no comment about them to anyone in the office, since they apparently had been there. As I passed back through the lobby, I was sure that they had gone down the front steps, for there were a few white boys and girls looking curiously toward Sixteenth Street, and there were some shrill whistles. But there was no other confusion.

Just before noon I was in the office again, and I asked Jess about the black students and was surprised to learn that he had not seen them. I went to the hall and brought Mary Ann Rath, one of the girls at the registration tables, back to the office, and asked her in the principal's presence if she had seen them. She replied that she had and that she had sent them to the office. The registrar heard us talking and came to the counter. Earnestine Opie—no one says *Miss* Opie—is a legend at Central. Two generations of students have admired her for her no-foolishness dealings with them, combined with her fabled memory for their names and faces and school records. "I'll tell you what happened," Opie said. She felt certain that the black kids had heard her tell a couple of boys from Tech High, who wanted to register at Central, that they would have to have transfers. She had explained to them that they would have to see the superintendent down at Eighth and Louisiana; that any student transferring from one Little Rock school to another had to get a transfer from there. Although she said nothing to the blacks, she felt sure that they knew that what she had said to the Tech boys applied to students from Horace Mann. So blacks had come to enroll but left without doing so, and there had been no "scene."

On Tuesday, August 27, Mrs. Clyde Thomason, identified as secretary of a newly organized segregationist Mothers' League for Central High School had filed suit in chancery court seeking an injunction against school integration. On Wednesday all teachers reported for duty. White teachers (only the administrators' and city-wide committees' meetings were desegregated) met at West Side Junior High School for the usual opening greetings from dignitaries and school officials. Mr. Blossom repeated the administrative message he had given the principals the week before. His popularity with teachers was made evident by their attention and applause. They considered him a man whose word they could trust and one who recognized teachers as individuals. Many teachers in the group probably looked on desegregation with disfavor. But only Central was to have black pupils; and Mr. Blossom had assured this group and others that the decision to begin desegregation at the senior high school level was for the purpose of having it affect as few people as possible.

After noon the Central High School faculty had its first meeting in its own school. There were many new teachers to replace those now at Hall High. I was glad to see so many young faces. The tendency of a stable faculty such as ours is to grow old together without realizing that we may be perpetuating a rigidity of form under the impression that it is education. On our faculty of ninety, seventeen were new to us, six of these teaching their first year. We now had twenty teachers under thirty—a good proportion, it seemed to me. But I wondered how these new people would accept the responsibilities of our school, what tasks they would assume, what ideas they had, how well they could handle classes, what they could teach. I would have felt more secure if the twenty teachers we had lost to Hall High were still with us. I knew their strengths and weaknesses—as they knew mine.

Jess Matthews' remarks on our desegregation were not specific. They couldn't be. He could not know whether Mrs. Thomason would be successful in securing her injunction or not. He said he hoped that by the time of our next meeting, on Friday, matters would be settled.

On Thursday he told me of a peculiar happening. I had never heard of Governor Orval Faubus' taking any notice of our school, even during the few weeks when his son had attended Central, the first year of Mr. Faubus' governorship. He had never accepted any of our invitations to appear on our stage at any of our programs. But now the principal had had a call from the governor's office, and it concerned a project of our student council.

In mid-August Margaret Reiman and Helen Conrad, the efficient faculty sponsors of the student council, had met with the council to plan the opening assembly for school and to prepare to welcome all students. Our new students who had moved to Little Rock during the summer would receive a particular welcome. They would be invited, as usual, to meet the members of the student council at their lunch period on the first day at school and be escorted to the cafeteria—a confusing place for new pupils. Our incoming tenth graders had already had an orientation and a guided tour of the building, but as one student council member pointed out, the black students had not. They would still be unfamiliar with our big building. So Ralph Brodie, council president, appointed a large committee to plan a preschool orientation for the blacks. One committee member asked whether Campus Inn, a snack bar and jukebox-equipped building popular at the noon hour, should be on the tour. Mrs. Reiman thought not, since it had already been cleaned and locked, ready for opening day. Some teenager remarked that it was just as well, since if the jukebox was available, some of the black kids might want to dance.

It was this remark that, distorted, evidently prompted the call from the Capitol. He understood, the unidentified caller said, that our students were proposing to have a dance for the Negroes, with racially mixed partners. Jess Matthews assured the caller that this was not in our plans and reported the call to Mrs. Reiman. The invitations from the student council, already written except for a date (because of the confusion of our legal situation), were not yet addressed; for Jess was still guarding, for their protection, the names and addresses of the black pupils who were to attend Central. He had told me only that there were to be nine.

Margaret Reiman did not have to look far in her student council to find the governor's source of information. The council representative for homeroom 151 was a daughter of Mrs. Margaret Jackson, whose name was becoming prominent in Mothers' League affairs. But it still seemed notable to Margaret Reiman, to Jess, and to me that the governor should be particularly interested in the Mothers' League, since he had not joined or attended our PTA when his son was in Central.

By afternoon on Thursday, August 29, the *Arkansas Democrat* headlines proclaimed that Judge Murray Reed had granted Mrs. Thomason's request for an injunction against integration in Little Rock schools. That ended any possibility of orientation of blacks before school opened. It also put us squarely in the middle between federal and state authority. The governor had been the only witness at the hearing. He had testified of weapons in the hands of high school boys and of gangs forming—matters apparently known to him alone. These accounts sounded to me more like fantasies from comic books than the behavior of the Little Rock adolescents I knew. In my journal I wrote: "Committee meetings, faculty meeting at school today. No plans for integration can be completed pending suits. Confused." But things had straightened out by Saturday, and that day I wrote confidently: "Federal Court in no uncertain terms ordered integration for Tuesday and enjoined all interference. Made the situation clearer, more stable." Everything was settled once more and integration assured for the first day of school.

Now, this day, Labor Day, was mine, to rest and to get ready for a new and exciting experience as a teacher. I was about to see what integrating a southern high school was like. So, as I relaxed at Smoke Hole, I was more excited than apprehensive.

Glen had stopped firing and was inspecting the sky, where the fog of the early morning had gathered in ominous clouds. Four miles of dust-deep roads lay between us and gravel, and the eleven miles of gravel were "under construction," so we needed to hurry out. We just made it to firm ground before the torrents fell.

Home, we read in the afternoon paper that the governor would appear on radio and television that night to speak on the integration crisis. I was out of patience with him for getting so scared over nothing, and I was tired from our long day. I had an exciting day ahead of me tomorrow. Anyway, what could the governor say, since the federal court had already spoken? I went to bed.

The Challenge

I waked a little ahead of the alarm clock's jangle on Tuesday, September 3. We were back on our school routine. At 6:25 Glen came to the kitchen and held out the *Arkansas Gazette* for me to read the headline: FAUBUS CALLS NATIONAL GUARD TO KEEP SCHOOLS SEGREGATED. Underneath was a picture of an armed guardsman on the front steps of Central High School.

We were aghast. Soldiers! Around a school! What for? To preserve order, the governor had said. How was order threatened? By the Mothers' League? I had never thought of mothers as dangerous. By the Citizens' Council? They had publicly declared that they were upholders of decency. By the children? We had never had to call on even the local police to handle any pupil at Central High School.

Glen and I asked each other these questions as we quickly ate our breakfast. I must get to school, I felt. There would be the daily bulletin to revise. We had written one on the assumption that our black pupils would be present. The *Gazette* said that Mr. Blossom had asked them not to come; but we had an equally unusual situation to prepare our pupils for. We had the National Guard. I left for school at 6:55.

There was almost no traffic as I crossed Markham and Twelfth, main streets into downtown. Everything was peaceful as I drove through the dewy September morning with its deceptive promise of a cool day. Things looked normal—until I got in sight of the school. Traffic barricades were across Fourteenth Street at the stadium corner, and a state police car was at the intersection. I controlled a wave of resentment. Telling myself that these men were acting under orders, I pulled up beside them, identified myself by name and position, and showed them my driver's license and my membership card in the Arkansas Education Association. The police let me drive on. Again, at the corner of Sixteenth Street I identified myself when another state police car stopped me. As I drove up the Sixteenth Street hill, I could see National Guardsmen in battle dress standing thick around the perimeter of the school grounds, their trucks and jeeps parked on the streets and behind the building. They had guns. I stopped at the entrance to the campus and again identified myself to the guardsmen. I parked the car in the teachers' parking lot. It was 7:05. This had been my school since 1930. Now I felt like a foreigner.

I managed to smile at the young National Guardsmen I passed at the back door as I hurried upstairs. The office was full of stale cigar and cigarette smoke. Guardsmen had been there all night. For headquarters they had appropriated Jess Matthews' office.

Jess looked stunned. However, he acted his genial self as he made arrangements to move the guard headquarters to the business office. He had managed to convince the officers that, if he were going to run a school, it would be necessary for him to get at his desk and his records.

J. O. Powell, the boys' vice-principal, had already been at school for an hour. He and Delbert Gordon, the custodian, had arrived simultaneously and had had a dickens of a time getting admitted. J. O. was busy getting the physical facilities of the school in some sort of order since none of our janitors, maids, and cafeteria cooks and helpers—all blacks—could cross the National Guard lines.

Jess discarded our "integration" bulletin and issued a new one to be read in all home rooms:

SPECIAL BULLETIN
Central High School   September 3, 1957
Students and Teachers:
This next announcement is *NOT* a topic for class discussion—
merely for your information. "We will continue school as in the past
until the question on integration, raised by Governor Faubus in his

television address last night, is legally resolved!" Students, you have the responsibility to yourselves and your families to go quietly about your business here at school. The Guardsmen who are stationed at our school are here to do a job, and you are asked to mind them and to treat them in a friendly manner and not interfere with them in any way. It is my earnest hope that every student in Central High School will carefully consider the above suggestions and cooperate in the peaceful solution of this problem. Good citizenship on the part of our students at this time will benefit everyone and will demonstrate to the world that Central High School students are law-abiding Americans.

> Best wishes for a successful year,
> Jess W. Matthews, Principal

The remainder of the bulletin was as it had been written originally, inviting new pupils to meet student council members at lunch; reminding council members to escort the new pupils; offering a prize to the student who, in greeting other students in the halls, was the fiftieth person to say HI! to one of the Mystery people; and asking for boys or girls to work at Campus Inn during lunch periods.

Teachers began to arrive, covering their nervousness with jocular remarks about how easy it had been for them to get by the guard—"Anyone could look at me and tell I'm a teacher!" Those who had walked to school had had to come not only past the guard, but through a crowd. Teachers who lived in the neighborhood of the school said they had been kept awake all night by the sounds of vehicles and men.

Margaret Reiman was worried about the flags. Should her student council boys raise them as usual—the United States flag to the right, the school flag to the left—at 8:45? Jess assured her, "Just as usual." And up they went, that day and every day (barring rainy ones) throughout the year. At eight o'clock I began helping new students fill out their registration papers, and I was busy until my first class began at third period.

I was pleased that thirty pupils were present in each of my English classes that morning. The new tenth graders, awed anyway by their new surroundings—the size of the school, and the unfamiliar teachers and routine—were further awed by the troops and the crowd in the street. The school windows are too high for a seated person to see the school grounds or the street; so outside noises were the only distractions. I raised my voice and introduced myself, collected and signed schedule cards, made a roll of the class, outlined the course, listed the materials and the requirements, and made a specific assignment for the next day.

A second special bulletin came around, asking teachers to eat their lunches in the students' cafeteria instead of the teachers' since three-fourths of the service personnel of the cafeteria had been barred by the troops. For the same reason we were requested to straighten our own rooms and close the school windows before leaving school for the day.

The first day of school is always a difficult one for the cafeteria and its patrons. Today, with only a skeleton staff, the cafeteria director had managed to get ready one hot dish—chili-mac, with slaw, fruit cobbler, and milk. Even with no one having to make a choice of food, the lines at the first lunch period inched along, and the warning bell rang with a hundred or more pupils still in the line, unserved. I circled the cafeteria, urging students to finish their meals before leaving, and issuing permits for them to enter their classes late.

During the thirty-minute break between the first and second lunch periods, cafeteria help and a few of us teachers managed to clear the lunch tables for the next serving. Again I issued a hundred or more permits to be late to class. During the remaining two hours of school the crowds on the corner across Park Street dwindled as they realized that no black students were coming to school today. I went home to read the *Arkansas Democrat* and find out what had happened out front. An eight-column streamer read: RING OF TROOPS BLOCKS INTEGRATION HERE. NO INCIDENTS REPORTED: OFFICIALS HUDDLE. In the story below this headline I read: "The Guardsmen were equipped with arms, some with rifles, bayonets, and night sticks." I hadn't seen any bayonets, but I hadn't been out on Park Street. A three-column head was over a Washington dateline: IKE ORDERS BROWNELL TO LOOK INTO FAUBUS' ACT: SEES "ROADBLOCK"; and a two-column head over a statehouse story: GUARD TO STAY "INDEFINITELY" SAYS FAUBUS. One-column stories were headed: MANN [the mayor] SAYS CITY WILL COOPERATE with the federal government, not Faubus, it seemed; 270 TROOPS ON

DUTY AT OPENING—CROWD OF ABOUT 300 GATHERS AS FAUBUS HALTS INTEGRATION: FEDERAL AUTHORITIES ARE SILENT; and GOVERNOR SEES TEST OF LAWS. Mentioned in the "crowd" story were the Reverend Corbett Mask of nearby Benton, who told the reporter that he had about twenty segregationists from Benton with him; and Mrs. Clyde Thomason, whose name I knew only from the stories of the Mothers' League. Hardly leading citizens, I thought, but we would hear from the other side soon, I was sure. In the *Democrat* pictures of Central illustrated STUDENTS MARCH PAST GUARDSMEN (I would have said amble); and KEEPERS OF THE DOOR, the guardsmen at our front entrance.

The headlines in the Wednesday morning *Gazette* didn't calm me: JUDGE ORDERS START OF INTEGRATION TODAY; FAUBUS ASSERTS THREAT OF VIOLENCE DICTATES HIS ACTIONS; and NATIONAL GUARD TO STAY. I was at school by 7:00 to help compose a special bulletin for the students, in case the black pupils were allowed past the National Guard. The regular bulletin, with its routine announcements, was already in the teachers' hands. This new bulletin read:

> This is a second bulletin to be read without discussion in your home room. Home room period will be extended till 9:05 this morning. Last night, the Federal Court ordered the Board of Education to begin today the integration of white and Negro pupils at the high school level, according to the plan of limited integration approved by that court and sustained on appeal. This Federal Court approved plan recognized the responsibility of the Board of Education to preserve the high quality of education in our schools. In order to carry out the directions of the Court, a group of qualified Negro pupils have been enrolled in Central High School this year. These students may be in attendance today, or at any future time. As a student in Central High School, you have certain duties to yourself and your school, and your community. You should know your responsibilities:
> *You have a responsibility to yourself*:
> a. Your first and immediate job is to get an education of the highest quality possible. Any disorder, confusion, disagreement, or quarreling at or around school will interfere with classroom work. Such disorder, disorderly gatherings, or excitement *anywhere* will make it hard for you to study. For the sake of your progress in school, refuse to be drawn into any disputes or disputing groups.

b. Any person interfering by word or action with the orderly carrying out of a direction from the Federal Court may be judged in contempt of that Court and will be subject to arrest and prosecution by the Federal Government. This is a serious offense and is punishable by fine, imprisonment, or both. Any name-calling, demonstrations, or similar disorder could be interpreted as contempt of court. This is no light matter.

You have a responsibility to your school:

Central High School has a reputation as one of the leading public high schools of the nation. It is important to each of us to keep it in that position. We can do that if each pupil and teacher will go quietly about our business here at school—learning and teaching. There must be no "incidents" at school.

You have a responsibility to your city, state, and nation:

The eyes of the nation and of the world are on our community during these days. The good name of our community will suffer if we become disorderly. How you or I conduct ourselves can help or hurt the reputation of our city, our state, and our nation. We can be known as law-abiding and peace-loving, or as quarrelsome and unintelligent. You and I can go about our business here and keep the headlines the kind that will make people want to live in Little Rock, Arkansas, or the U.S.A.—or, we can make people scornful of our community as a place where people cannot manage to live peaceably.

From the cooperative expressions we have heard from numbers of our students, we are expecting the whole-hearted cooperation of our student body in these matters of importance to their individual records, to the good name of our school, and to responsible citizenship.

Jess W. Matthews, Principal

Jess had instructed us in the office that when the black pupils arrived they were to be brought first to his office. But they did not come. Teachers, checking in, reported a larger crowd than on yesterday in front of the school. I looked out and saw the crowd. Lots of our pupils were on the school grounds, watching. Some would be tardy to homerooms, I was sure. J. O., who had gone out front to observe, came in about nine and remarked that it was "awful."

There were some tardies, most of whom explained that their parents had detained them in fear of "trouble." I met my classes—and again taught hard, all period. It was not my idea of good teaching to put on a one-man show, but with the windows up because of the warm weather, letting in the noise of several hundred people on the street outside, it was the best I could do.

The lunch hours were better, mostly because a lot more kids, forewarned of difficulties by yesterday's problems, brought their lunches in paper sacks.

After noon Mary Ann Rath came in, in tears; some girls in her gym class had taunted her because her father was on the school board. Until she told me, I had not known that the board and Virgil Blossom and their families were now under constant threat. Mr. Blossom had sent his high school daughter, Gail, out of town; and city police were guarding his home and those of board members.

It was only after I got home from school that I learned what had taken place in front of the school that morning. Headlines in the *Democrat* read: ARMED TROOPS TURN BACK 9 NEGROES AT CENTRAL HIGH; FAUBUS SAYS GUARD TOLD TO STOP NE-GROES; and FAUBUS PRAISED BY GRIFFIN (governor of Georgia). There was also a large ad for the Capital Citizens' Coun-cil, headlined "The Real Highest Court" and picturing Uncle Sam shaking his finger at nine black-robed men. The council declared itself "Dedicated to the Maintenance of Peace, Good Order, and Do-mestic Tranquility in Our State and to the Preservation of Our States' Rights." My journal reflects my desolation: "Home. Read the awful story. Saw the awful pictures—the dignity of the rejected Negro girl, the obscenity of the faces of her tormentors. Graded pa-pers to occupy my mind."

Thursday morning's *Gazette* had more pictures, more head-lines. I found a little comfort here and there. I was glad that I could not recognize the faces of any jeering pupils. They were not our student leaders, thank goodness. One of our former student editors had interviewed a group of student leaders, three of whom were openly hostile to the governor's action: "I don't like the idea of what Faubus is doing"; "Faubus made a fool of himself." Two thought that there might have been temporary trouble if the blacks had been admitted, but said that, although they preferred segregation, they had accepted integration. The two who had praised Faubus' actions unconditionally had asked that their names not be used. The *Gazette* also reported that the blacks would not try to attend today. I hurried on to school. Jess Matthews' regular bulletin began with a compliment—and an admonition:

We have been proud of the way our student body has reacted to the very intense situation which has confronted us since the opening day of school. The longer the controversy continues, the harder it will be for our students not to become involved. This is a time of testing. The law and its interpretation we must leave to authorities charged with those duties. The less we discuss these matters, the better. But we have an obligation of our own: to keep our feet on the ground and proceed with school. This, many of our students are doing. But actions and speech lacking in the courtesy and respect that educated people owe to *all* people have also been reported. What you do and say now becomes your record. We hope each student will keep a good one—one of which he will never be ashamed.

The largest crowd to date was in front of the school Thursday morning, many of them our own students. Alberta Harris, our drama teacher, came into the conference room for coffee, and we looked out the windows, across the sunny September lawn at a thousand people in the street. For the most part, they just stood, looking toward the school. Then something caught their interest toward Fourteenth Street, and the whole mass moved in that direction. Most of them must have had as little idea as Alberta and I what was happening at that intersection. But they moved that way, anyhow. The papers later told us that it was an angry verbal attack on Dr. Benjamin Fine of the New York *Times* and the other "Yankee" newsmen, one of whom asked the crowd whether their shouts to go home meant that he was to go to his hometown, Greenville, Mississippi. Then the mob surged toward Sixteenth Street where some black college students, who had come out of curiosity, had to be rescued by the guard. Alberta was fascinated. "You know," she said, "I've coached mob scenes in plays, but I've never actually seen a mob. Just look at the movement of it. I had no idea there was so much movement."

A mimeographed petition was being circulated by students at school, dated, Little Rock, Arkansas, September 5, 1957. It read, all in caps: "WE, THE UNDERSIGNED PARENTS AND CITIZENS OF LITTLE ROCK, DEMAND THE IMMEDIATE DISCHARGE OF VIRGIL T. BLOSSOM; ALSO THE PROMPT RESIGNATION OF ALL MEMBERS OF OUR SCHOOL BOARD, EXCEPT DR. DALE ALFORD." There was space for signatures, and signers were directed to return the sheet at once to P.O. Box 2478 at Little Rock. Dr. Alford was an opthalmologist who had been elected to the school board in 1956 without reference to integration. But, as the late summer crisis had developed, he had avowed himself a segregationist and sent his daughter to Gulf Park, a boarding school on the Mississippi Gulf Coast.

Jess responded to petitions and unacceptable school behavior with another special bulletin:

> Some special matters have come to our attention on which we wish to advise our students in connection with the tense conditions under which we are all working. These matters are of direct importance to your class and school progress. If you are concerned with these, and with your school record, please take note:
> 1. Colonel Johnson of the National Guard suggests, and I join him in advising students not to report to school before 8:15 if possible, and to come directly into the building as soon as they arrive. Considerations of safety and common sense dictate these suggestions. Furthermore, excitement and strife are hindrances to good school work.
> 2. Tardiness to school because of the delay of a student as a spectator or as a participant in demonstrations or gatherings will not be tolerated.
> 3. The right of any citizen to circulate printed matter or petitions is recognized. However, the circulation of such matter or petitions is a hindrance to class and school progress, and should not take place at school.

School maintenance, at least, was returning to normal. The black maids and cafeteria workers, having been properly identified, had been escorted into the building. Teachers were grateful to be able to eat in their own small lunchroom instead of in the noisy cafeteria; and so were a few of the National Guard officers, who were getting mighty tired of field rations. Lieutenant Bryce Allbright was one of these. Bryce had been a teacher—and a good one—at Central until the year before, but he had left teaching for a job that would better support his family. Now his National Guard unit had been called to duty at Central. As he came into the lunchroom, I thought he was not a little embarrassed in his present role. He stood twirling his billy club as we visited, and I couldn't resist teasing him. "Bryce," I said, "would you mind putting that stick behind your back while you talk to me? It makes me nervous." He blushed and complied. He got his lunch from Pearl Arrington, unstrapped his holster with its service revolver, laid it aside, and ate lunch with us.

After school I went to see my parents in their apartment east of Main Street. I had talked with them by phone during the week, but they needed the reassurance of seeing that I was all right. Mother was sure that Faubus had gone crazy. At home, I scanned the afternoon paper to see what had gone on in front of Central today and learned that Dr. Fine had been the special object of the reproof of the National Guard officers. My brother Bill called from New York. He had been horrified by the picture of a white girl screaming at a black girl in front of the school. I was glad I had English papers to check during the evening, to quiet my nerves.

Friday morning came. If we could get through this day, there would be respite for the weekend. Was the situation any better? The *Gazette* headlines didn't sound that way: BOARD SEEKS SUSPENSION OF U.S. ORDER; IKE SAYS HE WILL USE LAW; TELLS FAUBUS COOPERATE WITH U.S. There was a picture of General Sherman J. Clinger and Colonel Marion Johnson warning Dr. Benjamin Fine, and one of a girl (she had been absent from my English class on Thursday) circulating the petition to fire Mr. Blossom. In the "From the People" column the first letter, signed "Ten White Teen-agers," favored getting on with integration. Another letter, I noted with dismay, was from a man whom I knew as an officer in one of our leading churches, defending segregation and attacking the *Gazette* for its "unfair" reporting.

I went to school through the state police and National Guard lines. It is odd, I thought, how soon we come to accept the bizarre as usual. Most students seemed to be heeding our directions to come inside the building as soon as they got to school, and the crowd out front was small. It was almost time for my ten o'clock class when Jess came to my office with Colonel Johnson of the National Guard. With them, but not in uniform, was Sergeant Lawrence Gwyn, a special investigator for the state police. I remembered Lawrence as a former pupil of fifteen or twenty years earlier, but, as he reminded me, not as a star pupil in English. The officers wanted to interview and take a deposition from a girl who, they understood (from whom they understood it, they didn't say), had heard Dr. Fine of the New York *Times* offer a bribe to some boys to start a fight. I told the officers that they might interview the girl in my office if we first had permission from her mother. I reached the mother at the shop she operated in her home. She readily gave permission for her daughter to talk with the men, saying that her daughter had told her of the bribe, and that her husband knew of it, too, having been in front of the school each morning. I went to the study hall for the girl, a cute little blonde junior. I didn't remember her from last year, but she remembered me. She had been truant with a girl friend once last spring, and I had assigned her ten mornings in the early study hall to make up the time.

With poise and assurance this girl said yes, she had heard Dr. Fine offer some boys ten dollars to start a fight with some niggers. Yes, others had heard him offer the bribe, and she named some boys and girls. I did not know the boys she named. But I recognized two of the girls' names and doubted the reliability of their corroborative testimony. But Lawrence wrote up the testifying girl's account and had her sign it. "What did your daddy think of this when you told him about it?" one of the men asked.

"He said Mr. Fine had better go back up North where he came from or he'd find his throat cut." Lawrence did not add this statement to the account. He did ask me not to say anything of the interview—and I didn't.

The picture of the girl screaming after Elizabeth Eckford as she walked through the mob on the day the National Guard had turned back the black students had haunted me. No one seemed to be able to identify the girl—and small wonder. We were not used to seeing our students look like that. But by noon on Friday, I discovered she was someone I knew, and I sent for her in the afternoon. When she readily admitted she was the screaming girl I told her how distressed I was to hear it since hatred destroys the people who hate. She shrugged. Well, that was the way she felt, she said. Undeterred by her shrug, I said that I hoped I'd never see her pretty face so distorted again, that I never would have recognized that ugly face in the picture as hers. Wasted breath.

The first week of school was behind us. I had planned to brush up on English in the fall by taking a course in advanced grammar at the University of Arkansas Graduate Center. I saw no reason to change my plans, so I paid my tuition and put the course on my weekly calendar, for each Tuesday evening.

Sunday afternoon, Dr. Dunbar Ogden, a Presbyterian minister interviewed a group of students from Little Rock on television. I missed the show because Glen and I went on another muscadine hunt, but I read in the Monday morning *Gazette* that the students on the panel had been about evenly divided: "segregationists" and "moderates." The account of this program was overshadowed by other weekend headlines: JUDGE REFUSES DELAY IN SCHOOL INTEGRATION; BOARD STATES PLAN IN EFFECT; FAUBUS REMAINS FIRM. SAYS U.S. MUST GIVE IN; EISENHOWER AWAITS MORE LOCAL ACTION; and 8 ALDERMEN BACK FAUBUS.

Why didn't it rain? Rain might thin the crowds. It usually rained a lot during the first week or two of school, but our only rain had been on Saturday. How they trampled the lawns across Park Street! It occurred to me that had I lived in one of those houses I would be tempted to install a yard sprinkler and turn it on, full force, each morning.

And who were these people in the streets? Ruth Klepper Settle, vocal music supervisor for the schools, gave me a clue to what I had already suspected, that they were not all from Little Rock. Ruth and her mother lived just off Park on Seventeenth, a block from school, a street where many of the spectators were parking their cars. Ruth had suggested to her mother, Maud Henderson, an extremely alert octogenerian, that it might be just as well for her not to go out in her front yard, with as many hoodlums as there were on the streets now. So Ruth was a little disconcerted one evening when her mother began: "When I was out front this morning sweeping the walk . . ." Mrs. Henderson continued that some men came by who she was sure were out-of-town reporters. She gave them a "good morning" and commented on the number of cars parked in the area. "You know," she told them, "if I were back in the newspaper game (she had run a newspaper for years in Missouri), I would be interested in how many of these cars are not from our county at all." "How can you tell?" one asked. She told the reporters that all Pulaski County registrations began with the figure 1. They went off, making notes on license numbers. From time to time after that we began to have notice in the *Gazette* of our out-of-town visitors and where their cars had been licensed.

The *Democrat* on Monday afternoon and the *Gazette* on Tuesday morning had the pictures of black students turned back at North Little Rock High School. The pictures of the angry whites were just as horrible as ours. But there were two differences: no federal court order had been given to the North Little Rock School Board; and no state forces were there to prevent integration. The North Little Rock School Board just called off integration, in view of the opposition. On Tuesday, I wrote in my journal: "To school by 7:00 and got the coffee going. Crowd rather large, but tamer than yesterday. They applauded after the flag was raised."

Perhaps the crowd had applauded every morning, but I was where I could see it today. Geneva Howerton, from Room 245, which overlooked the corner of Fourteenth and Park Street, was absent today because her little girl was ill, and I took charge of her homeroom. The pupils and I stood with our hands over our hearts as the bugle sounded "Call to the Colors" and the flag went up out front. As we started the words, "I pledge allegiance to the flag of the United States of America," I heard clapping, and I looked from the flag to the mob; there they stood, applauding as if they were at a parade. The irony nearly overcame me, and I choked out the final words, "indivisible, with liberty and justice for all."

My "welfare children," who couldn't buy their own texts, were getting behind in their lessons because I didn't have second-hand books to lend them. Allsopp and Chapple, the downtown bookstore from which I had ordered new books for these pupils, reported that their black deliveryman couldn't get into the school. He could have, of course, if we had arranged with Colonel Johnson to provide an escort for him. But with other deliveries to make, and with the crowd's demonstrated antipathy to all blacks who appeared near the school, the deliveryman could not be blamed for failing to deliver the supplies. So I went to town myself for the books needed—this day and others.

On Tuesday afternoon the governor had accepted the summons to federal court. It seemed we were to have ten days of status quo. Jess Matthews decided before we left school to make no reference to the integration crisis in the daily bulletin on Wednesday but to concentrate on our winning football team. So the bulletin was written—"Let's back the ability of a great team with the support of a great student body."

My journal on Wednesday began: "For the first time, Mr. M. and J. O. not already at school by the time I got there. The situation apparently is stabilized for ten days, now. Crowd small, soon dispersed."

Our girls and boys had been pretty good about coming into school and not lingering in the crowd. This morning, more than one teacher on the north end of the building complained that a group of eight or ten boys and girls had been dancing rock and roll in the street under the eyes of TV cameras, as school began. I told one of the girls that Mr. Matthews had asked me to tell her that if she ever wanted to appear on a Central High School program again (she was a pretty and popular singer), she would have to stay out of street scenes. She was agreeable, saying, "Well, they just asked us to dance, and we didn't know you didn't want us to." Without a violent crowd to make news, the cameramen were pressed for interesting pictures.

The *Gazette* headline on Thursday morning was encouraging: GOVERNOR ASKS AND IKE AGREES TO TALK ON CRISIS. My journal reported: "At school at 7:40. No vehicles, few soldiers. A light rain began to fall. The knot of eight or ten 'watchers' scattered early." Gail Blossom, the superintendent's daughter, a senior and one of our cheerleaders, came to school for the first time since classes had started. Jess let me know that Gail was present and asked me to keep an eye out for any threat to her peace and safety. He told me that he had asked Bruce Fullerton and some of the other football "men" to do the same. I looked up Gail's schedule and made a copy for my purse. At the close of homeroom period I trailed after her for a few steps until I saw Bruce Fullerton fall in beside her. I went back to my office. I wasn't needed. Bruce, our star halfback, had me beat both in size and in prestige. At the end of the next period, I again watched for Gail. But here came Bruce, again. This time he did not walk with her and appeared not to be watching her. But he was only a few steps away as she went down the hall. Gail would not be threatened at Central, I felt sure.

Friday's headline announced that Congressman Brooks Hays would accompany Faubus to Newport for talks with Eisenhower. The reduction of the guard had a peripheral advantage in my field of responsibility. The propinquity of bored, unoccupied, anonymous young males had been almost too much for some of our girls, chiefly those who had never had the fun of being so attractive to the high school boys.

By Sunday Governor Faubus was back in Arkansas, but neither he nor President Eisenhower would comment on the conference. The headlines Monday did not sound encouraging: FAUBUS SAYS TROOPS TO STAY ON DUTY TODAY. HEDGES ON FORECAST; and he had told the TV audience in a Mike Wallace interview that violence was still a possibility. At school; there was some talk among the teachers that Faubus might withdraw the guard without warning and "throw us to the mob." I talked with Jess about a possible bulletin to teachers if the black children suddenly were permitted to enter, and we sketched it out to have it ready.

About midmorning J. O. and Jess apprised me of an anonymous call from an "engineer," who claimed that his son walked to and from school with some boys—Phil and Butch—one of whom had said that he had placed dynamite in a locker at school. Of course Phil and Butch had stayed home, and the caller said he had kept his son at home, too. But in his bigness of heart he had decided to call so that other people's children could be dismissed and not endangered. J. O. had had no success in locating the absentees Butch and Phil, and believing the call was an effort to close Central High School rather than integrate it, Jess suggested that we should keep school going but search lockers after school. The male staff members had spent one night the spring before searching the school after a nocturnal bomb warning. And a Nashville, Tennessee, school had recently been blown up—at night. There was a chance that we might be. But if we dismissed school for this warning, the violent members of our community would have a blanket invitation to threaten us daily, or hourly. We decided to wait till 3:30 to search.

In a special bulletin J. O. requested that students clear their lockers completely before leaving school and that they leave the lockers open. He gave as his reason a routine sanitation inspection for "rats and mice." I doubt that this annoying inconvenience fooled anyone, and of course, the subsequent search uncovered no dynamite, bomb, or other explosive device. But the bomb threat had cost Central High students one of their cherished possessions—the privacy of their lockers. On Wednesday, to facilitate any future inspection, each student was given a card on which to register his locker number and the combination of his lock. I spent most of my spare time that day returning books and other locker contents to Tuesday's absentees, who hadn't gotten the notice about emptying their lockers, or those who had ignored the notice. The janitors had cut off all locks not removed, permanently destroying them. The books from these lockers had been dumped, helter-skelter, on long tables in the conference room next to my office.

Jess Matthews had told me earlier in the week that he had had a written request from the nine black youngsters scheduled to join us—and a tenth one, Jane Hill, whose name we had not been given—for their assignments, so that they could keep up with their lessons while they were barred from attending Central. On this morning, Jess said, he was going to send for the teachers to whose classes these youngsters had been assigned, and ask them to write out lesson directions. He had already told me that I would have Carlotta Walls in my Period 3 English class and Jefferson Thomas in Period 4; but in general, teachers had not been told which of them would have black students in their classes. When the notice came to my Period 3 class, I looked at it with interest:

September 18, 1957

The following teachers are asked to see Mr. Matthews this morning for a very brief meeting at the end of Period 3. Please come to the office at this time.

Mrs. Donna Wells	Mrs. Carolyn Bell
Miss Maude Reid	Mrs. Mildred Stalnaker
Miss JoAnn Browning	Miss Vivian Daniel
Mrs. Dorothy Lenggenhager	Miss Irene Harrell
Mr. W. P. Ivy	Mrs. Govie Griffin
Miss Pauline Dunn	Miss Susie West
Mrs. Elizabeth Huckaby	Miss Carol Carter
Mrs. Margaret Reiman	Miss Margaret Stewart
Mr. Howard Bell	Miss Emily Penton
Mrs. Imogene Brown	Miss Margaret Dewberry

Miss Getha Pickens   Miss Jennie Perkins
Mrs. Mildred Dalhoff   Mr. Everett Barnes
Mrs. Helen Conrad   Miss Christine Poindexter

I could not see that any favor or discrimination had been shown in the assignment of teachers. There were first-year teachers and experienced ones; there was one who would be retired at the end of the year, and one who was barely twenty-one; there were three heads of departments, and some who probably would never be considered for any advancement. It included those who were segregationists at heart as well as some avowed integrationists, but all were professionals and would teach each youngster, no matter what his race.

The listed teachers reported to the principal's office, learned which black students would be in their classes, and were asked to make out assignments and give them to Jess by the end of the day, if possible.

On Thursday the first issue of the student newspaper, the *Tiger*, was distributed. It contained an editorial by one of the coeditors, Jane Emery, one of our top-ranking students, calling for calm and clear thinking.

A whole page of Thursday's bulletin had to be given to matters of locks, lockers, and "fire drill" regulations. We must be ready for a time when a bomb threat might have to be acted on as real. And Friday's bulletin would need to prepare the students somewhat for next week. The governor was to have his day in court on Friday. If the court should enjoin him from interfering, we might have an integrated school on Monday. I agreed with Jess's suggestion to emphasize law and order and educational progress. So his bulletin for Friday, September 20 began:

> How will you, as a student, and as a student leader at Central High School meet the challenge of the coming days?
> I have been proud of our student body during the three tense weeks since September 3. I am counting on the same steady, dependable, courteous and friendly spirit that has always been characteristic of students at Central in the days ahead.
> I believe in young people; in their respect for their government and for law; in their ability to adjust to changing times and customs; in their keeping their eyes toward the future, rather than the past.
> I believe in their concern for their education, for their school progress, for making a good record. That is why I believe you can meet

the challenge quietly, courteously, and with honor for yourself and for our school.

The bulletin got about the attention that adolescents generally give to the preachments of their parents and teachers. Their minds were on more important matters, anyway. The Tigers, unbeaten the year before and most of the year before that, were to play football in Texarkana on Friday night. All the cheerleaders and the pep squad and many of the students were leaving at noon by bus or car for the game. Jess hoped to go, too, if he could finish his court appearance in time. (He had been subpoenaed with others to testify in the injunction suit against Governor Faubus.) Jess confessed that his doctor had prescribed a tranquilizer to take before he had to testify; and Jess was sure he would need it.

At noon he returned to school to report that the governor's lawyers had walked out on the hearing, so he would have to go back and take the stand after court reconvened in the afternoon. The bus taking the parents of the football boys would be held for him so that he could see his son, Joe, the center, and the rest of the team play at Texarkana. Before school was out, we heard that Judge Ronald N. Davies had issued the injunction against Governor Faubus and the National Guard to cease interfering with the federal court's order for integration.

The *Democrat* headline Friday afternoon read: FAUBUS SAYS "NOW BEGINS THE CRUCIFIXION" (of himself, presumably). There was a picture of "Barred Students" in court, a boy in front identified as Terrence Roberts and a girl, Carlotta Walls. I looked at Carlotta with particular interest since she was scheduled to be in my class. Here was a tall girl, her head held high, her expression pleasant but serious.

My brother Bill, in New York, had become increasingly concerned for my safety. Things were bad enough in Little Rock, but judging from pictures in the New York papers, my devoted, sensitive brother saw me in constant danger and the whole of civilization threatened. So I wrote him on Saturday night: "Try to calm down a bit, Bill. You're getting ulcers, I'm afraid, over this crisis. This will pass, and there will be more. And I'm confident we can work it out. What damage has been done to Arkansas has already been done. Now, let's cool off. Love, Liz"

Saturday's *Gazette* had said that the governor, after the court's injunction, had withdrawn the National Guard, and it pictured a lone policeman on guard at Central High School. The *Democrat* that afternoon had a picture of Ashley Williams, the black groundskeeper, cutting the grass out front at Central where the guard had been. Editorially the Saturday afternoon *Democrat* said (and I think it was the last editorial in that paper on the school situation for the school year); "The immediate responsibility of all of us is to maintain law and order."

Sunday morning, the *Gazette* headline read: NEGRO GROUP UNSURE WHEN THEY'LL ENTER; but the *Democrat* was more positive: NEGROES TO ENTER CENTRAL MONDAY; POLICE ON ALERT. Separate stories bore the headlines: IKE PLEADS FOR CURBS ON VIOLENCE; and FAUBUS FEARS VIOLENCE.

Jess, J. O., and I met at school at two o'clock Sunday afternoon to make final plans for integration day, Monday, but we didn't have much to do other than go over Jess's bulletin:

CONFIDENTIAL BULLETIN TO TEACHERS

Little Rock Central High School   September 23, 1957

DO NOT READ TO STUDENTS

1. Although we are not anticipating anything but close cooperation from our student body, certain irregularities are possible during the days immediately ahead. If any situation develops whereby normal classroom procedure is disrupted, notify the office immediately. It should be made clear to all students at this phase of the transition that routine classroom order and policies will prevail. If a student leaves the room without permission, he should be told to report to the attendance office, sign out, and leave the building and campus immediately. Loitering in the vicinity of the campus will not be permitted. Negro students are to be treated with good judgment and professional impartiality. If they do not already know room locations, they should be given directions to their next classes.

2. It is especially important that all teachers assist, during the following weeks, in hall and corridor traffic control by STANDING AT THEIR DOORS between classes. Traffic should be kept moving, and students should be discouraged from congregating in groups and clusters in halls.

Jess said that the police would be at the school "in force" on Monday. We hoped that they would disperse the crowd in front, as the National Guard evidently had not been instructed to do. Jess didn't know whether state police would be available to help or not. No reporters, photographers, or other adults were to be allowed in the building. The coaches, who did not have homerooms, would be near entrances and in the halls during the 8:45–9:00 home room period. The black children should come directly to Jess's office when they arrived, to pick up their schedules. He was still confident that, if the police could control the outside situation, we could handle the inside.

I went on to a tea given by one of the girls' clubs, at Marietta Meyer's home. Mary Ann Rath told me that Marietta had been verbally harassed, after she had been quoted in the *Gazette*, among other students interviewed, as saying the governor "had made a fool of himself" by calling out the guard to prevent integration. Her father's firm, for which Mary Ann's father worked, had been suffering some business loss, because of Marietta's statement and because of Mr. Rath's position on the school board. This was a different Little Rock from the one that for so long I had thought I knew.

On Monday morning, September 23, I got to school at seven. Police, in their blue, short-sleeved summer uniforms, were everywhere. "I'm glad to see you," I told the policeman I met as I came in from the parking lot. "I don't know whether I'm glad to be here, though," he said. "Well, at least you're Little Rock men, and I'm glad of that." It occurred to me that the police could arrest troublemakers. The guard hadn't had orders to do that—just to keep out the blacks apparently.

In the office J. O. was talking with the police who were planning to set up a walkie-talkie somewhere on the roof at a point where the whole of Park Street, from the Fourteenth to the Sixteenth street corners, could be observed. Jess was checking over matters with the assistant police chief, Gene Smith, whose neat, muscular, gray-suited figure, topped by a narrow-brimmed straw hat, I was to see everywhere Monday. Teachers arrived, took their "Confidential Bulletins" from their boxes, read them, picked up the regular daily bulletin, and went to their homerooms. Only one teacher was absent, Sybil Hefley, who had gone with her family to the funeral of a niece in Russellville, Arkansas. Her substitute, Mrs.

Katherine Sprigg, went to Room 151, near the Fourteenth Street entrance. The coaches, in white duck trousers and white sport shirts, strolled about the upper hall, on the alert, visible, and with authority.

Jess had told me that the black students were to arrive at 8:45, just as the tardy bell rang for all students to be in homerooms, where the person in charge knew them individually, by name. Large, anonymous groups were to be avoided. At 8:30 I went out to the hall. I felt I couldn't stay isolated in the office any longer. The halls were noisy and full, as always at this hour. At 8:35 the first warning bell rang. I moved among the boys and girls collected in the lobby, seeing who was there. Some groups of boys, from their vigilance and aggressive manner, were evidently hoping to turn back any black students who came up the front steps, as North Little Rock students had done two weeks ago. The coaches kept the boys moving. When the 8:40 bell rang, most students left the lobby for their homerooms. The coaches urged the laggards. I took one boy to the office where he identified himself by his schedule as a student. I ordered one senior girl, who was still talking with her boyfriend in the lobby, to her home room. I was fearful that she might get caught in a scene. There are eleven outside doors to the building, and I did not know from which direction the black students were to arrive.

The lobby was now clear. The tardy bell rang and the flag went up. The coaches had gone out to the front steps and were looking toward the drugstore corner, Sixteenth Street. Coach Wilson Matthews came in shaking his head in disbelief, saying he thought some blacks were being killed. I went back into the office, sick, for I thought he meant our black children had been attacked.

Then down the hall came a group of black boys and girls, led by one of the student body officers, Craig Raines. Craig had been quoted in the *Gazette* interviews as preferring segregation, but he was a warm, sympathetic boy. "Mrs. Huckaby, these kids were looking for the office," he said, and went on about his business.

I said, "Come in, children," and led them into the principal's office, where they sat down, with a nervous giggle or two and considerable breathlessness. Then I saw that the smallest, a girl, had sunk down to the floor and rested her head on the seat of the chair. She seemed almost unable to breathe. One of the boys informed us that she had heart trouble. What a place for a child with a heart condition, I thought, as I sent for water and the nurse. Nurse Carpenter hurried in and took charge of Thelma, the ailing youngster.

Jess Matthews came in. He had been where he could check the Sixteenth Street entrance through which the black children had entered from the car that brought them. Whether the attack on the other blacks on the corner had been staged to draw the attention of the crowd as the children entered or not, the students had entered practically unobserved. The principal welcomed them to the school and led them to the outer office to Opie's desk to get their official schedule cards.

The thirteen-minute homeroom was nearly over, and teachers by now had read the principal's bulletin to the students. It was another request for good citizenship, and he also suggested that just before homerooms were dismissed for the morning fifteen rahs to beat the Istrouma Indians from Baton Rouge, Louisiana, would sound good.

A few cheers rang out from homerooms. It had been my suggestion that maybe letting off some steam in cheers might help lessen the tension, but perhaps I was wrong. Before the cheers, someone had already called to the street crowd, "They're in!" And the cheers were interpreted by the crowd and by reporters as sounds of disorder, even of violence, inside the school.

The bell for dismissal of homeroom rang, and the corridor outside the office quickly filled with students, some going as usual to classes, some milling about and peering into the office through the french doors to get a glimpse of the blacks, still at the counter near Opie's desk, out of direct view from the hall. Pupils in the hall began jockeying for a chance to make the next call at the three pay-phone booths. J. O. and Jess began dispersing groups, sending students on to their classes—or out the front door. The black boys and girls still stood at the counter. I had placed myself just inside the office door to keep out students who weren't supposed to come in. One boy pulled the door open and protested incredulously, "Mrs. Huckaby, are you going to let those niggers stay here?" "Boy," I said, "this is a *school*." And I pulled the door closed again. No one made a further attempt to come in, and of course I couldn't have stopped anyone who might have really tried.

After the tardy bell rang for the first class, I went out to encourage the girls to go to class—or leave school. "I don't know what to do, Mrs. Huckaby," said a girl who had served as one of my office monitors. "My mother told me to come home if the Negroes came." "Then, go on home," I advised her, "but sign out first in the attendance office so that we will know you have gone."

At 9:15, when the halls were clear, Jess Matthews sent the black students to the guidance director's office. Orlana Hensley, the director, talked with them briefly about their programs, distributed student handbooks, and told them how to find the room numbers of their classes. One of the girls wanted her schedule changed, but Miss Hensley said she would have to talk with her later about that. Usually, Miss Hensley sent a student monitor with late-entering pupils to show them the location of their classes. She could not risk that this morning; so she, Margaret Stewart (a counselor), and I took them in three groups and showed them the way. There were only a few more minutes left in the first class period, and all but one black student was in class. Miss Carpenter said she would see that Thelma, whose pulse was still irregular, got to her classes when she was able.

In a few minutes my English class was to meet. I found that Susie West, who taught on the first floor near the Fourteenth Street exit, had been sending for me. I went downstairs. The police were having trouble with some girl who kept running in and out of the school, screaming, and crying down the hall, urging other students to leave because the "niggers" were in. There was no girl in sight, now, and I could not recognize anyone in the seething, jostling crowd only a hundred yards outside Susie's classroom windows.

Back upstairs, the attendance office was beginning to have trouble. Esther Pickworth, fortunately, had extra help in Bonnie Brietz, who was to take over Esther's job as attendance clerk on October 1. A good many boys and girls had left school without signing out; a number of others had signed out on their own initiative. All telephone messages to dismiss certain pupils were being refused. Now, mothers were beginning to come into the school and ask to take their sons and daughters home. Some of these parents were frightened, some angry, some just stupefied by events they didn't understand. In each case, the attendance clerk would direct the parent to the proper room, instructing her to have the student come by and sign out. The police were allowing parents—but no other adults— to enter through their lines. We overheard parents say that radio and TV reports of "violence at the school" had alarmed them. A few, seeing the calmness inside, or having talked with their children and learned the truth, left their youngsters at school. But the line of upset parents was still lengthening as I went to meet my first English class of the day.

This class was a large one, every seat in the room assigned. In preparation, I had asked a custodian to bring in another chair, for Carlotta, and had placed it at the back of a row in a place where I felt the students who would sit beside and in front of her would be able to accept the contiguity.

I stood at the door. Carlotta came down the hall. No disturbance. I assigned her seat and signed her schedule card. We were working today on outlines for autobiographies to be filed in each pupil's folder in the guidance office, an annual English class project for incoming sophomores. I moved about the room, helping individuals with their outlines. Carlotta worked, too, though she had not had the preliminary instructions. Several pupils were absent; and as class went on, I dismissed one or two others whose parents came for them.

Period 4, now; Jefferson Thomas was to come this period. His seat was waiting for him in a group of boys. We worked on outlines of autobiographies in this class, too. Jefferson seemed more puzzled by the task than Carlotta had been. He needed help; but I could not turn my full attention to him. I must keep the whole class working. One of the better students in the class saw Jefferson's bewilderment and offered to help him. Most of the class were going quietly about their work. But one boy, as I passed, said to me with a sneer, "Jefferson Thomas—what kind of a name is that?" "The same kind as yours," I told him. But he didn't leave the class. No one left, except those whose parents came. When the period was about half gone, Opie called me to the door to say that the black students were being sent home and to ask if I could collect the girls. I had to tell her I didn't know where they were, and she said she would find out and go get them herself. I sent Jefferson to the office, and J. O. went for the other two boys.

As soon as the class bell rang at 11:55, I went to the attendance office to help. Parents were still streaming in. Bonnie Brietz, on a stool before the card file, was looking up each student's schedule as the parent waited. Bonnie's expression showed obvious disgust with the parent's actions. I tried to reassure one parent I had known from his childhood, but he said his wife was "about crazy" over what she was hearing on the radio.

By 12:30 Jess Matthews told me that it was at Chief Gene Smith's request that the black students had been sent home. The frantic parent situation was out of hand. Someone, not a parent, might be admitted, to attack or kill one of the children, or to set fire to or blow up the school. The police, Jess felt, had done a good job, but they had not been trained to handle a riot. Chief Smith had had to admit defeat.

Stories of the morning began to spread. Police had arrested a boy whom Jess had literally chased from the building. The girl whom Susie West had tried to get me to see and identify had finally been loaded into the police wagon and carried off. J. O. had seen two boys closing in on Jefferson Thomas and had sent them on their way. (They were part-time students with us, making up deficiencies necessary before they could take special training at Tech High.) After the black students had been sent home, Jess had gone out to announce the fact to the crowd, but they had howled him down in disbelief. Only when Opie had taken the megaphone and assured the mob that Jess Matthews was telling the truth, inviting them to choose two members to come in and see, did one of the women tell the crowd that they could "believe Opie." Did I know this woman, Jess wanted to know? No. I had never heard of her, but I was finding that there were a lot of influential people in Little Rock about whom I didn't know.

Doris Glenn added a note of humor. A mother had come to the door of her English classroom and announced, "I have come for my child." The "child," a big six-footer in the back of the room rose up. "Aw, Mom," he said.

I kidded Bruce Fullerton in the hall. "You mean your mother

hasn't come for you?" "Mrs. Huckaby, isn't it the silliest thing you ever saw?" he said in disgust.

The stream of parents slowed to a trickle during the afternoon. One youngish mother, leading a small child, came at the last period, looking for her son who was in phys ed. After being assured that he was in the stadium and not in the Field House, she left, and I knew that she had come there thinking the school itself would be blown up.

Jess issued a special bulletin for teachers to read at their eighth-period classes. He thanked the student body for their cooperation. The black students, he stated, felt that they had been treated nicely, but they declared that they would not return to Central until President Eisenhower assured them of protection.

I was exhausted by the time I reached home. The afternoon *Democrat*, under a headline VIOLENCE EXPLODES AS 8 NE-GROES ENROLL AT CHS; POLICE RESERVES CALLED, reported that "several fights broke out between Negro and white students in the corridors of Central High School after the Negroes entered," quoting as authority a student who had left the school. This was a lie—and not the last one reported by "a student." CROWD'S YELL TOUCHES OFF BRUTAL FIGHTING was the headline under a picture of a white man kicking a black. (This was part of what Coach Matthews had seen, I was sure.)

I lay awake for hours, going over and over in my mind our scandalous and humiliating failure. We had been lucky, indeed, to have no child injured. I could only hope that this would be the worst day I would ever have in my teaching experience. The challenge to the federal courts was clear. The governor had challenged them with the National Guard. Now the mob had challenged them with its rioting outside Central High School. It was bitter to have to admit it, but it was now Little Rock, Arkansas, versus the United States of America.

CHAPTER III

September 24–September 30

The Challenge Met

Tuesday, September 24 was quiet. Everyone seemed a bit shell-shocked from Monday's experiences. No more than twelve hundred boys and girls were in school. The night had seen much racial conflict, unprecedented in our heretofore peaceful city. The trouble had been largely rock-throwing; and though there had been forty-five arrests, no one had been seriously wounded. The black students were not in school, of course; but this comparatively calm day between the waves of the storm had to be one of planning. No one doubted that the United States government would meet the challenge of the state's governor. The morning *Gazette* had given us the news that the president had issued a cease and desist order to clear the way legally for sending troops, and that Governor Faubus had already challenged President Eisenhower's move.

Jess thought we should get substitutes for J. O. and me until things settled down. We called Wilma Means, and she reported to school by nine o'clock. I told her we would probably need her the rest of the week. But she was with us through May 27; and, except for a day or two when emergencies required Wilma to be somewhere else, I did not teach a class the rest of the year.

Imogene Brown, a soft-spoken Mississippi girl teaching with us while her husband served an internship at Arkansas Baptist Hospital, dropped by my office Tuesday morning to show me a sign that had been placed on her desk. It was crudely hand-printed on notebook paper: "NIGGER LOVEING TEACHER—MRS. BROWN." Imogene and I thought her best course was to ignore the thing.

Wednesday was PTA meeting day. The annual Open House, a night affair, had been canceled two weeks before. A smaller meeting, an afternoon tea, with one homeroom mother and all teachers, to plan the PTA membership drive, had been substituted. Today's lull gave me a chance to ask Lucille Barnett, the art teacher, to have name tags made for each teacher to wear at the tea. When Lucille brought me the tags I had no idea that they would remain unused for the whole year.

At noon we heard that the entire Arkansas National Guard was being mobilized and federalized. We knew, too, that federal troops would take over from the local police Wednesday and that the black students would attend school on Wednesday. Jess called J. O. and me to a conference to discuss the possibility of running the school with the black students present. I felt that if we were to conduct a normal school, the crowds must not be permitted to gather within a block of our classrooms. Jess thought someone in high authority, representing the federal government, should explain the situation to the student body so that they would know the seriousness of any actions in opposition to the federal court order. J. O. felt that guards of some sort must be stationed throughout the building. He thought it would take eight on the first and second floors to cover the two-block-long angled hallways, a smaller number on the shorter third and fourth floors to protect the black pupils from attack. He suggested that we have a thorough check of the building by demolition experts tonight as a safety precaution. The policy of not admitting reporters and photographers we agreed should be continued. Persons should be admitted to the building only after identification as students or teachers. Jess called Virgil Blossom and dictated our list to his secretary. Mr. Blossom would use our suggestions when he talked with the military.

About five o'clock Emma Scott, long-time dear friend and fellow teacher, now editor of the *Journal of Arkansas Education*, came by to visit with Glen and me as we sat on the front porch. As I started to tell Emma about the day before, our next-door neighbor, David Ray, director of the state's Exceptional Children's Colony, under construction at Conway, stopped in. I told them both what had happened at school. Mr. Ray shook his head. He had expected to integrate the Children's Colony, he said, but that was changed, now.

At my University Graduate Center grammar class that evening, some of the teachers in the class who had had to come across the river from North Little Rock reported that they were slowed by the movement of troops into Little Rock. At home, again I found sleep hard to come by. My thoughts were still busy with the day. Jess Matthews had tried to clear up in the bulletin he had written for Wednesday some of the wild rumors that had been circulating around school and around town. These ranged from the one that we had had the children locked in the rooms or in the building on Monday and refused to let them out to the report by the segregationist lawyer Amis Guthridge to the seven hundred persons at the meeting of the Capital Citizens' Council on Tuesday night that the Central High School teachers were going to walk out en masse in protest of integration. Jess's daily bulletin to be read on Wednesday, September 25 avowed:

1. There has been no violence in this building. No one has been hurt at school.
2. No pupil was forced to stay in school if he felt he must leave on Monday. High school pupils are past the compulsory school attendance law and are not required to attend school unless they so desire.
3. No outside doors of the school have been locked while school was in session.
4. No classroom door can be locked so that it won't open from inside.
5. No teachers have resigned.
6. All teachers are carrying on the school program with the welfare of all students in mind.

The *Gazette* named the 101st Airborne as the troops now in charge of Central and said that the black students would attend. I hurried to school to help with whatever changes we might have to make in our plans for the day. That Wednesday morning, September 25, troops were thick around the school—not just in front, as the National Guard had been. These were no lounging, half-trained civilians in uniform. These were armed professionals, moving with astonishing efficiency. The guards in the streets, for whom I stopped my car to identify myself, looked at my credentials thoroughly, but quickly, and waved me on. Soldiers were three paces apart along the sidewalks across the streets from the school. And there were no mobs in the streets. As I parked my car, I saw that the playing field behind the school was covered with military vehicles and gear: trucks, jeeps, field kitchens, and pup tents. Inside the school, too, was military order. Communication evidently was constant between jeeps patrolling the streets and the portable receiver in the hands of a sergeant in the office corridor.

Jess Matthews was worn out. He and J. O. Powell had been up most of the night conferring with the deputies of General Edwin Walker, commander of this military district, and making the physical arrangements required. General Walker would address the student body at nine o'clock. The black students would be escorted to school but would not arrive until after the assembly.

Jess introduced Captain William Madden, who would be in charge of operations in the school. I gave the captain a copy of our faculty roster for identification of teachers as they entered, along with the page giving the bell schedule for classes. J. O. sent Mr. King, of the custodial staff, to the parking lot to identify the teachers' cars as they entered.

The PTA's teacher-parent tea scheduled for the afternoon was called off when fewer than a dozen mothers would agree to come.

Jess asked me to help him with what he would need to say to introduce General Walker. He wanted it brief and factual, and he handed me the morning *Gazette*, which gave a résumé of the military background of the commander of this district.

The bell rang for the thirteen-minute homeroom. While the halls were clear, Jess escorted General Walker from the office to the assembly stage. The bell rang for the assembly. Some students—attendance was about like the day before, eleven or twelve hundred—evidently were debating leaving. J. O. and I moved through the hall urging them to go to their regular assembly seats—or leave school. Only a few left. One boy, a black-jacketed fellow who looked older than a high school student, couldn't name his homeroom or his teacher when I asked him. I was certain he had no business there but trouble, and I asked him to leave. He left, under the scrutiny of a sergeant.

The assembly began with the usual, but always impressive, ceremony: the call to order by the student body president, Ralph

Brodie; the presentation of the flags; and the pledge of allegiance. Ralph then presented Jess, who introduced General Walker. I listened from the hall. General Walker's voice was good, his tone firm, as befitted a commander. He reviewed the facts of the Little Rock school integration case. It was a clear summary. I looked around the auditorium. It was too bad that so many of our pupils, particularly those who needed to hear this factual presentation, were absent.

Lovey Pettyjohn, Jess's secretary, slipped in from the office. "I don't know what to do about this call," she said. "The FBI says the White House wants to know whether the Negro children are in the school yet or not." She could not answer their questions, or even be sure it was really the FBI calling. I beckoned one of the FBI agents, and he went to the office phone to take care of the call.

General Walker finished his brief address with a solemn warning to students not to interfere with the carrying out of the orders of the federal court. The student body stood for the retirement of the flags, and Ralph dismissed the pupils to their first class.

Most of the students went on to class. Some lingered uncertainly or belligerently in the corridor. "If you're not staying in school, go sign out," we told them. About eighty signed out.

I imagine that I have seen hundreds of pictures of the black students escorted by the 101st into Central High School. These pictures all show the Nine walking up the front steps. But none is the picture as I saw it from the inside of the lobby. Through the open doors at the far side of the lobby came a double file of nine black children, with a protective line of fully armed guards on each side of them. They paused at the center of the lobby, just where the low step-up divides it, while a photographer from the 101st took the official picture, which I have never seen, but which will show the entrance of the group as I remember it. Jess Matthews stepped forward. "Well, good morning, boys and girls; this is the first class period, and you all know your way to that class. You may go to class, now," he said. And off they went, in various directions, their individual guards behind them.

Opie had given me a copy of each child's schedule on small, individual cards. These cards, worn and dim, were still in my purse at the close of school on May 27, having been consulted almost daily after September 25. This morning I toured the school each period, beginning with the classroom on the first floor near the Fourteenth Street entrance where Melba was in English class, and ending on the third floor two blocks away on the Sixteenth Street side where Elizabeth was in American history class. There was no disorder anywhere. The guards who had followed the black children were standing at ease in the corridors near the rooms. Other soldiers were here and there in the halls. On the stairway landing where they could see Park Street at Sixteenth, soldiers were watching what must have become the notorious "bayonets in the backs" picture: two laughing girls, absent from school without their mothers' knowledge I found later, being moved along by soldiers with bayonets pointed toward them.

At eleven-thirty Jess called J. O. and me into his office to tell us he had just had another anonymous call that the school was to be blown up at noon. We couldn't afford to risk this one; he rang for a fire drill.

The drill, though it was our first of the year, was orderly. With the rest of the office force, except Jess and J. O., who stayed to show the demolition squad around, I went to Park Street, directly in front of the school. Down the middle of the street was a cordon of troops. Across the street the newsmen and photographers found the fire drill a real bonanza. They moved up and down the sidewalk, looking for classes that had a black member, taking pictures, calling out questions. A military helicopter hovering overhead attracted attention from the soldiers. Bruce Fullerton and others from a senior math class exchanged learned comments about its mechanism. One platoon of soldiers was relieved by another. Their movements were efficient and precise. These were effective soldiers. No mob, such as we had had in front of the school two days ago, could break through them. I was not frightened for our pupils today.

Though we had never had such a long fire drill, three minutes being the usual duration, our kids weren't anxious to get back inside school. This was a wonderful show for them. We were outside for thirty minutes before the recall bell sounded. When we got inside, it was time for the first lunch period. I arranged with the guards to have Carlotta, Melba, and Gloria, brought to my office. I wanted to go with them to the rest room to be sure that they were all right there, and to take them to the cafeteria, since they had never been there. I couldn't ask a pupil to escort them, as I would have done with the usual new student. I felt that it was too dangerous.

The guards waited in the front hall while I went with the girls to the lavatory near Room 220, then followed us as we went to the cafeteria. As the girls entered, (the guards stayed in the cafeteria corridor) they were met by white girls who asked them to sit at their table.

The second lunch period was just like the first, except that I thought I would never get Thelma, Elizabeth, and Minnijean to the cafeteria. Minnijean wanted to find a locker first. Then she took an unconscionable amount of time primping. I was afraid there wouldn't be time left from our brief lunch period for the girls to get even a sandwich and a coke. I finally got my charges to the cafeteria door and remarked laughingly to Captain Madden, observing from the hall in front of the cafeteria, that I might have to put dynamite under Minnijean, she was so slow. As I said it, I was appalled at the ineptness of my remark.

At the last class period Billye Jean Spotts, a senior who was my office monitor, told me that things had gone "just fine." She said one of the girls (Gloria) was in her gym class and she was very sweet. "We asked her to play on our softball team."

At the end of the school day, the black students, followed by their guards, gathered in the corridor outside Jess's office. From there they were escorted to a waiting car. Preceded and followed by jeep loads of soldiers, the car moved away from Central.

The *Gazette* on Thursday morning quoted an unnamed teacher as saying that there had been no trouble in the classrooms; that things were "mightly calm." It also said that the black students, with the exception of Melba, reported no incidents against them. Melba had spoken of one boy who "made a speech" and walked out of class when she entered.

My journal for Thursday, September 26, reads:

101st Airborne on hand, performing with efficiency. . . . Atmosphere more relaxed. Fewer guards accompanied blacks in. No demonstration by students. . . . Pencil thrown at Melba in Miss Dewberry's class. Lipstick writing, "Nigger go home," on rest room walls. "Central High Mothers" evidently putting on a telephone campaign to scare women from sending their children. . . . Some positive items reported, too. Colored and white at one table in the cafeteria at first lunch. Grace Dupree told of her home room president shaking hands with Ernest Green as they were introduced.

Margaret Duggar had asked me to talk this morning with one of her students, a bright, but rather erratic girl in her home room, who had announced that she would no longer pledge allegiance to the flag after what the national government had done. Of course, no one wanted to force the girl to say the pledge; but I did give her a little sermon about remaining faithful to her country even when she disagreed with policies. And she finally said she could do it. The next week she dislocated her finger playing volleyball and was in pain. The field army doctor came to her aid and corrected the dislocation, even offered to take her in his jeep for X-rays. I suppose the point is that I was glad to see her able to accept assistance from a representative of her government.

The *Gazette* on Friday morning reported that the governor was calling for calm and order but also voicing resentment of the "occupation." On a televised interview he had shown the now famous picture of school girls with "bayonets in their backs." But the perimeter of patrol by the troops had been moved a block away from the school in each direction. The guard about the black children was not so tight. They were not surrounded by soldiers as they came up the front steps. There was only a slight rise in the volume of noise among the pupils gathered to watch as they came in. Separate guards did not follow the black pupils from class to class. Melba came by my office alone at noon wondering whether I thought it was safe for her to go down to lunch, and I assured her it was. Most of our hard-core segregationist children were not attending school these days.

The eighty boys and girls who had signed out and left school when the 101st had escorted the blacks into school had been barred from class until they had conferred with one of the vice-principals. A few girls returned this Friday morning, and I interviewed each. I confined my questioning and admonition to the point of good conduct in school, under whatever circumstances. No penalty was assigned for their absence. We were anxious to get the boys and girls back in school and proceeding with their educations. As public school teachers and administrators we felt that education was our major responsibility and integration a secondary problem in the social revolution of our times. Our daily bulletin had instructed homeroom and classroom teachers to see that parents were aware of those pupils remaining absent from school. Since much of the disruption of class work this week was acknowledged to have been because of parental concern, teachers were urged to be lenient (within the limits of their endurance) in permitting those absent, but not truant, to turn in back assignments and makeup work.

During Friday morning General Walker paid a visit to the school. Jess sent for me to come to his office to meet the general, Colonel Kuhn, and some other staff members. I attempted my usual chatty greeting to the visitors at school but quickly sensed that it was hardly suited to this example of the military personality on duty. So abrupt! So businesslike! Only Gilbert and Sullivan could have done justice to the scene, I thought, with supressed laughter. Jess sent for a copy of the first issue of the *Tiger*. He also wanted to show the general the story of the arrival of the 101st, written for next week's issue. The general, though he was in a hurry, waited for it and asked Colonel Kuhn to let the public relations officer check through it. I hardly thought Jess meant to present it for censorship, as the general seemed to think was in his province. At any rate, it appeared, as originally written, in the next *Tiger*.

Because Central was to play football against Istrouma High of Baton Rouge on Friday night, we held our first pep assembly on Friday afternoon, just after the second lunch period. Several of us teachers were in the auditorium early, since this was to be our first integrated assembly. I watched the four black children who were in my section of the auditorium find their assigned places with their homerooms: Melba and Thelma in groups next to the south wall, Minnijean in the center of the auditorium to my right, and Ernest with his senior group down front. There was no disturbance. A teacher was with each group, and she knew her own pupils.

It was a good assembly. There was a clever pep skit. Then the organized cheering began, led by our girl cheerleaders. The students (there were fourteen hundred in school by now) needed to let off steam, and they yelled, sang, and clapped with the cheer leaders and the band. I watched Ernest's back as he clapped to the music with the other kids. I wished we could make this his school to be proud of. I wished he could go to the football game tonight. But I knew these wishes were impossible for now—maybe for all year.

The pep assembly closed, as always, with the student body standing and singing the school song, "Hail to the Old Gold, Hail to the Black." I wondered who else noticed the ironic pun. The kids streamed out of the auditorium past me as I waited for the last to leave. Captain Madden was standing across the hall, his face alert but expressionless, as befitted a man on military duty. I smiled and assured him he could have relaxed since there was a teacher in there with each home room group, and he said, "Why didn't some-one tell me that? I could have enjoyed the assembly, then."

At three-thirty school was over for the week. The Nine as-sembled as usual near Jess's office, to go with their guards to their station wagon and its escorting jeeps. "See you at the game tonight, Mr. Matthews," said Ernest, with a twinkle in his eye.

On Saturday the *Gazette* reported that J. Edgar Hoover had been annoyed by one of the "outrages" Governor Faubus had cited in his inflammatory speech on Thursday evening, the TV appear-ance in which he had shown the blown-up picture of the girls "with bayonets in the backs." Mr. Hoover was irked at the Governor's charge that the FBI had "held two girls incommunicado for hours" while questioning them. Mr. Hoover named the girls who had been interviewed and who had reported the "outrage." They were two young friends I had scolded recently for their language and for their conduct with National Guard soldiers at the drugstore corner.

The Saturday afternoon *Arkansas Democrat* had a story about a group of women from the "Mothers' League of Central High" who had gone to the Governor's Mansion in the morning to petition the governor to call a special session of the legislature to close the schools. The girl who had testified to the state police in my office about the New York *Times*'s Dr. Benjamin Fine offering bribes, was pictured hugging Mr. Faubus as the Mothers delivered their peti-tion. The *Democrat* on Sunday morning predicted that the call for the special session was "just hours away."

On Sunday I went to church with Father. Mr. Ruffin, the associate pastor of the Second Presbyterian Church, offered a beautiful prayer asking forgiveness for all of us for the violence of the week. Then Dr. Boggs, the pastor, gave an explanation to his congregation of a series of rumors of a week ago. A call had come to his office on Saturday, the 21st, from a man who gave a name and Lake Village, Arkansas, as his home. He had told Dr. Boggs that two busloads of blacks would attend the Second Presbyterian Church on September 22 because of Dr. Boggs's stand for integration. Since he doubted that the call was authentic, Dr. Boggs had called the Presbyterian minister in Lake Village to ask about the person whose name had been given and found that no one by that name lived in Lake Village. Nevertheless, the ushers were prepared to seat the black worshippers, if they should come, down front at the east side of the church. Of course, none arrived. The Capital Citizens' Council had listed fifteen leading ministers of the city: Presbyterian, Methodist, Baptist, Episcopalian, Lutheran, and Disciples of Christ, and had suggested that blacks be urged to attend their churches. Dr. Boggs's name had headed the list.

On Monday night, September 30, I wrote in my journal:

> A rather peaceful day, but busy, since I spent most of it making a study of the reasons for absence of the 470 absentees. 290 of them are out possibly because of integration. Military atmosphere further relaxed. If any incidents happened, they were unreported. Mr. M. observed a boys' gym class (without guards, today) in which Terrence Roberts seemed to be in the middle of a friendly basketball game.
>
> After school J. O. said the 101st was pulling out, federalized Guard moving in this afternoon.
>
> Sleepy tonight. I think I'm beginning to relax—I hope not too soon.

CHAPTER IV

October 1–October 27

Precarious Balance

Tuesday, October 1, was not a good day at school. The efficiency of the U.S. 101st Airborne, which had effectively removed the mobs from our streets and had given our students the feeling that no harassment of the black students would be permitted, had given us a false sense of progress toward the solution of our problem. We administrators, anxious to have control of our students returned to the faculty, had asked that the federalized National Guard troops, who were to have full responsibility for security beginning today, stay as much in the background as possible: some in the back office, some in the teachers' conference room off the main hall, and some reserves in the old shops in the basement.

We knew that we did not yet have a stable student body for although more pupils were returning to school each day, they were the more aggressive segregationists—and obviously, the ones who cared least about their studies. Our worst error in judgment had been in underestimating the opposition to integration. The local leaders of that cause were, in general, not people one would call the backbone of the community. But they were well organized. And we did not understand that their lack of stature was fully compensated for by backing of the elected leaders of state government and—a realization that was much slower to come and even more bitter to accept—by the decision of the federal government, under various political pressures, not to act further in this crisis unless it was forced to do so. The "troops" had been a political mistake, and the

Eisenhower administration apparently did not want to make others.

The withdrawal—to Camp Robinson, only a dozen miles away—of the 101st and the substitution of the federalized National Guard did not change the attitude of those who resented our "occupation." On Friday we teachers had been issued mimeographed passes, signed by "Barker Sp. 32." One teacher arrived early each morning wearing hers pinned across her dress front, daring anyone to challenge her. Once a friendly, cheerful person, she now came into the office with her face frozen, never speaking to me unless I spoke to her first. She identified me I am sure, with those twin evils, integration and occupation.

This Tuesday morning was more disturbed than any since the Nine had been brought to school by troops. A large crowd of boys and girls at the front entrance to the school were shouting names and attempting to block the black students, as they came up the broad steps, throwing pencils at their backs as they went through the halls. Harassment continued in some of the classrooms when the teacher turned to the board.

After the eleven o'clock tardy bell, Elizabeth Eckford came into my office, red-eyed, her handkerchief a damp ball in her hand. I motioned her to the chair beside my desk, where she was screened from view and reached for the middle lefthand drawer of my desk for the Kleenex. But Elizabeth refused the proffered kerchief with a shake of her head. "I want to go home," she said. Her story was one that became too familiar during the rest of the year from all the black children: at first the name-calling, thrown objects, trippings, shovings, kickings were done by strangers. Later on they could recognize their assailants, for most of them were repeaters.

It would not do for one of the Nine to leave. It would make it harder for them to return; it would prolong the necessity for armed guards; it would put pressure on everyone involved, from the president on down. I argued. I appealed to Elizabeth's courage, the courage that I knew she possessed. Pictures on September 4 of this lone, proud child, turned back by the Arkansas National Guard and followed and screamed at by the insane mob, had received international attention.

I finally persuaded Elizabeth to stay and walked with her to her history class. Her next class was on that same floor, and I went back down the corridor, asking those teachers who would be likely to look out for her welfare to be especially alert as she passed: Helen Conrad, Margaret Reiman, Betty Young. Some I did not ask because I did not know how they felt about Elizabeth's presence— some, because I did know.

Back in my office I had a call from a mother who wanted some advice: should she keep her daughter, a prominent senior, home on Thursday? Some of the students, she said, were calling around to get all the pupils to agree to come to school on Thursday and then walk out in protest over integration. She didn't want her daughter to walk out, but she didn't want her to be left in school if most of the others walked out. I advised her to send her daughter to school and told her that we would get to work on the problem here. Inquiring of other girls in the office, I learned that they had heard of the walk-out. Then a gym teacher came by to tell me that she had heard of a planned walkout; so I went to Jess. He would make a positive statement in tomorrow's bulletin, he said. Anyone involved in such a walkout would be suspended.

After the closing bell for the day I asked Elizabeth if she weren't glad she had stayed at school. "No, I'm not," she said, forlornly. And the other girls had their troubles to report, too: milk bottle caps thrown into their food at lunch, for instance.

After school we wrote the bulletin for Wednesday. As always, we tried to have something constructive to say. But the events of the day called for some prohibitions, as well. We assured those students who had been attending school regularly that they need not be concerned about receiving full credit for their work since our school remained fully accredited by the North Central Association; college entrance credit had not been affected by the crisis of the past weeks. We warned them that to walk out would bring suspension and that readmittance would be only on approval by the Board of Education. The bulletin urged teachers to be at their doors as classes passed and to exercise special vigilance during the next few days.

Before I left for my grammar class Tuesday at seven, the radio was reporting the news that Governor Faubus had agreed to a proposal of the southern governors for terms for removing the troops, promising protection for the integrated school. But I heard on the ten o'clock news that Faubus was hedging on his part of the bargain so that it was no longer acceptable to the president. We were just where we had been, or perhaps a little worse off.

I didn't have a very good night, but I was at school as usual by 7:30. As 8:00 approached, I became more and more nervous, for the National Guard brass was with Jess in his office, and J. O. with them; and the crowd on the front steps was getting larger by the minute. The black kids were due at about 8:20. Remembering the petty mistreatments of the day before, I felt that someone in authority should be out there, but I confess I was afraid to go. I had always thought of the *taste of fear* as a figurative expression. Now I knew differently. Fear tasted *brown*. And it provoked other sensations, too. My mouth was dry and my stomach was turning over. But at 8:15 there was still no sign of the conference in the principal's office being over, and I knew I had to go out front.

At the main-floor entrance the mass of students on the porch was too thick for me to push through, so I went down stairs and out the door that led to the bottom of the south front steps. The Nine students had just gotten out of their station wagon and started toward the building. I planted myself at the bottom of the steps and looked up at the jeering group of boys at the top. I didn't know one boy in the bunch. I was vainly trying to memorize faces or shirt plaids or colors. I was relieved to learn later that a photographer from the 101st photographed the scene from just behind me, from which J. O. was able to identify most of the boys on the front row. I recognized two girls, looking on from the side.

The black students, realizing that their usual entranceway to the school was blocked, veered toward the nearest door, at the south end of the building on Park Street. "Get those coons!" yelled one of the boys, and the pack started down the steps. "Go back!" I said in my loudest and firmest teacher voice to the first, the second, the third, and the fourth boys down the steps. They ignored me, and one of the girls started down, too. But when I called her name, she stopped and went back up the steps.

Reentering the building, I heard no sound of disorder, merely the usual before-school noise. By now the conference with the officers was over, and I told Jess what had happened.

It was nearly time for homeroom, and I hadn't even unlocked

my office door. As I turned the key in my lock, I became aware of a scramble of boys coming up the steps from the first-floor hall. A pack of boys was chasing Terrence Roberts and Jefferson Thomas, and just as I looked, one boy kicked Terrence, and another shoved the books from Jefferson's arms and started kicking them across the floor. Without thinking, I seized the arms of the two boys at the head of the attack and escorted them into my office. I didn't know them, so I demanded their library identification cards, which I took with me as I escorted the boys to the main office. I was wondering where the men from the National Guard were when I saw a group of them looking on from the door of the conference room next to my office. None of them had made a move toward the scramble I had interrupted.

Jess Matthews interviewed the white boys, who felt they were fully within their rights in making things as miserable as possible for the "niggers," who had no business in the school. The principal suspended them and ordered them to get their books and leave. I went back to my office to catch my breath and check up as usual on absentees.

Just before the tardy bell rang for the ten o'clock class Melba Pattillo and Minnijean Brown came in and asked me to change a quarter, which I did. Only after they had walked out the door did it occur to me what they needed the change for. I looked out into the hall and, sure enough, they were starting into the phone booth in the front hall. I stopped them before they had finished dialing the number, and they told me they were calling Mrs. Bates, the NAACP president. Things were just too rough for them at school; the National Guard was not making any effort to protect them and they were going home.

"But don't you think you should talk with the principal first?" I asked. They hesitated, then agreed, and we went down the hall to Jess's office. He asked me to get the facts about what had happened to the girls that morning. I quote from my report to him, the first of a long series of such accounts that would pile up during the year:

> Melba was very much upset. She said she had had no physical injury, nothing except some crowding, pushing, and shoving. She said she felt that the remote areas needed more protection, the south end of the building, the third floor, etc. She said that as she had walked

from the south end of the building's third floor to the north end, pencils were thrown at her, and there was noise and jeering. She said there had been a big change in the atmosphere yesterday and today, and that it was worse today. She feels that more guards—or different guards—are needed.

Minnijean said that before school all the guards seemed to be concentrated on the second floor in front of the offices. She was followed from the second floor to 301 by two girls, one very short, and four boys who jeered and were abusive. She replied by calling the small girl a midget, she said.

Outside the lavatory near 220, one girl deliberately ran into her, Minnijean said. She walked up to a guard who seemed to be "in command" and asked for more protection. He said that he had to follow orders.

Melba added that many white students had been friendly, but that they had explained that they were as afraid of the "tough" students as the Negroes were.

Jess told the girls, after they had given me their account, to go into the back office where they were free to use the phone. One of the boys—Ernest, I believe—joined them, and Jess and I left them, to report to Mrs. Bates we supposed. Then Jess called the military to come to his office.

When General Sherman Clinger, in command of the federalized National Guard, arrived, he and Colonel Ernest McDaniel met with the three black children, Jess, J. O., and me in the back office. The youngsters had talked with Mrs. Bates; and they insisted that they would have to go home if they were not to be better protected.

I almost felt sorry for General Clinger. I was sure that the integration of anything was distasteful to him. He had been in command of the Arkansas National Guard when it barred the Nine under the governor's orders in September. Now he found himself "federalized," under General Walker's and President Eisenhower's command, charged with seeing that the black students were protected in school. He was almost querulous as he discussed the matter.

I spoke up to assume some of the blame and the responsibility, admitting that we had been too confident of our ability to control our own students and had even suggested the less obvious role for the guard. I did not add that we hadn't expected the guard to stand idly by if trouble occurred.

General Clinger asked Colonel McDaniel whether he had men to handle such a situation. The colonel said he had none trained, but that he would call in a platoon from outside duty and assign two guards to each black pupil. We set up a meeting in Room 134 for the assignment of the guards. While Colonel McDaniel ordered his platoon, I collected the other black children: Elizabeth from 302, Gloria from gym, etc. Melba, Minnijean, and Ernest called Mrs. Bates and told her what was being done for their safety.

It is always a pleasure to see a man of decision and force of character at work, and such a man was Colonel McDaniel. I have no idea what his political or sociological views might have been. The only other place I have seen him is as an official on a football field. But this one morning I felt he was a man I would like to have around in any crisis that called for action. Into Room 134 came a platoon of the National Guard in fatigue uniforms. Most of them were of high school age or just over that, from what sections of Arkansas I do not know. Colonel McDaniel assigned two of them to each child, saying, "You are to protect them, if it means walking shoulder to shoulder with them the rest of the day." There were no further incidents that day.

By the close of school it was cloudy and raining. I sat in Jess's office discussing the day's events and pondering the contents of tomorrow's bulletin. Suddenly we were jarred by an ear-splitting blast of sound. Dynamite! And then we laughed. It was thunder.

On Thursday morning Captain Madden of the 101st, who had not been at school since the federalized National Guard officers took over, walked up to the office counter. "I want my readmittance slip," he said, grinning. He was not absent again until the end of November, when the 101st finally got to return to Fort Campbell, Kentucky.

New instructions had been issued by the military district for handling disturbances at school: "Should military personnel on duty in the school observe an incident which takes place or should an incident be reported to military personnel on duty, the soldiers concerned will immediately intervene, quell the incident, and escort the offender(s) to the principal's office."

Our daily bulletin took notice of the threatened walkout and of Wednesday's disturbances reminding teachers to check attendance carefully all day and to call absentees. And to students Jess directed a sharp rebuke: "A few students gave Central a real black eye yesterday when they attempted to harass Negro students entering and attending classes in our school. Disciplinary action will be taken against any student or any group of students who deliberately heckle, shove, or otherwise intimidate any student in school. This type of behavior must stop."

Our main concern this Thursday was the organized walkout. There is something appealing to all youngsters, especially teenagers, about cutting school. It is the natural assertion of their independence, their right to establish themselves as adults by choosing where they go. That, entirely aside from their feelings about segregation and integration, would be a force pulling them into any walkout. We did not really know just how strongly our students felt about integration, or about desegregation under military supervision. And, no matter how they felt, we did not know how many of them could withstand the pressure of other teenagers, the taunts of "chicken" or "nigger-lover," or possibly even the physical threats of the organizers of the walkout. We just didn't know what to expect.

We hoped we could identify those who walked out, though with an already abnormally long list of absentees we might not. Nurse Carpenter was prepared to refuse permission to check out to any boy or girl who reported to the health room as "sick" in an effort to join the walkout and still maintain a clear school record. With her long experience in dealing with high school kids, Miss Carpenter had a reputation for being hard to fool. "They'll have to be stretcher cases to get out through my office today," she promised.

The walkout was scheduled for nine o'clock, at the end of the homeroom period. At nine, Jess Matthews, J. O. Powell, Captain Madden, Mrs. Charles Stephens, PTA president, and I were near the front doors. The hall filled with a milling, uncertain group. We took no part in it, except to be there and prevent a traffic block in the hall. I heard Barbara Barnes, pretty and popular senior cheerleader and an officer in the non-school-connected Youth Center, urge one boy, "*Please* don't leave"; and I am sure other of our student leaders must have been giving the same word. It appeared to me that not many left. There were ten other exits from the school;

and I thought other students might have left through those. Since this was meant to be an organized defiance, however, most of those leaving should have used the main door.

The bell rang for class, and the stragglers left the hall. I went back to my office. In the outer office sat Elizabeth Eckford, who had slipped in, unnoticed, as I stood in the hall. "I was afraid to go through that bunch," she said. I didn't blame her, but the corridor was clear, now, so I sent her on to her study hall. Elizabeth, I realized, was the most emotional one of my charges.

Some teachers, already bringing in reports of absentees, knew of pupils who hadn't been in school since the Nine came, but who had come this morning specifically to walk out. Among these was a junior, the daughter of Margaret Jackson, president of the segregationist Mothers' League of Central High School. This girl had frankly told her teacher about her reason for attending. Strangely enough, her younger sister, a tenth grader, was in school today, and did not join the walkout.

Captain Madden reported that observers for his group had seen about 150 pupils leave the building, and half of them apparently finding their numbers so few, had just walked across the grounds and reentered the school through another door. According to the captain, the group that really left went across Park Street to the vacant lot on the corner of Sixteenth Street and staged their demonstration, including the burning of a black effigy. The guard broke up the demonstration and brought one girl back to the principal's office for "rabble rousing." The girl was one of those the governor had previously named as having been held "incommunicado" for hours by the FBI.

I began the all-day task of determining which students had actually walked out. Ironically, the chief obstacle to an accurate check was also a contributing factor to the failure of the walkout. All seniors were scheduled to take the American Council on Education Psychological Examination, required by the University of Arkansas and other state colleges for admission. Our seniors realized its importance to them, so almost all of them stayed. Since the seniors stayed, most underclassmen stayed in school, too.

But complicated test scheduling did hinder my checking. I could not automatically list as walkouts all seniors marked absent after homeroom. First I had to know whether they were in the ACE testing room. Then I had to check whether they attended classes after they took the test. I was still checking at home at 11 P.M., but I finally had a fairly accurate list of seventy names that I turned over to Jess on Friday.

Probably a few more names should have been on the list. An occasional teacher may have overlooked the presence of a pupil in homeroom and thought that pupil had been absent all day, not walked out. As always, some parents covered up for their children. One or two girls, refused permission to leave by Miss Carpenter, left, anyway, and their mothers insisted they were really sick. I assigned them to report five mornings to early study hall for failing to sign out but did not list them as walkouts since that would have implied that their mothers lied. Some parents, too, insisted that their children had not actually come to school to attend but had stayed on the outside to watch; or that they had come into the school just to get books to study at home because they were sick.

My brother Bill called me from New York on Thursday evening. The New York *Times* had carried the item, picked up from Wednesday's *Arkansas Democrat*, about my "rescue" of Jefferson and Terrence. That story had its origin in Mrs. Bates's report, not from the school. As a member of my English classes, Jefferson Thomas was able to identify me by name. At least one other teacher, Zinta Hopkins, had corralled the harassing white boys on Wednesday morning at the north end of the first floor and had rescued Terrence and Jefferson. But they did not know her name. So name-starved were the news agencies because of the ban on reporters and photographers in the building that they played up this minor matter as international news. Friends visiting in Montreal sent me a clipping from a French language paper about Mme. Elizabeth Huckaby. I had done what any experienced teacher has done a dozen times: broken up a fracas before it could get serious. Only the circumstances of our unique crisis made it news.

On Friday, notices of suspension from school were mailed to the seventy walkouts. All were barred from attending classes, pending satisfactory conferences between their parents and Mr. Blossom. None would be allowed to return before three days; and none could return without a formal readmittance letter from the superintendent. At school we noted a few defiant Confederate flags and caps among the kids, but very few. One or two boys had made paper hats with "101st" printed across the front, in mockery of the troops. But all-in-all, we felt that we had won in this walkout skirmish.

The movie star Julie Adams (she had been Betty Adams when she had attended Central a few years back) was in town visiting relatives and had called Alberta Harris, her former drama teacher in Central, deploring what the political tug-of-war had done to the good name of her school, her home town, and her state, and wanting to do something to help. Alberta arranged for her to appear briefly at our pep assembly Friday afternoon. In her talk, Julie Adams commended the student body (most of them, that is) for their calmness and good behavior. Many of our hard cases were absent, suspended for their walkout of the day before.

So the school week ended. On Saturday morning Glen and I left home at 4:15 for a squirrel hunt at Smoke Hole Club. At 5:45 Glen put on his hip boots to wade across the tupelo gum sloughs and hunt on the islands up Bayou Two. I always hunt with him; but this morning I couldn't. I was exhausted, physically and emotionally. I stretched out on the car seat and dozed till the chill of the October morning crept into my bones. At sunup I moved to the canvas reclining chair, pulled a blanket over my knees, and leaned back, limp, just looking into the treetops above me and down the slope to the edge of the swamp. I saw a gray squirrel come out of the tupelo gums in the swamp, hurry through the big white oak, then the hickory, then the red oak, by his familiar path into the dogwood over the woodshed, just twenty steps from me. He made his breakfast on dogwood berries for fifteen minutes and never knew I was there. He left, undisturbed. When Glen came in with his morning limit of squirrels, I was still sitting. On Sunday I wrote Bill:

> Smoke Hole Club
> 6 A.M. Sunday
> October 6, 1957

Dear Bill,
   Glen and I came down here early yesterday morning. He has hunted squirrels and is out again this morning, but I have just rested. It just about takes Saturday and Sunday this fall to collect myself for the other five days. And I hardly see Glen otherwise.
   One inevitable result of all this stew centered around nine boys

and girls is the harm it is doing to the personalities of some of the children. Some of them are, through no fault of their own, acquiring a feeling of too much personal importance. It is not within the conception of most adolescents to see that the might of the U.S. Army, at $100,000 a day, is not being spent to protect a few *persons*, but an *idea*. And of course they can't see what I see: that until we can work up to a point of their being inconspicuous, their case will never be won. Again, it's not all their fault, but the fault of everyone. Still, until I see evidence to the contrary, I think the Governor will have to bear the major blame—for these children, for a crippled school for eighteen hundred others, for fear, hate, and suspicion in a community and state, and for a disrupted economy in Arkansas and comfort to the international rivals of the United States.

Radio news, which is the only kind I have had since Friday, gives the big play to the Russian satellite. We'll be glad to take second billing for a while.

A substitute teacher will take my classes for the third week. I hate not to teach, but I'm busy every moment with something connected with the crisis. The remarkable thing is that so many teachers, pupils, and activities proceed and do so well. Classes are making progress in math, science, English, history, etc. Our football team won its 25th consecutive victory (over a three-year period). And I am sure we have at least twelve hundred pupils who haven't missed a day, in spite of parents' urging, in many cases, to stay home and avoid trouble.

One parting remark. The big "assists" I have had all fall are the support of my family and friends—and two mighty comfortable pairs of school shoes.

Lovingly,
Liz

Monday, October 7, began our sixth week at school, the third one of integration. It was a rather uneventful day, the only disturbance being some jeering remarks directed to the guards. But at noon the radio and the early edition of the *Arkansas Democrat* reported a ridiculous charge by Governor Faubus that military guards were following the black girls into the girls' gym dressing rooms—a charge with undertones of sex to titillate the prurient. We were new, then, to the technique of the Big Lie. Like all big lies, this one had a built-in usefulness: no denial could ever be as effective as the original lie. This is a fact of the propaganda device.

On Tuesday I took up the investigation of Governor Faubus' false accusation. Captain Madden requested that I interview the girl reported to be the source of the tale about guards in the girls' dressing room. The girl said she supposed a remark she had made at Period 2 gym to her girl friend must have been overheard and repeated by Mrs. Jackson's daughter. She said Carlotta Walls's guard followed Carlotta to the landing of the stairs leading to the dressing room. The girl said she remarked to her friend that she didn't see why the guard came so far with Carlotta; that none of the girls in gym would hurt her, and that if the guard stayed on the landing, he might see into the dressing room.

Further questioning revealed that the guard had never stayed on the landing; he was never there when the girls left the dressing room for the playing field. Before the investigation ended, a general, a colonel, Captain Madden, and lesser officials participated in the investigation—tracing routes to the gym, measuring, taking photographs, coming and going by helicopter. But no evidence was ever uncovered to substantiate the girl's remark. Rumor had it that a captain of the Arkansas State Police bragged that he had dreamed up the girls' locker room accusation. He was named later by one of the segregationist kids as their liaison with the governor.

My journal for Thursday noted: "To school by 7:30 as usual. Routine sort of day. With the 'protection' one forgets the submerged violence. Negro children being entirely ignored, it seems. Those who would be friendly to them have been frightened out of friendliness by the rough and vocal (and often anonymous) minority. Attendance near normal."

In the office hundreds of letters had accumulated—more than we could ever afford to answer or buy stamps for. After going through them I stuffed heaps of them into a box and wrote a summary report on them to Jess. Viewpoints in the letters ranged from the most violent segregationist to the most ardent integrationist. They came from all over the United States, from most of the European countries, South America, Asia, Canada. In my report I emphasized the sympathetic letters and quoted little from the harshest critics. Jess had enough of those at home.

Friday, October 11, I called, in my journal, another "more or less routine day, under the circumstances." Melba Pattillo was absent; flu, I discovered, was the cause. But military intelligence needed to know the reason for any black student's absence.

Crudely lettered notebook paper was taped to the walls. "Go back to Africa Niggers" read one; and "You are now walking through the halls of intergrated L.R.C.H.S. courtesy of N.A.A.C.P." read another that I pulled down. A sign in light pink lipstick on the wall of a rest room booth exhorted: "Nigger go home or youll be sorrow."

That week completed the first grading period. Aside from the problem of assigning grades, we had other problems. As segregationist parents realized that the black students were to stay in school under federal protection, pupils were being withdrawn daily. Often we did not inquire the reason for withdrawal. "Opposed to Integration" on their permanent records might some day embarrass some of these students, should they become more enlightened than their parents. One father, withdrawing his two children from school, asked that we put in the record the reason for his children's leaving our school as "federal dictatorship." We put it in the record. Some children had just quit coming to school or had failed to return to school after the blacks entered. We could not talk with children whose parents had no telephones, although some of these pupils had borrowed their textbooks from the PTA-funded supply for indigent pupils. We made a list for Mrs. Paynter, director of attendance for the schools, to investigate. On this list, too, were children whose parents did have phones but who had been so abusive when teachers called about their absence that the teachers refused to inquire again. We asked that parents either return their children to school or give us authority to drop them from our rolls. School law in Arkansas did not require attendance at the high school level.

Friday's regular bulletin, which again asserted that the principal would not tolerate hoodlum tactics and wisecracks to a soldier or other students, attests to continued tension.

Our "protection" remained about the same. Captain Madden had associated with him for learning the routine a Captain Leon Stumbaugh of the federalized National Guard. Elements of the 101st were still about. The blacks' station wagon was escorted to school by jeeps. All the black kids were trailed, but at a distance, now, by guards, who followed them from class to class but remained outside in the corridor, as always, during the class periods. We had had a succession of FBI agents in the building. One, who

Central, for more than a half a century Little Rock's largest high school. During the 1957–58 session its students numbered eighteen hundred.
JEFF BULLARD PHOTOGRAPH

Colonel Marion Johnson, under Governor Faubus' orders, blocks entry of the black students, September 4. Three of the students shown are Carlotta Walls, Gloria Ray, and Ernest Green.
ARKANSAS DEMOCRAT

Elizabeth Eckford being turned away from Central High on September 4.
ARKANSAS DEMOCRAT

Elizabeth Eckford, followed by the mob on September 4.
UNITED PRESS INTERNATIONAL

Amused as these girls appear to be, this photograph created a furor and was used by the segregationists as evidence of mistreatment of white pupils.
ARKANSAS DEMOCRAT

Nine black students enter Central for the first time. They were slipped in through the Sixteenth Street side door on September 23. Gene Smith, assistant chief of police, is in the foreground.
ARKANSAS GAZETTE

Seven of the Nine enter Central under guard. From left, Terrence Roberts, Elizabeth Eckford, Melba Pattillo, Gloria Ray, Thelma Mothershed, Carlotta Walls, and Minnijean Brown.
ARKANSAS GAZETTE

Elizabeth Eckford waits for the bus, surrounded by reporters and hecklers. Behind her (in bowtie) is Benjamin Fine, education editor of the New York *Times*. Grace Lorch, back to camera, befriended Elizabeth.
ARKANSAS GAZETTE

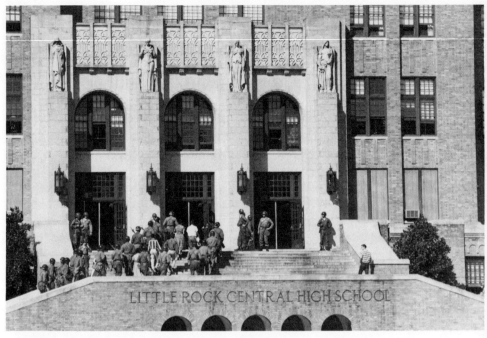

Black students enter Central High on September 25 under armed guard.
LARRY OBSTINIK PHOTOGRAPH

The author faces hostile white students as they confront the Nine on October 2, after the federalized National Guard took over, briefly, from the 101st.

The author, vice-principal for girls at Central during the troubled year.
CENTRAL HIGH YEARBOOK

J. O. Powell, vice-principal for boys.
CENTRAL HIGH YEARBOOK

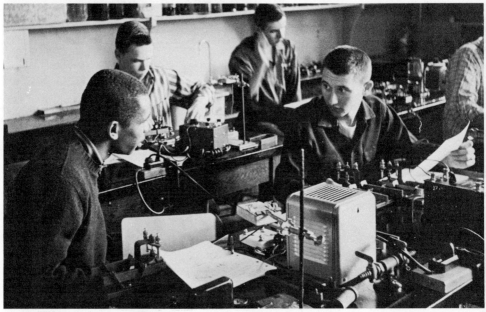

Integration at work. Ernest Green in the physics lab with fellow classmen.
GERTRUDE SAMUELS

had been there for only a few days, was a former student body president of Central. We were glad to see him, and he, us. But he was in a tough spot. His uncle was one of Governor Faubus' key men; and no doubt our graduate's relatives had little sympathy for his mission at Central. Whether this had anything to do with the brevity of his stay, I do not know. A Mr. Pryor stayed around all year, inconspicuously going in and out of a back office. He was not FBI, but had something to do with "intelligence."

The *Arkansas Gazette* and the churches provided the only moderate leadership in Little Rock. Saturday, October 12, was observed as a day of prayer in most of the large churches, cathedrals, and synagogues. But on that same day a large group, principally very fundamentalist churches, were praying for segregation, "according to God's Law." Lots of local people belonged to these fundamentalist churches.

Local courts had not acted against the people charged in the disturbances of late September. The cases had been passed, a rather normal procedure for cooling off feelings; but certainly there was no vigorous support of order in the community.

At school, the week of October 14 was full of normal activity under abnormal conditions. The PTA membership drive was in progress. Mrs. W. Myer Smith, the membership chairman, and her faithful group, Mrs. Charles Stephens, Mrs. Grainger Williams, and Mrs. Jay Heflin, were always there, with about twenty others who came, a few each morning, to check on the progress of the campaign and to accept membership fees turned in by homerooms. The 100-percent membership goal in the PTA, which actually meant only one adult member for each student in school, seemed unlikely. And the prospect of an integrated membership made the 100-percent goal improbable, it goes without saying. *Occupation* was a prickly subject; some parents whose children kept on attending school declared they would never enter the building while the federal government *occupied* it. Captain Madden did a magnificent job of public relations in trying to overcome this handicap—being charming to the ladies and making himself and his men useful to them by moving blackboards, setting up the daily chart of progress, and running errands. One handicap to the PTA drive this year was irrelevant to integration. The transfer of so many of our pupils to Hall High School had effectively reduced the number of parents who had the means to support the PTA and the leisure to work with it.

The second Monday of each month is faculty meeting day. When we assembled at 3:45 in the club room, Jess Matthews was high in his praise of the faculty. And their fortitude had been remarkable. Eighty-nine teachers; their ages twenty-one to sixty-five; their teaching experience, none to forty-five years; their viewpoints, extreme conservatism to moderate liberalism, had been at school every day for six weeks, with the exception of one day each missed unavoidably by two teachers. Evidently we were a tough bunch.

On Tuesday, report cards were circulated for the recording of grades; and on Wednesday the cards went home in the hands of pupils. By Tuesday, too, we were having to send dozens of pupils home from school with sudden high fever. A nationwide epidemic of flu had struck us, including Terrence Roberts and Melba Pattillo.

On Wednesday I wrote Bill:

> We can't see our way any further, here, than day to day. Over a hundred of eighteen hundred pupils have withdrawn from school, some of them to country, consolidated schools (not comparable in their standards to Central), some to live with relatives in other towns or cities, and some just quitting school. These latter, many of them, would have found a pretext to quit before the year was out, having about reached their level of educability. Of the approximately seventy we suspended for their part in open defiance, fifty have been readmitted by Mr. Blossom and a dozen are in the list of withdrawals.

I noted that only nineteen boys and girls were being withheld from attendance because of integration. These figures were fresh in my mind because I had spent most of the day sifting the list. But I also compared Little Rock to Nazi Germany, citing the leaders in school and town silenced by physical threats, principally to children, and by economic boycotts; second-rate professional people doing the big talking for the rough and rather inarticulate mob.

On Thursday and Friday I taught my two English classes while Wilma Means took Bonnie Brietz's place in the attendance office. I was glad to see my classes again, but I was disappointed to see Carlotta and Jefferson more isolated than ever. The chairs around them were vacant. Unhappy, I returned to my office in time to be shown a brown paper sack found in a rest room. Inside the sack was a pint fruit jar filled with a colorless liquid. There was a foil-wrapped cylinder in the liquid. We hurried the mysterious package to the military for a check. The liquid in the jar was water. The foil-wrapped cylinder was a brown glass pill bottle with a screw top, filled with water, too, as it was analyzed by Govie Griffin, our chemistry teacher.

By now, half of the 101st had gone home to Kentucky, and all but five hundred members of the National Guard were being defederalized, the papers reported. But the governor said that Central High was still "occupied."

On Friday two teachers came to me with problems about Minnijean Brown. The problems were usual ones, made unusual only by the special circumstances of Minnijean in our formerly all-white school.

Shortly after entering Central, Minnijean had been allowed to change from French to speech. Her problem in French, besides its difficulty, was at least one overt class antagonist, a boy. There had been a scene one morning, when, according to one version, this boy had refused to move his feet as Minnijean went to her seat and Minnijean had stumbled over them; the other version said that Minnijean had kicked the boy. According to both accounts an exchange of uncomplimentary remarks had resulted, and Minnijean had stepped to the door and summoned her guard. Carol Carter, the twenty-one-year-old French teacher, had sent the guard on his way, saying that she should handle the situation in her own classroom. But the boy was not an easy pupil to handle, especially for a young woman only two or three years his senior, teaching her first year. So Minnijean had her schedule changed. French was too hard, anyway, she said, especially under Miss Carter, a Phi Beta Kappa with rigid standards that even the best pupils found hard to meet.

Mickey McGalin, Minnijean's speech teacher, had assigned Minnijean some study material when she entered the speech class six weeks late. Then she had put Minnijean in a desk chair outside the classroom door to take the test on that material while the class went on presenting some individual speeches. Minnijean, Mickey thought, must have used her notes to look up answers on the test. What should she do about it? I told Mickey that what I had usually done in such cases was not to make an issue of the situation if it were one in which I had given the student the clear opportunity to use outside help, as Mickey had in this case. I added that in the future I would be careful not to give the same opportunity. In the meantime I would work with the pupil toward good daily preparation of assignments and toward an increase in confidence in her own ability. Mickey agreed. But she went on to remark that she was finding a lot more angles to this "integration thing" than one could foresee.

Susie West, Minnijean's English teacher, came in with the same sort of problem as Mickey had brought. When spelling test papers had been passed to the front for checking, Minnijean's could not be found. At the end of the class period it appeared on the teacher's desk with the other papers, all words correctly spelled. What should she do? Just watch more closely to be sure there was no fraud, by or against Minnijean, I suggested.

The week of October 21 was a real scramble, just to keep up with attendance and health office records. Flu absented almost five hundred pupils on Monday, and I taught my classes again to let Wilma Means help Bonnie Brietz, just back from flu herself, catch up on attendance records. Tuesday was a rainy day, "a good day for inside duty," according to Captain Madden. Nearly six hundred pupils were absent. On Wednesday we decided that we had passed the worst of the flu crisis, since our absences dropped back to five hundred.

The PTA members, their drive even further hampered by the huge absences, closed their effort on the 23rd, having reached 90 percent of their goal. All the black parents had joined. Daisy Bates, president of the Arkansas NAACP, had joined through Jefferson Thomas's homeroom. Margaret Jackson, president of the segregationist Mothers' League of Central High School, had joined through her younger daughter's homeroom. And in the rivalry to win the prize for the highest percentage of memberships in any homeroom, W. P. Ivy's Room 341 had taken up a collection to buy additional memberships and had sent membership cards to Governor Faubus and President Eisenhower.

The military had been chafing at our inability to handle the integrated situation without their help, an attitude that was understandable but unrealistic, in view of the governor's continued stand. They called for a conference to consider a list of proposals that in essence, would stop the guard from following the black students in the building; stop driving the children to school with convoy guard; and reduce the obvious guard at the school.

They wished to consider our reactions to these proposals and the reactions of Mrs. Bates, the black children, their parents, and the white students. What problem areas did we foresee? When did we think this program could be put into effect? Additional questions concerned the attitude of the PTA, teachers, student organizations, and school departments and the role they might take.

I had jotted down some notes to talk over with Jess Matthews before the conference. I felt that one of the weaknesses of the school board's position was the lack of a real public relations expert to handle its desegregation news. If the guard were to be stopped from trailing the students, teachers must be at their doors between classes and must stop all incidents immediately. Pupils involved must be sent home until a conference could be held with their parents. The black children's lockers must be where they could be observed, particularly before and after school. Some of the black pupils would resist a reduction of their guard because they would feel insecure, one or two because they would miss the feeling of importance a guard gave them. The reaction of our students to a normal situation would, for the most part, be good, I thought. I felt that the PTA should meet to talk about these problems. Our faculty should be brought into a discussion, and the student body organization should be a forum for such a discussion. Eventually I would realize that some of my ideas were as unrealistic as those of the military.

At 10:00 on Thursday morning Jess Matthews, J. O. Powell, and I went to Mr. Blossom's office. At 10:30 we moved on to the military district headquarters in the 555 Building on Broadway. There we sat with General Walker and assorted officers of his command. General Walker listened to what we had to say. He even teased me a little about being able to handle a riot single-handed. He had heard of the happenings of October 2, no doubt. He was much less brusque than I had tabbed him at our first meeting. As he cupped his hand behind his ear, to hear better, he seemed even avuncular. I almost liked him. Returning to school, I was amazed to see the school still running with the three principals absent for a couple of hours. The attendance office sent me notice that Minnijean Brown had been tardy to classes five times without excuse. That meant an automatic assignment to early study hall for one morning. I made the assignment and went personally to Margaret Baker, who kept that study hall from 7:30 to 8:30. She was not happy about the prospect of having Minnijean in the early morning study hall. Her usual occupants of that study hall were the hard cases of the school, those pupils, principally boys, who were being punished for various infractions of school rules. Keeping down misbehavior in that group with Minnijean there would be too much to expect of a person with less moral force than Margaret. I felt sure she could handle it. But Margaret told me on Friday that she didn't think she could manage a like situation again, and she asked me to have any future black girls who had to come early to report to my office.

As the military studied the implementation of their return-to-normal plan, the newspapers reported the reorganization of the League of Central High Mothers. Mrs. Margaret Jackson was president. On the board were Mrs. Anita Sedberry and Mrs. Margaret Douglas, each with a son in Central, and Mrs. Hilda Thevenet and Mrs. Marjorie Masters, who had no children yet in Central, but whose children were due to attend in a year or two.

In the hall J. O. Powell had stopped a boy carrying signs proclaiming REFUGEE FROM OCCUPIED ARKANSAS, a sentiment also seen on bumper stickers about town. J. O. asked the kid what he was doing with the signs, and he said he was selling them. He seemed amazed when J. O. told him that selling things or distributing unauthorized printed matter at school was not permissible, and he volunteered he got his supply from Mrs. Jackson's daughter. I asked the girl to take the signs home, and she agreed. The next day her mother withdrew her from school. Now we had neither daughter of the president of the League of Central High Mothers in Central.

I summarized the week in my letter to Bill:

Sunday evening
October 27, 1957

Dear Bill:

I am enjoying the "Nine Who Dared" series that you are sending. The first one I passed on to Captain Madden of the 101st (in charge of safety of the children at school), Mr. Matthews, and J. O. Powell because it reported some incidents which had not come to our attention. The others I shall file in the Guidance Department where a folder is kept on each of our students. Their counselors might find the background material interesting. The articles are somewhat romanticized, as they would have to be to be readable. By now I could add a few footnotes that are too realistic in one or two cases. New experiences almost daily for this ex-English teacher. (A substitute teaches my classes.) Thursday I sat in an hour-and-a-half conference with Mr. Blossom, Jess, J. O.—called by the general and other high brass. Purpose: getting the Army out of the school as soon as possible. The General is being pressed by the (national) Administration, of course, since it feels that it's losing ground in the South over the "occupation". We at school feel that as long as the Governor is fulminating, no one has been indicted in the community for conspiracy, and the community is still listening to the segregationist radicals, for the Army to pull out would be dangerous. You'll note that the escort to school was abandoned Friday and the children aren't being followed from class to class. I look for some more open harassment of the Negroes tomorrow, since our hard cases will feel that the relaxation of the guard gives them more openings. With each week that passes, though, we will be on firmer footing with our own pupils, knowing them by sight and having a sort of classroom grip on them. Anonymity is the best cover for cowards, and the pupils grow less anonymous to us as the weeks pass.

Lovingly, your sis,
Liz

Steady Progress– Nowhere

The return-to-normal plan had begun without notice on Friday. All the black children arrived by civilian transportation, their parents and adult friends forming car pools for them. Only Minnijean, Melba, and Jefferson were followed from class to class by guards. The others had felt that they didn't need them. Carlotta had always outdistanced hers, anyway, with her swinging, athletic gait. Her guards referred to her as the Ridge Runner. Thelma Mothershed was so tiny and timid that she didn't invite difficulty. Gloria Ray, luckily in classes where she had good acceptance, was also careful; she never tried to cross the flow of student traffic until she could do so without personal contact. Melba and Minnijean walked across it when they needed to, just as the white students did; their contacts, however, caused resentment as those of white students did not. Elizabeth was more anxious to be independent than safe. Ernest had an even disposition, not easily ruffled; and Terrence, with his high intelligence and sense of humor held his head high and attended to matters in hand without inviting trouble. Jefferson's difficulties came mainly from his tentativeness, a manner that tormentors often respond to with cruelty.

By Monday the knowledge of the relaxed guard would be general. So in the daily bulletin for October 28 we tried to strike an optimistic but positive note:

Except for the flu, we had a good eighth week of school. It is a pleasure to see more and more of our students assuming responsibility
for their own conduct. Under the present circumstances, and following the disturbed conditions in our community, each student needs
to exercise more care than usual; for rudeness may easily be interpreted as disorder. The aim of all of us must be to return to our
usual situation, in which each Central High School student follows
the rules of good citizenship in a democratic school: that is, that
each student conforms to the rules established for the good of all,
and that each student respects every other student and his rights.

On Monday, at the beginning of the last class period, a guard
brought to my office a girl who he said had shoved Elizabeth
Eckford at noon, or, rather, had shoved a friend into Elizabeth, who
had then turned and grabbed the arm of the girl whose shoulder
had hit her. The two white girls had run off before the guard could
stop them; but he had watched for them, and now he brought in a
short, round-faced girl whom I came to know well before the year
was over. Now, she insisted that she and her girl friend were just
playing. I sent for her friend. She was a tall, pale, passive girl, with
a peculiar sway-backed walk that swung her hips in a way that
often got attention. She had a slow, sultry smile, with which she
responded to wolf whistles or remarks. This friend agreed that the
girl the guard had brought in had shoved her into Elizabeth, and
she held out her arm to show me where the black girl had
scratched her. I saw a faintly pink line, but the outer skin was not
broken and no blood drawn. I took the two girls to the bench in
front of the principal's office, leaving them while I told Jess the
story. We agreed that the two girls should be suspended. Then I
ushered the girls in.

The girl who had done the shoving repeated the story, protesting that she "loved Negroes," would probably go to school with
them in Arizona or New Mexico when she moved there later in the
year. She assured us that she and her friend "played rough" all the
time in the halls. Why, only yesterday the friend had shoved *her*
into Ernest Green and she had said "Excuse me" and he had said
"Certainly." The second girl was silent, except to agree with the
first that they played rough in the halls.

Jess sent the girls back to the bench while we conferred. We were sure that the target of their shoving had been Elizabeth, but it seemed to us that the girl who got scratched had probably got the worst of the encounter and that we might avoid a blowup and gain some peace and quiet about school by putting them under a peace bond, so to speak. Every "arrest" by a guard was just another challenge to the segregationists in the community. We recalled the girls to the office and warned them that any further aggressive acts would make them eligible for suspension.

The next day I realized that I had made one bad mistake. I had not called in Miss Carpenter to inspect the scratched girl's wounds. Never again, whether there was any visible hurt or not, did I make this mistake. The girl's mother reported to the papers that her daughter had been "scratched and clawed by a Negro girl" in school, so badly, in fact, that she had taken her to the hospital where she had been given a tetanus shot.

On Monday, Superintendent Blossom, J. O., and I met with the black parents, who had asked for a progress report. We arrived at the Administration Building at 4:45, just as some of the children and their parents got there, in two or three cars. Upstairs in the school board meeting room Daisy Bates, there as the children's sponsor, was distributing the fan mail of the day to her charges, each of whom already had a large group of pen pals and an extensive foreign stamp collection. As I recall, Elizabeth Eckford's grandfather was there, Gloria Ray's father, Melba Pattillo's mother, Minnijean Brown's mother, Ernest Green's mother, Thelma Mothershed's mother, Carlotta Walls's mother, and Jefferson Thomas's mother. I noted in my journal that I liked them all. I do not remember that anyone had much to contribute to the conference. J. O. and I spoke briefly about our willingness to help with any hard spots at school. Mr. Blossom spoke, more at length, about the responsibilities of the Nine and their parents. Perhaps the meeting gave the parents a better knowledge of those persons charged with the school protection of their youngsters.

As we left, at 6 P.M., Minnijean came up to me in the parking lot. "Mrs. Huckaby," she said, "can I be in the Christmas program? I need to know as soon as I can so I can get a white dress." When I asked Jess about it the next day, he said he would talk with Mr. Blossom and try to decide as soon as he could.

The deep fears and prejudices that made an issue of Minnijean's singing with her class on the Christmas program were further illustrated by an anonymous call to Jess, warning him of a situation he needed to attend to right away: a girl who belonged to the National Honor Society was sitting next to Ernest Green every day at lunch; it looked like a love affair, and Mr. Matthews needed to break it up. I made a trip or two to the cafeteria at noon and saw white students at the table with Ernest, Carlotta, Gloria, and Melba; but the socializing was quite general, and I reported this to Jess. But the anonymous prodder called again, and he asked me to speak to one of our top-ranking students, an independent, liberal-minded, attractive girl who had evidently been named as being too friendly.

Jess asked me to talk to the girl, and I did. But her only response was a direct gaze and the twitching of her upper lip. I felt like a heel. I believe, now, it would have been better to have let her parents deal with the matter as they chose. Josephine Feiock, her homeroom teacher, knowing nothing of the anonymous calls, had reported that the girl was being snubbed by her peers, among whom was a boy whose father was a prominent businessman in Little Rock and a member of the Citizens' Council.

Jess talked with Ernest and advised him to arrange, always, to have one of the black girls sit beside him at lunch so that any other girl who sat at the table would be insulated, so to speak, from criticism. I noticed that Ernest followed this suggestion—as he did every other one that was given him throughout the year.

On Thursday, October 31, Jess, Orlana Hensley of the Guidance Services, and Josephine Feiock of the English Department left for the annual Freshman-Principals Conference at the University of Arkansas in Fayetteville. That left J. O. and me—and the army—in charge of Central. We had only minor incidents; five white kids, walking five abreast down the hall asked Minnijean, who was standing in the middle of the corridor, to move. Minnijean reportedly replied, "Go to hell," and a small disturbance ensued. Five abreast was no way to walk—unless you wanted trouble. The middle of the corridor was no place to stand. If the racial element had not been present, nothing would have happened. But it was there; so we had the challenge, and the response. On Friday, Melba Pattillo said that someone in her homeroom had shoved a chair into her back, and, later, that she was the target of spitballs. But our biggest administrative problem, on Friday, was to get substitute teachers. Flu had finally struck the faculty, as it had struck the students earlier. Jess returned Monday to a short week because schools were to be closed on Thursday and Friday for the State Teachers' Association meeting.

But the events on Tuesday proved that our progress was principally a matter of crossing off the days and not of solving our problems. A girl came to the health room before school to get treatment for facial scratches. She reported that she had been in a fight with some black girls on the South Highland bus on her way to school. The bus inspector had taken down the Central girl's name, she reported, but the black girl had refused to give hers.

I reported the incident to Mr. Blossom's office and to Dr. L. M. Christophe, principal of all-black Horace Mann High School, and to Edwin Hawkins, principal of all-black Dunbar Junior High. Mr. Hawkins called back later to report that he had identified the girl with whom our student had had the altercation. He and I agreed that counseling was the only action we should take in the case. I can't say I was sorry when I was unable to reach our girl's mother by telephone. Her daughter had been in the walkout, and I was pretty sure what the family's attitude toward the fight would have been.

In late morning a guard reported that he had intervened in a scene in the lower hall. A small white girl had called out some obscene remarks to one of the black girls. As the guard came up to ask the name-caller to come with him to the office, one of her companions, a boy, had grabbed the guard's arm and the girl had escaped into the lavatory. The guard said he knew where to watch for the small girl in the afternoon, and he would let me know where to find her.

After lunch the guard returned to tell me that the girl and one of her friends had exchanged clothes at noon in an apparent attempt to confuse him; but he knew which girl he wanted.

As the afternoon classes began, the guard came back to tell me that the girl he wanted was in the sewing class in Room 405. I was just leaving my office with him to see which girl he meant when

Grace Dupree, the teacher in 405, came in with the girl, who, Mrs. Dupree said, reported that a guard was chasing her. I recognized the girl, behind in school for her age and with a truancy record. I took her to Jess's office. She was defiant. She had a right to say anything she wanted to. Minnijean was a nigger, and she could call out about her if she wanted to. She had changed clothes with her friend (the girl who had testified to the state police about Dr. Fine of the New York *Times*); but that had nothing to do with the case. She and her friend changed clothes all the time, and they had planned to do it today before all this came up. As she talked, she became more excited, almost hysterical. "I hate niggers!" she screamed. Jess, despairing of getting anywhere with her, sent her home, and he asked me to call her mother in for a conference.

At the beginning of the last class period of the day, Minnijean came to my office and waited ten or fifteen minutes to see me. She reported the affair of this morning with the small white girl. After I heard her report, I asked whether she wasn't missing an American history class, and sent her on with a late-to-class permit. After school, Margaret Stewart, Minnijean's history teacher, asked me whether it had been necessary for Minnijean to miss part of her history class. The class had been told yesterday that they would have a test today, and Minnijean had missed half the test. Minnijean, Miss Stewart said, was not making any effort to get her history lessons, and this was not the first test she had missed. Miss Stewart thought Minnijean was "soldiering on the job," and I was inclined to agree with her.

On Wednesday morning, the small girl's mother came with her to school, and we conferred with the principal. This Minnijean was a troublemaker, the mother said. Her family had deliberately moved into the Central High district, she asserted; and on the day the Negroes had come to school to register, Minnijean had picked a fight with white children on the drugstore corner. (These assertions were without any factual basis, so far as we could tell, but were typical of rumors spread by the Mothers' League.) We had never heard of these charges, naturally. Her daughter, the mother asserted, was not happy in Central and was after her mother all the time to let her go to California to her father, though her stepfather was better to her than her own father had ever been. Her daughter had been "chased by a Negro" when she was a small child, the mother said, and had always been frightened of them.

I went to the bench outside the office to bring the girl herself into the conference. She had disappeared, and I finally found her with her clothes-changing friend in the phone booth in the hall. I scolded her for leaving the bench and took her into the principal's office. She would not agree to anything. She would call people anything she wanted to, she insisted. That guard had no right to stop her. She hadn't used any words she shouldn't—just *nigger*. And Minnijean had insulted her one time and called her a midget. (I remembered.) The girl cried and railed in her high, whining voice. Jess told her mother either to take her home or make her behave. He had no further time for hysterics. Later in the morning the mother got a weak agreement from her that she would stay clear of the black students. She had no classes with any of them. Then the mother said her daughter was too upset to stay at school the rest of the day and took her on with her.

Captain Madden came to my office mopping his brow. The pair had talked with him, the mother demanding to know what words her daughter had used that were so bad yesterday. "I told her that I couldn't repeat in her presence the words the sergeant had reported. She said her daughter didn't use profanity; but before long the girl let out a string, and I said, 'Madam, it was something like that.'"

By the end of the day, we were ready for the two-day respite from school offered by the Arkansas Education Association meeting. There had even been some evidence on Tuesday that not everyone in Little Rock was crazy, for six of the seven Little Rock city director positions had been filled in the election by Good Government candidates, who had defeated, by narrow margins in some cases, the segregationist candidates of the Citizens' Council or the Mothers' League.

After the holiday, Monday passed rather peacefully. But before school on Tuesday morning a girl, recently readmitted after her part in the walkout, came to the health room for treatment of her eye—a sty, she said. But to a skeptical Miss Carpenter, who examined the eye, she admitted that she had got the injury as she boarded a bus for school. A black had "picked a fight" with her, she said. She was the second of our returned walkouts to report an out-of-school racial fight. In neither case was the black a CHS student.

On Tuesday afternoon, just before the seventh period, while Jefferson Thomas stood facing his locker, a white boy whom he didn't recognize came up, turned him around, and knocked him flat.

By Wednesday morning all the kids in the school knew the identity of the boy who bragged that he had struck Jefferson. He probably couldn't have brought himself to hit Minnijean, though he had been one of the boys in the corridor confrontation with her on October 31. When Jess Matthews sent for the boy and asked him whether he had hit Jefferson, he denied it. Jefferson could not identify his attacker, and there were no witnesses.

This boy was ordinarily a likable, pugnacious, off-beat sort of kid, not quite good enough in football to make the team, where he would have been kept under control. I had known him from his junior high days, for his father and my husband had occasionally played golf together. I had taught one of his uncles a few years before in Central. As this boy walked through the hall between classes this morning, I watched him—and he watched me. I knew what he had done, and he knew that I knew, as did many others. At noon, he raised himself in my estimation by going to the principal and admitting his deed. He was suspended. And the next day's bulletin was still reminding teachers to stand at their doors and observe the halls between classes.

I had been searching my mind for a project that might give some of the high school students some perception of the fact that the prevalent local view of integration was not the only one or even the most widely accepted one. The scheme I came up with was not very effective, but it was the only one I was able to devise during the whole year.

Each Wednesday morning before school I had been accustomed to meet with the Pentangle Board, made up of two representatives from each of our five service clubs for junior and senior girls. I had not called the group together so far this year, for I could not take before-school time for meetings. But now it occurred to me that these girls might learn something from reading and answering some of the letters we were receiving from foreign countries. They would find little international approval of what had happened, though the tone of the letters was more in sorrow than in anger. After all the girls had read, with many exclamations of surprise, some of the letters from far-off places, they devised a form letter, much too long, apologetic, and uncritical of state authorities; and it ended with pious platitudes. But when the composition committee read us the letter, I questioned only one phrase, that describing the mob in front of the school in September as people who wanted to "stir up trouble." That was how I saw them; but I was aware that the Mothers' League and the Citizens' Council had declared that the crowd was made up largely of parents and citizens concerned for the safety of children, or merely curious. I wanted to find out what these girls thought. They insisted that the mob was made up of troublemakers. So their wording remained in the letter, which follows:

Dear ———:

We received your letter concerning the Little Rock crisis and sincerely appreciate your interest. We realize that it is inevitable that your comments were based on newspaper reports. We were shocked at them ourselves. Because most of us were inside the school continuing our daily work, we could not observe any of the violence and were therefore unaware of the incidents which have caused you to be alarmed.

The disturbing reports which you received concerned only a small number of our population. The violence was confined to a small area and appears to have been started by those wanting to excite trouble. These acts, unfortunately, were fully reported but did not necessarily reflect a true picture of our community.

Because reporters were not allowed in the school, there was little mention of the majority of the students, who objected to violence, regardless of their own opinions. They sought to continue their education in the usual manner, to conduct themselves properly, and to accept the laws of our country. We are writing you, not to deny the unfortunate conflict, but to reveal a clearer picture of the situation.

Today, Central High School represents an ordinary school of our nation. Our educational program has not been changed, and the students continue enjoying their activities such as sports and club organizations. Although the nine Negro students are facing a difficult situation at Central this year, they are attending regularly and progressing in their classes.

In closing, we of Central High School sincerely hope that this letter will help you to form a clearer conception of our actions. What the world needs now is a "peace that passes all understanding"; many students at Central are working toward that peace. Although problems arise, we must all forever strive for peace throughout the world and understanding between people and nations.

———, Secretary
Pentangle Service Board

Perhaps the only good result of the project was a bit of education for the ten or twelve girls who read the foreign letters. Some of them received pleasant replies. In May, Mary Ann Mathews, president of the board, showed me a scathing response from Heidelberg, Germany, asking for more truth and less piety in reply to his letter. I told Mary Ann to reply or not, as she and her parents might think best.

My attention on Wednesday morning was not all directed to the Pentangle Board as they read and exclaimed about the letters they were to answer. I had the door to my office open so that I could see across the hall and into the auditorium where the cheerleaders, promoting attendance at the football game for Friday night, were admitting ticket holders to an early-morning pep dance. On Monday, Mildred Cromwell, one of the cheerleaders, had asked Jess what he thought about admitting Carlotta Walls and Jefferson Thomas, who both "just love to dance." Jess had asked my opinion, and I had said that I thought it was their privilege as much as anyone's. But I warned Mildred that some kids would quit dancing if Carlotta and Jefferson joined the group. Mrs. Baker, who supervised students at noon at Campus Inn, had told me that all jukebox dancing had stopped there on the one occasion that Minnijean and Melba had wandered in. I told Mildred that, if dancing stopped, it would be up to the cheerleaders and their boyfriends not to leave the black couple dancing alone on the stage. She agreed.

Evidently the news had gotten around for a crowd gathered in the auditorium, and Captain Madden was watching from the front hall. But the two black kids did not show up, possibly because of the attack on Jefferson Tuesday.

Also on Wednesday, we braced ourselves for the first PTA meeting of the year, two months late. Ordinarily the entire PTA met in the auditorium for the business part of the meeting and then moved to the separate, smaller meeting places for class-level panels. But this year, Mrs. Stephens, the president, her program chairman, and Jess had decided that a better plan would be not to have a general meeting but to go directly into the small groups, moving the officers from group to group to carry on the business, hear the minutes, and approve the recommendations of the board. There were rumors that some members might stage a walkout if blacks came, and to divide the group into three sections might diminish the effect of any such demonstration.

As a member of the panel of teachers before the tenth grade parents, I met with that group in the main auditorium. Two black parents, a man and a woman whom I didn't recognize, were already seated near the front when I entered. Twenty-five or thirty other parents were there when the meeting opened, and about a third of Central's faculty. The PTA officers presented the business to this section first. Another black parent came in and sat near the back of the auditorium; I recognized Carlotta's mother. The officers, after completing the business meeting, moved on and our panel took charge. Afterwards I spoke to the couple down front, who identified themselves as Elizabeth Eckford's parents. I told them that we were glad to have them but that, since Elizabeth was a junior, they would have found the junior section more informative than this tenth grade group. They asked where that group was meeting and left to join it; but it had already broken up. When I told Jess of the Eckfords' mistake, he said it was probably a fortunate one. A mother in the junior group was all ready to lead a walkout if any black had come to the junior section. But the only black parents to attend had come to the tenth grade meeting.

At the end of the week, the 101st troops were leaving Little Rock, their stay prolonged past the most pessimistic prognostications. On the calendar on my office wall, Captain Madden pointed out to me the date he had thought they would be able to leave when he had arrived on September 24. That date was October 1, a date that was more than six weeks past. Our "return to normal" was painfully slow.

Many of those who had worked with Captain Madden had become very fond of him. We saw in him not only an efficient, capable officer but an appealing young man. He and I had collaborated on one nonracial problem, in our different ways. A senior girl, the prettiest in school in Captain Madden's estimation, had become the object of the affections of a young private who had been at Central briefly with the first contingent of the 101st. The girl's foster mother called me about the romance, which she felt had become too serious. She had no objection to the young man, except for his precipitousness. He had returned to Little Rock over the weekend and insisted that the girl marry him at once. The girl was agreeable, but her parents were not; and there had been a family fuss. The young soldier (a letter had been intercepted) was trying to get his girl to run away and marry him in Kentucky. I suggested that the mother talk over the problem with a counselor at the Family Service Agency, and I told her that I would ask Captain Madden to counsel with the boy. "Counsel!" barked Captain Madden. "I'll give orders!" And so he did, with the result that the boy was restricted to base and reduced in rank for leaving Kentucky on a weekend pass not valid for a trip to Little Rock. A footnote: The girl soon married another young man, one whom she had known for a long time, and dropped out of school.

Captain Madden was homesick and anxious to get back to his wife and two small sons, and to get acquainted with his baby daughter, born a couple of weeks before he had to come to Little Rock. He had told me about his mother in South Carolina, a "bridge-playing Presbyterian." I had taken Dr. Boggs, the Presbyterian minister and a South Carolinian, to the back office to meet Captain Madden one morning when Dr. Boggs had been the speaker at the Chapel Club.

We who knew him wanted to wish Captain Madden luck as he went back to Fort Campbell, although some faculty members had never spoken to him, feeling so strongly about his unit's "invasion of states' rights." Nevertheless, the office force invited all teachers to drop by the conference room between 8:30 and 10:30 on Thursday, November 14 for coffee and doughnuts. Miss Carpenter bought toy stuffed tigers for the captain to take to his little boys. J. O. Powell fixed up a mock Arkansas Traveler certificate, like the ones the governor's office handed out to favored persons. About half the faculty dropped by to tell Captain Madden goodbye.

Later in the morning Mary Ann Rath came to my office with

Minnijean Brown, who was crying. "Mrs. Huckaby, you talked to me when I was upset this fall, and I thought you could talk with Minnijean," said Mary Ann. She was one of the few white girls who continued to walk down the hall with Minnijean.

Some girl whom Minnijean believed to be her friend had cut her as they passed in the hall. "I guess it was because she was with her boy friend, and he doesn't want her to be friends with Negroes," Minnijean sobbed. "I'm just tired of it all." I gave my sympathy, but told her that being tired of it all was not reason enough to give up now. Poor Minnijean; affectionate, impetuous, undisciplined, she needed so much help, and there were so few to help her.

The vice-principals had told the black children to report hard spots around school. Gloria Ray stopped by to tell me of a boy in her homeroom who, the week before, had called her a nigger and threatened to kill her. This morning, as they left assembly, the same boy had shoved her into the wall. Margaret Stewart, her homeroom teacher, knew the boy, and she was careful to see that he did not bother Gloria in or near homeroom again, though we heard of him in other places.

Vivian Daniel came to tell me of a boy who had asked her in front of the homeroom whether "a nigger girl had a right" to elbow him. As one of the walkouts, his opinion on integration was on the record. But he said he had not started the trouble, that it had happened as he went into the office before school to see Mary Meltabarger, his history teacher. He said he didn't know the black girl's name; but when he described her, members of the homeroom said it was Carlotta. I called the boy in to ask for details. He disclaimed any intention of implying that the elbowing was deliberate, and I dropped the matter. I thought it most unlikely that Carlotta would know anything about such an incident.

Melba and Ernest also reported situations that might be leading to trouble. Ernest reported to me because J. O. was in and out that day, to the hospital and back, for his wife, Velma, was hospitalized after suffering a miscarriage.

I met my English classes myself in the library on Thursday morning to help them choose biographies to read outside class. After describing some of the books available and showing the class where they were to be found, I watched the youngsters go to the shelves to inspect and choose books. Carlotta, in my first class, got up quickly with the others and went right to the shelves with the rest. In my next class, Jefferson hung back from the rest and finally wandered off to look through books in a far section of the library. Carlotta was somehow more confident. But after all, Jefferson had been decked once.

On Friday morning before school, when word was brought to me that some girls were fighting in the first-floor hall, my heart sank. When I learned that one white girl had hauled off and socked another white girl in a scuffle over a bit of gossip, I felt an odd relief. I had almost forgotten that the kids at Central could have trouble that wasn't racial.

But that day there was racial trouble, too. Melba reported that two boys from her homeroom waited for her almost daily outside the door and cursed her as she entered. I passed the report on to J. O., who talked with the boys. That seems very little to have done; but had we accepted reports about the actions of whites toward blacks without witnesses, how could we have failed to accept unsupported reports of whites about blacks? Had we ever begun accepting those reports without teacher verification, they would have been manufactured so fast and would have been so heinous that, in no time at all, no black student would have been in school. To protect the Nine from such tactics, we frequently had to leave them vulnerable to indignities, except for the vigilance of teachers and guards.

Today was Color Day at school, with all the pupils wearing the school colors, black and gold. For those who came to school by oversight without the colors, the student council had provided gold streamers printed with a pep slogan in black. One segregationist girl challenged Minnijean's right to wear her streamer as she entered the cafeteria at noon. So Minnijean tore off the streamer, threw it down, and stepped on it. She could do nothing to please her classmates.

For Color Day, homeroom doors were decorated in competition. Marie King's homeroom door depicted the members of the Little Rock Tiger football team descending by parachute (a reference to the 101st Airborne) to conquer their rivals, the Pine Bluff Zebras.

Captain Madden, leaving at noon, admired the decoration so much that Miss King's homeroom packed the poster for him to take with him to Kentucky. With Captain Madden's departure, the federalized National Guard was now in complete charge at Central.

Because of the change in command, we rather expected trouble on Monday, November 18. But nothing unusual happened; nor was there trouble on Tuesday. On Wednesday the only unhappy report was from Elizabeth Eckford, who was shoved during her gym class. The girls in the gym dressing room sometimes sang songs, she said. Elizabeth's eyes twinkled and she giggled briefly. "Some of the songs are really funny," she said. Too bad the girls wouldn't allow themselves to get to know Elizabeth. She thought the same things funny that they did.

Jess was in low spirits on Wednesday. One of his student friends, the same boy who had reported to Mrs. Feiock about the white girl's fraternization with the black students at the lunch table, had shown Jess a petition being circulated by the Capital Citizens' Council asking for his dismissal for "selling out to the Virgil Blossom crowd" and misrepresenting incidents at school. Jess had always been a hail-fellow-well-met person, genuinely fond of lots of people and enjoying their expressions of approval. This public expression of disapproval, however insane it was, really hurt him.

The news on Wednesday that the local judge, Harry Robinson, had freed thirteen men charged with violence in the September disorders outside the school was disappointing, though not unexpected. We were still confident that there would be federal action against the inciters of the violent rejection of the orders of the federal court. The new attorney general, William P. Rogers, it was true, had been rather quickly approved by the Senate, an indication to some observers that a deal might have been made. Surely, though, the federal authorities would maintain order, even without troops. We would just have to wait and see.

All week long there had been a stir of talk among the kids at school about the junior talent assembly, which was in preparation, the question being whether Minnijean Brown was to be on it. And would she sing "Tammy"? Our vocal music teacher, Naomi Hancock, told me that Minnijean had a good voice, and because of her talent she was probably better accepted in Glee Club than in any other class. I suspected that Minnijean had promoted the story of her plan to try out, partly from a real desire to be on the program and partly to tease. The segregationist pupils were promoting it, too, for an issue. At least two among them, a boy and a girl, both popular entertainers, had said they would not sing on the program with Minnijean. But Helen Hazel, the teacher in charge, had told me that Minnijean had not even registered to try out, and the date for such application was past.

The try-outs were to be held in the auditorium after school. I stood at my door in the hall across from the auditorium, as usual, observing till the last of the black students went past from their lockers to their car at the Sixteenth Street exit. Minnijean, Melba, and Thelma walked by slowly. I saw Minnijean hesitate at the door, looking into the auditorium. Both Melba and Thelma were arguing with her and shaking their heads, but Minnijean still hesitated.

I walked over. "*Can* I try out, Mrs. Huckaby?" Minnijean asked. She was teasing me, I knew. She probably was not even aware that the deadline for applying to try out was two days past, for Minnijean was careless of such formalities. But she wanted, desperately, to do something before the student body that she knew she could do well, and I wished that I could help her.

"You know as well as I do that it wouldn't do, Minnijean," I said. And the girls went on toward the exit.

On Thursday a guardsman brought a poorly dressed, overweight, and thoroughly distraught girl to my office. He had seen, inside the door of her locker as she opened it, a hand-lettered poster on newsprint, reading IKE FOR DOGCATCHER—PD. FOR BY DAISY BATES.

The girl wouldn't look at me. "Go on and expel me," she said, sitting with her back toward me. I told her that I had no intention of expelling her. I merely wanted to point out that we could not have public disrespect for the president posted in our school. Speaking to her back, I tried to calm what was evidently genuine hatred and terror. "I hate those Yankee soldiers," was her only response. I dropped the poster into the wastebasket and sent the girl on to class.

Early Friday morning Glen came in, grinning. "Sis, look out the window." The ground was white with a thin layer of snow. At school, the snow made a change in plans necessary. The football team was to play in Blytheville that night. As usual, a bus load of cheerleaders and pep squad members was scheduled to follow the team, leaving the school at 2:30. The snow, which extended into northeast Arkansas, would make some highways slick, and Jess moved the bus's time of departure to noon so that it could proceed more slowly. And he made a last-minute decision to ride with the girls and their faculty sponsors. On a previous trip this year, the girls had taken some rude heckling about our integrated school, and at Blytheville, in the East Arkansas cotton-growing section of the state, they might meet this rudeness again.

School moved peacefully this day. After the last pupils, black and white, had left, I went to the main office. A call had just come in from Jess, who had been upset by a radio report he had heard from a Memphis station about a rock-throwing fracas at Little Rock High. J. O. had assured him that our snow was all gone, that no such fight had taken place here, but that the afternoon paper reported an incident near North Little Rock High in which students there had injured a passing black woman by hitting her in the eye with a rock encased in a snowball. Bad as that was, Jess was relieved. It hadn't happened at Central.

TROOPS COST 3.4 MILLION the *Arkansas Democrat* headlined on November 22. The story carried the by-line of a reporter whose brother was one of our segregationist students. The article cited as authority "a source close to Governor Faubus." Sunday's *Democrat*, November 24, mentioned a new prospective date for the special session of the legislature to be called by Faubus to enact anti-integration laws: LEGISLATORS SEE SPECIAL SESSION IN MARCH.

It looked as if we might make it to the Thanksgiving holidays. And we almost did. But at the end of pep assembly on Wednesday, November 27, Minnijean came by my office to report that she had been kicked as she went to her assembly seat. She showed me the large red spot on her leg. J. O. talked to the boy she accused, but he denied it. There were no teacher witnesses, so it was his word against hers. The only sure thing was that Minnijean had been kicked.

Our Thanksgiving holidays could be days of thankfulness that we had no school and for two days had no school problems. Tuesday's *Arkansas Democrat* had carried a picture of an ahead-of-time Thanksgiving dinner given the CHS Nine by Robert Gray, a Canadian public relations man, at which the blacks were quoted as "thankful for America." This ironic declaration was relieved by a quotation from Melba Pattillo. When the host asked her whether she wanted white or dark meat, she said she would take hers integrated—some of both.

On Monday, December 2, one of the teachers who had a daughter in school brought me a copy of a mimeographed letter that the Mothers' League had sent to parents of our pupils:

November 29, 1957

Dear Friend:

"When evil men conspire, good men must get together." These were the words of a great English statesman, spoken to his people in dark and troublesome times. We face such times today. Never has there been such a conspiracy of evil forces confronting free men. A divine providence, it seems, has decreed that a most critical phase of this conflict is to be fought in Little Rock, Arkansas. We are now in that conflict. A staggering force is before us.

We must awaken, arouse, and alert those who do not as yet understand the wickedness of those forces arrayed against us. The control of our schools, the education of our children, the sanctity and dignity of human freedom—everything that free men hold dear is in process of being gradually taken away from us. This is being done in the name of Brotherhood, piety, and law and order.

Monday night at the Legion Hut at 24th and Wolfe Street, Little Rock, Ark., at 7:30 P.M. the Mothers' League of Central High is having a most important meeting. Won't you please arrange your affairs so that you can be present this Monday, December 2.

WHAT CAN I DO ABOUT IT?

This question is usually asked in a sense of helplessness and futility. At this meeting Monday night we are dealing specifically with this question. The meeting is open to everyone who believes in States rights, racial integrity and that our public schools should be kept segregated. Rev. Wesley Pruden, pastor Broadmoor Baptist Church is our speaker. His subject "SHALL WE QUIT THE FIGHT—WHAT IS OUR HOPE"

We sincerely hope you can be present and bring a neighbor with you.

Mothers' League of Central High

The *Student Directory*, published by our student council, containing the names, addresses, and phone numbers of our students, was proving a handy mailing list for the Mothers' League. Segregationist youngsters, and probably oldsters, were using it, too, to harass the black students at home. Having their names included, to treat our students alike, in Central's directory, was making their phones instruments of torture to interrupt their studies, keep them and their families awake at night, and subject them to profanity and obscenity, all by anonymous callers.

On Monday, December 2, there was more National Guard brass at school than usual. The last unit of the 101st had flown back from Camp Robinson, Arkansas, to Fort Campbell, Kentucky, two weeks after they stopped appearing at Central. There had been rumors of some sort of demonstration to celebrate that complete withdrawal, but none developed. The brass went back to headquarters, and we went on with school.

On Tuesday I called in Carlotta for a conference. She seemed to me the black girl most generally accepted by all the students. She was such a good sport, it was hard to see how anyone could work up much steam for hating her. Besides that, she was a good student and went her own way independently. In our conference she offered no complaints. Under my prodding, however, she finally mentioned some boys and a girl or two in her biology class who said unfriendly things to her, and two boys in her English class who threw paper wads and small objects at her when Mrs. Means wasn't looking. One of these boys was extremely small for his age, and it seemed to amuse Carlotta, somehow, that he would throw at her. "He's so *little*," she laughed.

On Wednesday morning, as the Pentangle Board members worked at answering the foreign letters, one of the girls asked, "Is it true, Mrs. Huckaby, that fifty more Negroes are going to enroll at Central at midterm?" "Why, certainly not," I said. "No one ever transfers from one high school to another at midterm, except in an emergency." It was one of those rumors constantly being circulated to keep feelings stirred up.

The popular girl singer accepted for the talent assembly came to see me about her number on that program. She wanted to sing an Ertha Kitt impersonation of "Saint Louis Blues," but the teacher in charge of the program wondered what I thought of that. "Absolutely, no," I told her. "Now, if Minnijean Brown could be on the program and sing what *she* wanted to, I wouldn't object." The white girl claimed, at first, that she didn't know of any white singers she could impersonate, but she eventually found one.

On Thursday, December 5, Melba Pattillo asked the principal to let her drop French and take speech. She had dropped chemistry to take French earlier in the year after her late entrance had put her so far behind in chemistry. Although Melba protested that her previous speech training would make catching up in speech easy for her, Jess would not approve another change. He allowed her to drop French; but she was assigned an extra study hall in its place.

Since Minnijean had asked me about her appearing with her choral group on the Christmas program, Jess and I had discussed the matter several times, with Naomi Hancock, the music teacher, in on some of our talks. Jess had said no to her appearing on the evening program before the PTA, feeling that the kind of adult crowd we would have would be out of our control. He was still considering the possibility of letting her be in her group on our student assembly program, when Naomi reported that Minnijean herself had decided that it would not be wise for her to appear on the stage. So it was something of a surprise when I got back to school on Friday, December 6, from the luncheon meeting of the Family Service Board (the first time that year I had felt it possible to leave school for this civic responsibility) to find Minnijean in Jess's office asking him whether she could appear on the assembly program. He told her that he had understood that she had decided not to and that that was his decision, too. After the conference, he told me that he was sure that Minnijean had been told to ask him that question. He knew that I had felt all along that she should sing with her class at assembly. It was just part of her being in school, it seemed to me. But Jess said that some things had been reported to him by boys about what might happen if she did appear; and I did not question his decision.

A week and a half was left before the Christmas holidays. As was customary at Central, homerooms were planning Christmas gifts of large baskets of food and small gifts of toys to needy families. I was supplying names and addresses of these families from among those with youngsters in our school, carefully preserving their identity from other children by giving the information only to the homeroom teacher. Our students have always been so generous with their gifts that I needed to supplement our list of families with additional names from Goodfellows and Family Service, and from grammar schools and junior highs. For years, one homeroom or another had sent a basket to the family of the black woman who worked for Opie. Opie, herself, always supplemented the food basket by adding shoes and clothes bought for the big family of youngsters; and she placed the name of the family with Goodfellows so that the mother could pick out toys there.

This year, for the first time, I struck a snag in these arrangements. Opie's cleaning woman was the only black on my list, but I soon found that no homeroom would take a black family to help. Our recipients had been of both races in previous years with no questions or objections. I began to be aware of the change in attitude when one teacher came in to ask me point blank whether the family I had assigned her homeroom was white. It was. I knew her feelings well enough not to assign her homeroom a black family. But the teachers I did approach about Opie's maid were not encouraging. "Of course I'll take the family; but I'll just have to keep it a secret from the homeroom that they are Negroes. Otherwise my youngsters won't help," said one. I couldn't agree to this subterfuge. I would just call Goodfellows and make an exchange with them: if they would supply this family with Christmas dinner, we would take, in exchange, two of their white families.

I called Mrs. Loyd Watt at Goodfellows and made my proposal. She was apologetic. "We're not registering Negro families this year," she said. "There are too many objections. No one will give if Negroes are registered. I can give you the phone number of a Negro agency that is going to list their own people if you want it." I didn't. Poor Little Rock. We had sunk even further than I had realized. I told Opie, and she said she would take care of the maid's family herself, somehow.

On Monday, December 9, Jess had alerted me for a conference

with Minnijean's mother. She had asked that J. O. Powell be present, too. Jess presumed that the Christmas music program would be the subject of the meeting. Just before the time for the conference, he came down the hall to tell me that not only Mrs. Brown, but also Daisy Bates was waiting in the office to see us. He was upset about Mrs. Brown's bringing Mrs. Bates. He didn't mind conferring with any parent; but Mrs. Bates was not a patron of the school. However, he would go ahead with the conference.

Mrs. Brown began the conference directly by saying that she and Minnijean were very much disappointed at Mr. Matthews's decision not to permit Minnijean to sing with her group on the Christmas program. She advanced, as part of her argument, the fact that it was a scheduled class activity, that it would mean much to Minnijean, that her classmates in glee club recognized her ability to sing, that Christmas was a time of goodwill. All her arguments were valid. To them, Jess replied that, in his judgment, her appearance on the program would be unwise under present circumstances.

Mrs. Bates joined the discussion. The chief point she wished to make was that Mr. Matthews lacked control over the students; he failed to enforce discipline. Here, I came to his defense, telling Mrs. Bates what I believed to be true: that with anyone else as principal of Central, the school would have gone to pieces in September or October. It was teachers' and pupils' loyalty to him that had kept them on the job during those days. Mrs. Bates then further chided us for not doing anything to educate our pupils to accept integration. To this I pointed out the difficulties and dangers to which we were being subjected merely for complying with it. It was evident that we could not hope to succeed in any education more pointed than our continual reminders of the duties of good school and community citizenship, which had been our almost daily effort through the school bulletin and through counseling.

Mrs. Bates kept returning to the discipline theme. Minnijean had been kicked, and nothing had been done about it. Jess said he *had* done something about it: that the matter had been investigated and was still under investigation; that the boy suspected had been questioned, but that since he would not admit the act and no teacher had witnessed it, we were unable to support the charge.

I broke in here to say that Minnijean herself had not followed up on her responsibility in the matter. On last Friday morning, just as the assembly was starting, she had come to my office to say that she could point out the boy who had kicked her. I did not want to disrupt the program by causing the stir that my entrance and her pointing an accusing finger would have done; so I asked her to go back and note the seat number of the boy she wanted to point out and to tell me just as soon as the assembly was over. She had not come back.

Mrs. Bates and I were doing most of the talking, a tendency I have in any conference. Our discussion was amicable, though we expressed different viewpoints, each with conviction. I realized that I was talking too much and fully expected Jess to tell me so, in a nice way. The conversation was still going on when the bell signaled the end of the class period. Jess excused himself hurriedly and made a brief excursion into the outer office. He had suddenly remembered, he told me later, that the boy who had knocked Jefferson down and had been readmitted to school, had been assigned to report to the bench outside his office because of some misbehavior unconnected with integration. This boy was not one he wanted to overhear our conference, even through a closed door.

I could see why Mrs. Bates was successful as president of the state NAACP. She was a good infighter, persistent, intelligent, unintimidated—a woman who had made a choice of this career fully aware of its dangers to her person and also its rewards in prestige and in service to her people. As we conferred, she had a notepad and pencil in her hands, which she later showed me to be marked only with doodling. I showed her mine—also doodling.

J. O. had sat silent all the while. Mrs. Bates asked for an expression from him, and he gave a brief statement of his ardent desire to help solve our problems but of his inability to suggest workable solutions. Mrs. Bates and I talked some more, but I don't recall that either of us said anything significant. I finally told Mrs. Bates that I was sure that she and I had different goals in mind for the Nine; that her goal was specifically the advancement of the colored people, but that mine had to be the advancement of the human race, to which both she and I and the black and white children all belonged. And since my field was education, my immediate goal was having the black children in school as just ordinary children. Mrs. Bates smiled and said she appreciated my attitude.

On Tuesday morning Minnijean came by, I was sure at the prompting of her mother or Mrs. Bates, to tell me that the boy who had kicked her had been sitting too far toward the middle of the row for her to get his seat number on Friday, but that he was sitting to the left of the teacher. I checked with Mrs. Barnett and learned that the boy to her left was our suspect and that the teacher had placed him beside her because of my report to her.

Later in the morning J. O. told me that he had the boy sitting on the bench in the office. He wanted Minnijean to see whether this was the right boy. I sent for her and asked her to look at the boy on the bench. She came back and reported that this was the boy who had kicked her. But when J. O. asked her whether she was sure that he had done the actual kicking, she said she couldn't be sure. The kick had come from a group of boys behind her, and this boy's comments to her afterward made her think he was the one taking credit for it. As we pointed out to her, her uncertainty was hardly sufficient evidence for the school to suspend the boy, though his guilt seemed highly probable.

I kept Minnijean for a while to discuss with her her lack of acceptance in Central and what we could do about it. She was too impulsive, too ready to come back at people, too unprepared to accept the heavy responsibilities of her difficult situation. It was hard to censure the language the group of students had used to her in the hall the other day—when she came back at them with similar words. I told her that I was aware of the constant strain she was under and even agreed that she was reacting as a sixteen-year-old might be expected to; but she had a job to do at Central that required the poise of a diplomat. She must try to teach herself not to react so fast. She needed, instead, to report offenders to us so that we could warn them and watch them.

I talked with Minnijean, too, about her attitude toward the federalized National Guard. Since they were not professional soldiers, they had not been as well trained as the 101st, and their performance in the early days of their assignment at Central was certainly not as efficient. But I was afraid that she was letting her resentment of their role in the governor's command to turn away the black students from Central on September 4 make her resent individual guardsmen who had had no part in that action. I reminded her of the uncomplimentary comparison she had made, in the presence of one man from the guard and one from the 101st, the day she had signed out ill and her mother had picked her up at the Fourteenth Street entrance. It was not a diplomatic thing to do, to antagonize those on whom you had to depend. Minnijean said she saw what I meant and would try to watch her speech.

By this time the last period had begun, and I hurried her on to her American history class. Jess and J. O. came in to discuss the kicking incident further. It was one of those troubling matters in which we were morally certain that we knew who the guilty party was, but the evidence would not hold up under the challenge that was sure to follow a suspension. While we were talking, I saw Elizabeth Eckford come into the outer office; but, seeing that others were with me, she left. When I was free, I sent for her. She said she had just come in on impulse and that she had decided it was really nothing.

Jess was sure that the segregationists would make much of Mrs. Bates's visit. Sure enough, Tuesday afternoon's *Arkansas Democrat* had the story, an inaccurate report, as usual. Mrs. Bates and Mrs. Brown had come, so the paper reported, to protest Minnijean's not being in the junior talent assembly. Another headline in the paper was more threatening of our future, in my opinion: [Attorney General] ROGERS TO LET CHS CASE REST.

On Wednesday morning I found out what had brought Elizabeth to my office the afternoon before. Shirley Stancil, one of the counselors, came in to report that one of her counselees had asked to see her because she "might be in trouble." She told Mrs. Stancil that in her 7th period gym class some of the girls had been pushing Elizabeth as she left class and that she happened to come up behind Elizabeth just as Elizabeth kicked back at the pushers. Having received Elizabeth's kick, this girl kicked Elizabeth in return. Now she was afraid that her segregationist actions and speech, reported in the press earlier this year, might get her into trouble. Mrs. Stancil had advised the girl to report the incident to me, but she had not.

I called in Elizabeth and told her what I had been told. She gave me her account, which was that there had been three kicks: the girl kicked her, she kicked the girl, and the girl kicked her for the second time, with the remark that "no nigger" was going to kick her. I asked Elizabeth, if she could, to avoid physical retaliation so that we could be in the clear in labeling these occurrences as attacks, rather than scuffles. Elizabeth said these kicks happened all the time. I asked the gym teachers to watch more closely.

After I insisted that the black girls keep me aware of their troubles, I had reports from two of them on Wednesday. Carlotta reported that on Tuesday of the past week, December 3, a girl whom she knew by sight but not by name had tried to trip her as she went into the cafeteria. And on Monday afternoon, the 9th, two boys had bumped into her hard enough to spin her around as she went from the exit to the street. A guard had previously reported that incident, and a boy had been questioned about what he called an accidental bumping.

Gloria reported that the boy from her homeroom who had given her trouble before had again bumped her, this time as she went to her locker, slamming into her hard enough to knock her across the hall and into the lockers on the other side of the hall. I reported the incident to J. O. He arranged for the boy's mother to have a conference with Jess, at which conference he was warned that he would be suspended if he bothered the black children again. J. O. quoted him as saying that he had been "fighting niggers" since he was five years old.

Thursday was a bad day. School had barely started when Jess called me to his office to hear a report from a boy of an incident that he said had happened the day before after school and that had had consequences this morning before school. The boy had been parked on the south side of Fourteenth Street, waiting for his mother to come out of West Side Junior High School where she was on the staff. Another boy and a girl were in the car with him. A car carrying some of the black students from Central, with an adult driving, came by. On the far side of this car, facing toward the boy's parked car, was Minnijean Brown. The boy said she smiled at him; and when he did not smile back, she made a vulgar gesture. This infuriated the boy, and when his mother came out, he told her. She advised him to forget it. This boy said that he had never been involved in any harassment of the blacks at school or anywhere else. He said his companions in the car saw how angry he was, but he thought they probably had not seen Minnijean's gesture.

This morning he had met two boys (both had been involved in our integration difficulties) at the drugstore and told them of the incident. They then went with him to the third floor of the school to hunt for Minnijean. When they found her, the boy accused her of making the indecent gesture at him. He said she at first admitted it. He told her that he would knock her teeth down her throat if she ever made that gesture to him again. Then, he said, she called the guard and denied the act in his presence. The guard had brought the boys to the office.

I interviewed Minnijean in my office about the matter. She said her first knowledge of it came during the morning. She was walking with Ernest Green down the third-floor hall. As Ernest stopped at his locker, the bunch of boys surrounded her, and this frightened her. She said she had never consciously seen the accusing boy before, and she denied having made any gesture to him. When the boy had become threatening to her that morning, she had asked the guard if he was just going to stand there. When I told Minnijean the boy's version of the incident, she said she didn't recall seeing any car parked on Fourteenth Street as they passed. Minnijean said that frequently kids who want to torment the blacks followed them in a car down Fourteenth; so she always noticed a car behind, but not one parked at the side. She had noticed the car behind them the day before with a boy and his mother in it, and at first she had thought that this was the one the boy had been talking about. But she had not spoken or gestured to anyone except those in her car. She said that she was laughing and talking to Melba, who was on the right of the rear seat. "You know, Mrs. Huckaby, we're always so glad to get away from this place that we laugh and sing and act silly all the way home," and she smiled. She always waved her hands as she talked, she said; but she made no vulgar gesture. "I would certainly have to be crazy to do that!" she declared.

After Minnijean went back to class, I called the boy's mother at West Side to tell her what had happened at school. She minimized the incident and said that she had told her son that he had probably imagined something as directed at him that was a chance occurrence. She had told him to forget it, and she deplored his having approached Minnijean at school with those particular boys at his side. She said her son had been highly emotional since his bout with rheumatic fever last year.

I talked with the boy before school was out. He was still convinced that Minnijean had insulted him and that the other events were as he had described them. I advised him to forget the whole matter as soon as he could, since even if his interpretation was correct, no insult could have been directed toward him as an individual.

Terrence Roberts' English teacher, Imogene Brown, had come in during the morning to tell me that she had observed an act of hostility toward Terrence for the first time in her class. She had looked up in time to see a girl throw a wad of paper at him. Mrs. Brown made no comment at the time, but kept the girl after class to ask her why she had thrown at Terrence. The girl said it was because he stared at her. Mrs. Brown said that Terrence's behavior in class was always correct, that the only time she had seen him look in this girl's direction was after her missile struck him, and that the class as a whole ignored him. Terrence went quietly on his way, making top scores on every test and written assignment.

Now, throwing paper wads is often an attempt to get someone's attention. I wondered about this girl's subconscious feeling about Terrence. He was a tall, good-looking boy, with an intelligent, mobile face and an attractive smile. Could this girl be resentful of her true feeling for Terrence?

I had dreaded the prebasketball season pep assembly to be held after lunch Thursday. Jess and the superintendent had kept up their attendance at Rotary Club each Thursday, between twelve and two, attempting to maintain their relationship with the business and professional leadership of Little Rock. Therefore Jess would not be in school for this assembly, which was to be in the Field House so that the team could run through a few plays after they were introduced. That meant that the students would have no assigned seats, but would sit as they chose in the stands, without teachers being in direct control of those boys and girls whom they knew, as they knew their homeroom students in their assigned assembly seats in the auditorium. From some of these anonymous groups, assembled in the bleachers by affinity, there was likely to come trouble.

The assembly was just as bad as I had feared it would be. Elizabeth, Thelma, and Minnijean were sitting on the front row of one section I noted as I entered the Field House. No student was beside them or immediately behind them. Shirley Stancil, Zinta Hopkins, and I went to sit beside them as a sort of insulation from trouble. As the pep assembly started, students were disorderly, yelling, but not following the cheerleaders in their patterned cheers. A group of senior boys in the north section were noisy and vulgar. They began to sing, raucously, "I'm dreaming of a white Central." Paul Magro went to stand in front of the group to stare them down. Shirley Stancil pointed out in the center of the group the boy who had made Minnijean miserable in the French class. When the assembly was over, it was a relief to know that the student body would now be in smaller, manageable classes rather than this disorderly mass. We should never have held the assembly in this place, even to see the team in action.

I found Melba in my office when I got there. She had wisely elected to sit there rather than go to the assembly. Jefferson Thomas had stayed in the boys' health room.

Shortly after classes resumed, J. O. asked me to check with Minnijean about a report made to him by a National Guardsman that, as he was standing on a stair landing observing the outside traffic of students coming from the Field House back into the main building, he heard what sounded to him like, "you son of a bitch" and turned to see that it was Minnijean who had spoken. I waited until ten minutes before school was dismissed to send for Minnijean so that she would not miss too much of her history class. She said she had spoken aloud as she passed the guard, in resentment at his not being attentive, as she saw it, to his duty. He ought to be watching the corridor, she thought, not outside. She denied saying the words he thought he had heard and declared that her remark was, "I could do a better job than that." I reminded Minnijean that she was in no position to criticize the guard, for she did not know what orders he had been given. In whatever role the National Guard had been here this fall, they had taken an oath to obey their commanders. I also reminded her that, although she, personally, was not the cause of this man's being away from his home and normal occupation, it was her safety he was guarding. By this time Minnijean was in tears and begged to be allowed to see the captain and apologize to him and to the guard. I took her to Captain Stumbaugh's office. He told her that the guard had been instructed to watch the outside passageway, where he *was* watching. Minnijean made a sincere apology and asked to see the guard. But he had left for the day. She said she would apologize to him tomorrow.

On Friday morning Minnijean came in to tell me that the guard she had wanted to apologize to was not here today but that Captain Stumbaugh had told her that he had conveyed her apology and that the guard had sent word that he held no grudge. She told me that she intended to apologize when she saw him again. So Minnijean's impulsiveness was still making trouble for her. Her contrition was admirable, but restraint would be better. She needed to learn that, fast.

Friday's *Arkansas Democrat* proclaimed: QUESTIONING OF STUDENTS DEPLORED; MOTHERS' OFFICIAL CHARGES MRS. BATES IN ON GRILLING. The article, under Bob Troutt's by-line, said: "Closed door grilling of students occurred following alleged mistreating of two Negro girls during gym class." It went on to report, with Mrs. Jackson of the Mothers' League as authority, that "several of the students have been punished with five days in early study hall." Buried, five paragraphs down, was the denial by school officials. More tales, made up from a combination of youngsters' reports of Mrs. Bates's school visit and the kicking episode in gym—about which no white student had been questioned. The *Democrat*'s headlines would be remembered, the denial forgotten or discounted.

Jess had asked me to be present at the Christmas musical for parents on Friday night. He wanted me there, I could see, in case "anything happened," which meant, I supposed, the attendance of black patrons. I attended. The program by the music and drama pupils was lovely; the crowd of parents was large and appreciative of their children's performance; there were no blacks present.

Glen and I took to the woods and swamp for the weekend. It took all Saturday and till noon on Sunday to calm me after the concerns of the week. By Monday morning I felt I could face those concerns again. This last week before the Christmas vacation would be only three days long. I hoped we could make it.

Monday morning brought Jess a registered letter from Mrs. Jackson repeating her charges that girls were being "grilled" by Mrs. Bates. She demanded that she, or some other member of the Mothers' League be present if Mr. Matthews found it necessary to let Mrs. Bates grill any others. In the same mail came a letter from a man who had been arrested in the disorders around school at the time the 101st had moved in. After his conviction on the charge of obstructing the army, the man had appealed, hoping the Arkansas Supreme Court would rule that the use of federal troops was a violation of citizens' rights. Now, in his letter to Jess Matthews, this man demanded that, if the principal found it necessary to question his daughter in Mrs. Bates's presence, he be called first. I helped Jess draft a reply to the letter, telling him that it had never been necessary to call in his daughter for any purpose, that she had a good school record, and that we would continue the same policy we had always followed: if any person other than a school official wanted to talk with a student, the parent's permission was secured first. Mrs. Jackson's letter did not warrant a reply.

Jess was aware that, as large as Central was and as scattered as the teachers were in a building two blocks long and five floors high, the faculty might be just as vulnerable to the propaganda of the Mothers' League or the Citizens' Council as the general public was, since many of them had no firsthand knowledge of the facts. So he invited Mr. Blossom to come to our faculty meeting to report on the matters of fact that were being distorted by the Mothers' League and published in the *Arkansas Democrat*. Mr. Blossom came. He related the circumstances of Mrs. Bates's visit to school; he denied that any pupil had been assigned to early study hall for any racial disorder; and he assured the teachers that no person on legitimate business at school was being denied entrance. Mr. Blossom also commended the teachers for their professional attitude and their performance as teachers during the strenuous fall term. After the meeting several of the teachers told our principal that Mr. Blossom's statements had been helpful. I talked a little with Josephine Feiock, chairman of the English department, about whether informing the faculty of incidents as they happened would be either feasible or helpful. She could not see that it would help. She said she had never seen any racial incidents and rarely heard of them.

Tuesday, December 17. Chili day in the cafeteria. Theo Weekly, who had been a chef at Central for almost as long as I had been a teacher there, made wonderful chili. Without fail, chili was on the lunchroom menu each Tuesday, and only on Tuesday. So unvarying had been this custom that it had been my usual illustration to my English classes of a syllogism: Major premise: Every Tuesday we have chili at school. Minor premise: This is Tuesday. Conclusion: I can buy chili for lunch today. If I teach deduction in the future, I shall use a different example. This one has acquired racial overtones.

We had a quiet morning, but near the end of the first lunch period Jess sent word for me to come to his office. When I walked in, I gasped. There stood two junior boys whom I knew only by sight as members of the a cappella choir and the Key Club quartet. Both stood with hands held stiffly out from their sides as chili dripped down from the gray, sleeveless pullover of one and the long-sleeved white cardigan of the other, and down their slacks. Neither boy was angry—merely sheepish looking. And in the corner of the office sat Minnijean, the picture of dejection. The principal asked Minnijean to tell what had happened.

She had had chairs shoved in her way as she passed between tables in the cafeteria many times, and she had warned the shovers that they might get something dropped on their heads, she said. Today, several chairs were shoved her way, pulled back, and then shoved again. She had dropped her tray, on which she had a bowl of chili. Mr. Matthews asked her whether she had thrown her tray. She said she had not thrown it, but she had held it over the boys' heads and dropped it.

One of the boys said that he *had* moved his chair out from the table, but, seeing that it was in Minnijean's way, he had moved it back. The other boy said that he had not moved his chair, but that the boy across the table from him had put his feet against the chair and kept pushing it out in the way. Both boys made an effort to excuse Minnijean, saying that she had been annoyed so frequently that they didn't blame her for getting mad, and that she might have dropped the tray accidentally. I felt that the dropping of the tray might have been impulsive, but hardly accidental.

The boys were sent home to clean up. Minnijean was angry with herself, saying that she had promised her parents and friends not to get into any more trouble. She said she might not come back to school after Christmas. She wanted to call her mother. I took her to my office to call; her mother was not at home. Minnijean then wanted to talk with Elizabeth Eckford, but I discouraged her in this. I didn't want Elizabeth associated in the minds of students with the chili-dropping incident.

The principal came to my office to tell Minnijean that she was suspended from school. To be readmitted, she would need to apply, with her mother, to the superintendent, Mr. Blossom. The minimum length of a suspension was three days; and since we had only one day before the Christmas vacation, the two more days would take us to January 6.

By this time, Minnijean's mood had changed to resentment; things happened to her all the time and no one got suspended for them, but when she did something, she got suspended.

I had walked with Minnijean to her locker to get her books and her wrap, and then on to the Fourteenth Street exit, after she said she would just walk home when she hadn't been able to reach her mother by phone. Students were all in classes, but I wanted to be sure that she left the building without retaliation from some white supremacist student who might be in the hall. As soon as Minnijean left the grounds, she would be safe, for in Little Rock no one paid any particular attention to a black girl walking along a sidewalk. It was only in school that she was resented.

News of the chili incident was in the *Arkansas Democrat* by 2:30 P.M. The school had refused to give the names of pupils involved, but "other sources" had named Minnijean. One of our students, no doubt, had used the public phone in the hall to call in the news, whether directly to the newspaper or to the Mothers' League, we didn't know. I wrote in my journal that night, "This bowl of chili, no doubt, has been heard around the world." And from this time on, each racial incident was given this on-the-spot, if biased, coverage.

At 3:45 an irate mother called me to say her daughter had just called from school to say her coat was missing from her locker. She had been reading that Minnijean had been sent home and implied that she'd stolen her daughter's coat. I protested that Minnijean was not that kind of person. To this she replied, "Oh, they'll all steal."

At the main office, Jeanne McDermott, the staff member in charge of the switchboard and the lost-and-found enquiries, said that the student who had been on duty there at the end of school had told her that a girl she didn't know had come in to inquire about a coat, but that she had to turn back to the switchboard momentarily and the girl left without giving her name or describing the coat. Shortly after four, I called the girl's home to get a description of the coat and further details of its loss so that we could follow any clues toward recovering it. Yes, her daughter was home, now, the mother said, and continued, "She's been telling us what went on at school today." I assured her that I was aware of what had gone on, but I wanted to know more about the coat. "Oh, she has it. Her girl friend had got it out of her locker for her."

In addition to the chili story that evening, the *Democrat* ran a story on the circulars being distributed by the Capital Citizens' Council giving sheriff's office pictures and photostats of the state police record of Daisy Bates, a record of such incidents as were classified as criminal only if the person involved were black: "gambling," etc. The circular repeated the charges that Mrs. Jackson's letter had made of Mrs. Bates's grilling Central High girls, and it ended with the question, "Who is running Central High School? Blossom or Bates?—or both?" The *Democrat* said that Amis Guthridge had refused to reveal where the police record, ordinarily a confidential matter, had been secured. The effect the circular sought was guilt by association, the school officials with a "criminal." Again, our Central High School student directory had been used as a mailing list. Several copies of the circular were brought to us by parents. Each envelope bore a stamped medallion inscribed "Remember Little Rock." Under the caption was the drawing of a soldier prodding the backs of two girls—two of those September 25 truants. We were to become familiar with this stamp, used on all Mothers' League and Citizens' Council mail, and even adopted for use on all its official mail by the state of Georgia!

Wednesday, the last day before the Christmas vacation, was a tense one. It is never a restful day, that preholiday one, with the inevitable relaxation of rigid discipline. Student committees from homerooms were going and coming, taking boxes of food to needy (white) families. There was added restlessness, too, because of Minnijean's chili dropping and because of the Citizens' Council circular. Seven of the Nine, all except Minnijean (who was excluded) and Melba braved the day.

Before homeroom that morning, a small, pleasant-looking junior girl brought me a letter that her homeroom teacher, Sybil Hefley, thought I should see before she mailed it. The girl explained that her hobby was getting autographs from authors. She had written to an author, probably one who wrote teen-age stories for magazines, asking for her autograph. The author, noting that her correspondent was a student in Little Rock Central High School, and probably seeing an opportunity to get some material for a story, had asked the girl for some of her opinions on our integration. The girl showed me her typed reply.

Her letter began with the statement that, although some people might have changed their opinion since September, the majority still felt the same way. I asked the student what way they felt and how she knew. The majority were very much against integration, she was sure. I told her I thought she should qualify her statement by saying that it was her opinion, not based on any survey. The letter went on to charge that the publicity put out by the North had been unfair, showing the kind of schoolhouses Negroes were attending as shacks. She said she was enclosing a picture of Horace Mann High School, which the Negroes would be attending if they were not at Central, and that it was much newer, finer, and more modern than our school. It was completely air-conditioned, she wrote.

I asked her how she knew about the pictures of the shacks. Why, a traveling man had told her daddy about them, she said. She had assured me that the first part of her letter was factual; so I pointed out to her that, as a reporter of facts, she should not include that statement as her own observation. The inclusion of the picture of Horace Mann High School was good, I said; but she would have to cross out her last sentence about the school, for it was not air-conditioned. She was amazed; someone had told her for a fact that it was.

The rest of her letter, the girl said, was her own opinion. To her northern correspondent she wrote that she was opposed to integration because race-mixing was against God's law. Of course she was interested in the "Negro's soul." Like most southern people, she really "loved Negroes," but she did not want to go to school with them. Here I stopped her. Which ones did she love? She looked puzzled. For instance, did she love the nine who attend Central? Oh, no ma'am! she said, with horror. Did she have a Negro servant at home of whom she was fond? She couldn't think of one. I told her to say whatever she felt.

"Of course I do not believe in violence," the letter continued; "but if the guards were removed, I guess I would join the rest of the kids in getting the Negroes out."

"What would you and the other kids do?" I asked.

"Well, anything to make them miserable," she said.

"Wouldn't that be violence? I wonder whether you don't mean that you won't use violence as long as you are prevented from using it. But no matter. I think the person you are writing to will understand."

I complimented my visitor on her spelling and punctuation and general sentence structure, but I told her that I thought her principal need in composition now was to learn how to sort out facts from opinions and how to test her opinions by standards of reason. She thanked me and left with her letter.

No incidents were reported that day—just tension. We had extra federalized guards on hand. Three-thirty, finally. School was out for a long two weeks, till January 2. "Merry Christmas!" the passing students said to me and to each other as I stood outside my door, in the hall. "Merry Christmas!" I replied. "Merry Christmas!" the black students replied to my greeting, the only one they had on that corridor since I was the only teacher there and no student spoke to them.

CHAPTER VI

January 2–February 10

A Target Selected

The new year, 1958, as it began at Central High School, seemed distressingly like the old one, with the same turmoil and undercurrents. On our first day back at school, a dainty little baton twirler who was in my fourth period English class came in to tell me that Mrs. Jackson had called her the night before to ask her to give evidence.

"Evidence of what?" I asked.

"Oh, of what goes on at school," she said. "Like my gym class. She asked me if I was one that Daisy Bates had questioned, but I told her, 'No, ma'am. She has never questioned me.'"

I assured her that no one else had been questioned either, to my knowledge, certainly not at school. She said she had just seen it in the paper. I told her that I knew no other name to call these statements but lies.

The girl went on to tell me that her father, a member of the state police, had not been at Central in September, but that he had heard a lot "on the other side" and had told her to talk to Mrs. Jackson if she wanted to. But she liked me and had decided not to go to the meeting of the Mothers' League to testify. She said that her parents had kept her out of school at first for fear of violence, but now she thought she would get along in school all right if it weren't for Minnijean. She was Minnijean's gym captain, and Minnijean would never dress out properly. She either didn't have on tennis shoes, or she wore a sweater instead of a blouse; she felt that Minnijean was entirely too touchy—kept feeling she was being picked on when no slight was intended. As her captain, the girl said she was scared to make Minnijean mad by reporting her for failing to dress out properly.

I told my young friend that she was expected to do her duty as gym captain and report Minnijean's failures just like any others. I had already assigned Minnijean to early study hall on another matter, and I would assign her for gym failures if they were reported, just as I assigned others.

The youngster went on to say that having blacks in school sometimes made her so nervous that she couldn't study. I asked her why; and she said for fear they would harm her if she did anything they didn't like. But she said she really enjoyed hearing Jefferson Thomas make a book report in her class. She could just listen to him for hours. "He's really smart," she said. She told me more of her telephone conversation with Mrs. Jackson, who wanted to know from her whether I was "for the Negroes." The girl had tried to defend me, saying I treated them like everyone else in my class, and that when there were any blacks in my office, I was only doing what it was my business to do and I'd be fired if I didn't. I thanked my pupil for her concern for me and told her to tell Mrs. Jackson whatever she knew to be true, if her parents wished her to "testify."

After homeroom I found a note in my box from a girl asking for an early conference and stating that she was in study hall at Period 2. This was the girl who had told the state police that Dr. Benjamin Fine of the New York *Times* had offered a bribe to some boys to start a fight with some blacks. She was also the girl who, on September 23, the first day the Nine attempted to attend Central after the governor withdrew the guard, had been taken away in a paddy wagon by the city police for creating a disturbance in the street in front of the school. I sent for this girl. She just wanted to know, she said, why she was being kept from performing on our school programs. I told her that it was because her name had been before the public in an unfavorable light in the early days of our desegregation disorders; and that it was not our policy to put such students on programs representing our school. She said her parents particularly resented her not having been given a part on our Christmas programs and that her parents were "going to do something about it." I told her that the ban on her appearance was supposed to be for one semester, only. She asked me whether I would put the reason for the ban in writing; I told her I would not. She said she didn't feel that what she had done had hurt the school. Was I referring to the time that she had hugged the governor? I told her that the publication of that picture did not hurt the school, and that she had not been identified by name in that picture, anyway. I suggested that she might talk with Mr. Matthews, and she said that she would like to.

I called the principal, and he came to my office for the conference. We went over the same ground again, one of us mentioning the paddy wagon which took her off after her hysterical behavior on September 23. Our persistent questioner justified her recent conduct, saying that she had never "done anything to niggers." I corrected her pronunciation, here, and her grammar in another spot. I admitted her contention that she had not been in the October walkout, but then she had not been in school all that week. She said she would never agree to stop working on the outside for segregation. I told her that we were not seeking to control her ideas or her actions or what organizations she worked for, but that we would not tolerate anything at school that disrupted the process of educating *all* our students. (More "testimony" would be available at the Mothers' League that night, I was willing to bet.)

Jess agreed that the ban on her stage appearances would be over in time for her to be in the Key Club Capers, and that she could begin to rehearse for that program now. We looked at the calendar with her and noted that there were only eight more days of school this semester. The girl left the office, hinting vaguely at some things about the school and us that had come to light during the Christmas holidays.

Later in the morning the girl's father called and said he wanted to ask me a question. I asked whether he knew that his daughter had had a conference with the principal and me already; and when he said he did not, I referred the call to Jess. Jess told the father, who talked calmly, that ruling pupils out of public appearances because of actions that reflected on Central had been our long-time practice.

At 10:15, while Carl Vaught, Don Dugan, Jane Herrick, and Don Fowles, at home from college for Christmas, were sitting around my desk visiting with me, Jess called to say that the switchboard had just had a warning that a bomb would go off in the building in two minutes. He said he was sure it was a hoax. I laughed and replied that two minutes wasn't enough time for us all to get out, anyway. By 3:30, Jess had decided that the call had been intended to force us to call a fire drill, which would turn into a walkout.

J. O. reported during the day that a knot of people had gathered across the street as they had during the pre-101st days. The *Democrat* in the afternoon identified them as members of the Mothers' League, who stated, "Our mission is accomplished. We just wanted to demonstrate that the guard is still necessary."

Jess showed me a collection of letters he had received during the Christmas holidays. One was a registered letter to which Mrs. Jackson's name was typed, but not signed. It made the ridiculous charge that Jess Matthews had banned the singing of "the beautiful and time-honored Christmas song, 'White Christmas.'" I had seen the same letter run as a paid ad in the *Democrat* on December 23 under a streamer, GOODBYE "WHITE CHRISTMAS" AT CENTRAL HIGH SCHOOL, and followed by the invitation: "If you would have us continue publishing ads of this nature, giving information the race-mixers are trying to conceal—send a contribution to Freedom Fund for Little Rock, Box 842." But Jess, who hardly knew one tune from another, had no idea that gym teachers had been frowning on the song because the segregationist students were parodying it, "I'm dreaming of a white Central."

On Friday morning, January 3, Jess called early to say that his mother, who had fallen and broken her hip on Christmas Eve, had now developed pneumonia. He planned to take the next plane for Kansas. I assured him that, since everything that *could* happen at Central had surely happened at least once, J. O. and I should be able to handle any eventuality. J. O. suggested we divide the work: "You do the greeting, and I'll do the groaning."

My brother Bill had been visiting our parents in Little Rock for the holidays. At noon, he came out to Central to lunch with me in the teachers' lunchroom. Afterwards, he sat down in my outer office to visit with Ann Williams, my office monitor, and Robin Woods, who had dropped by to talk with Ann. Jefferson Thomas came in to ask whether he could study in my outer office, as he sometimes did to get out of the hostile halls at noon. I took him back to my inner office and asked him whether he wasn't going to eat lunch. He said he didn't want any. J. O. strolled in. Someone had twisted the handle off Jefferson's locker, and J. O. wanted to make other arrangements for him. I remarked that my office was rather full, and J. O. took the hint and suggested that Jefferson come study on the bench outside *his* office. I was genuinely afraid for the two girls to be seen sitting with Jefferson in my office, for both of them were known antisegregationists and might easily become physical targets.

After school, Elizabeth Eckford dropped by. She apologized for coming so often, but I assured her that I didn't feel she was coming too frequently. She said that except for some broken glass thrown at her during lunch, she really had had a wonderful day. I made a note of the glass throwing to pass on to Mrs. Means, who supervised behavior in that part of the cafeteria at noon.

Captain Leon Stumbaugh had said he was keeping his fingers crossed up to his elbows, hoping there would be no incidents so that he could go to his home in Clarksville for the weekend instead of having to go out to Camp Robinson and write reports till midnight. As I left school, I asked him whether his crossed fingers had worked. They had, though Jefferson Thomas's ride hadn't come for him yet. He had asked the sergeant to stay with Jefferson till it did come.

Bill came over to eat supper with Glen and me. He looked glum. He said it had probably been a mistake for him to go to Central today, it affected him so strongly. When he had gotten to Mother and Father's, who should come in to visit but an elderly distant cousin. She stayed for an hour and a half, talking incessantly of how she resented the federal guards at high school; of how she loved Louise, the black woman whose help she and Mother shared and who "knew her place," on the bus and elsewhere; and of how sure she was that "they" were going to "get that uppity nigger girl"—Minnijean—when she came back to school. Bill said he had blown his top after she left, for she had also talked piety and church. Bill wept as he said, "Liz, seeing that scared, frail child [Jefferson] at school and then hearing this, I just couldn't stand it. I got sick at my stomach." I told him that I shared his feelings, though I was over the sick-at-the-stomach stage—*had* to be, to stay healthy and on the job.

After supper, our neighbor Eleanor Cooke dropped by to visit. Her talk, being sympathetic and light, cheered us up. She gleefully told of the Christmas card she had sent Julian Miller, president of the Citizens' Council and a fellow communicant of hers at Christ Episcopal Church. She had bought the card in the church office and had signed her name to it. The greeting was illustrated by four tiny angels holding candles, one of the angels black.

On Monday, Jess's mother was improved, so he was back at school. Virgil Blossom had called me on Friday to ask me to attend a conference on Monday at five with Minnijean and her parents about her return to school following her suspension. Jess felt that his attendance at the conference would make too many officials to confront one pupil and her parents; but he suggested that I talk with Minnijean's counselor and all her teachers about her educational progress.

Orlana Hensley, her counselor, said she had talked with Minnijean an hour before the chili incident and had told her that she was not achieving up to her ability. I asked Miss Hensley what tests she had of Minnijean's ability. She said, only her reading ability, which was well above her grade level. Her grades for the last six weeks were four D's, and a B in glee club. Orlana said that she had told Minnijean that reports from her teachers seemed to indicate that she had come to Central more with the idea of getting attention than of getting an education.

Margaret Stewart said that Minnijean was failing American history for the current six weeks, and that would mean failure for the semester, which she could reverse only by making C or better next semester. Margaret was distressed at Minnijean's failure. I already knew some reasons for it: her failure to secure a text, partly because of being dilatory; her absence from class on test days, once because she reported to the health room ill on that day, once to come to report an incident to me. Margaret thought Minnijean still didn't have a textbook of her own but was borrowing Elizabeth's to bring to class. In class, Margaret said, Minnijean was unresponsive and dreamy; and when she made a comment, it apparently was a quotation from what she had heard another student say rather than from any study she herself had done.

In typing, Mildred Dalhoff thought Minnijean was doing well, though her late entry into class had slowed her progress. Once, Minnijean had asked to move her assigned place in typing because the girl who sat next to her was so *good* in typing! Mary Ann Rath had offered to let Minnijean sit next to her; but Minnijean's place in class was already so favorable, near the door at the front of the room and in a rather isolated group of four typewriters, with fine girls at the other three, that Mrs. Dalhoff had persuaded Minnijean to stay where she was.

Susie West had no complaint about Minnijean's class behavior, now. She was not doing *good* work, but she was preparing such assignments in English as memory work and even coming to the front of the class to recite memorized poetry, as the others did.

Micky McGalin said that Minnijean's attitude in the speech class was defensive. She usually came in and sat, biting her nails, taking offense at the evidently accidental moving of a chair in her direction, which set her to crying, disconcerting the girl who had stumbled over it and was turning to say she was sorry.

Naomi Hancock said of Minnijean, "Well, you know she has a really lovely voice." Minnijean's behavior in glee club had been too effervescent at first, according to Mrs. Hancock. She had wanted to corner groups of girls to talk with them and show them jitterbug steps. But she had settled down into a very acceptable pattern of behavior, following class procedures and learning with the rest of the girls.

I asked Mrs. Hancock whether she could have misunderstood Minnijean when she told her that she had decided not to appear on the Christmas assembly program, since Minnijean's mother and Mrs. Bates had said she meant only the night program. Mrs. Hancock was sure that Minnijean had meant both the night and the school assembly programs, for they had talked a long time about the possibility of her appearing next year; and Mrs. Hancock had even wondered, with her, whether, for the sake of her voice training, she might do better to return to Horace Mann, where she would certainly be in the a cappella choir.

Govie Griffin, Minnijean's homeroom teacher, said she had reproved Minnijean for her behavior in homeroom in the early days of her attendance: her frequent trips to the teacher's desk to make inquiries, her quickness to accuse persons of not treating her fairly. Minnijean now kept her assigned seat in the homeroom and did not attempt to attract attention.

Mr. Blossom asked me to come to the administration office ahead of the Browns. He wanted to ask me whether I thought we were making any progress at school in adjusting to desegregation. I told him that the only progress I could see was the result of custom, which was making the blacks less conspicuous. He asked about faculty attitudes. I felt they were good; even the teachers most disturbed originally about integration were not quite so much so, now. I mentioned my fear for the poise of one of our best teachers but felt her more relaxed, even willing to speak to me. I told Mr. Blossom that I could name more teachers actively with the program than against it, and that it was cheering to see the young teachers on the positive side. He wanted to know whether his appearance before the faculty had helped, and I assured him that it had. I had heard several comments to that effect. I also thought that the Christmas letter, signed by the superintendent and each member of the board, had had a morale-building effect.

Mr. Blossom then turned to the case at hand. He said he had thought a suspension of seven to ten days for Minnijean was in line with suspensions he had given others and asked what I thought. I mentioned two things: Minnijean should not return on a Tuesday, for that was chili day in the cafeteria; but since we were to begin midterm tests on Tuesday, the 14th, she should be back in school before that date. He suggested that Monday, the 13th, would be about right. I spoke of the possible danger to Minnijean upon her return, quoting my elderly relative's remark that "they" would "get" her if she came back.

The Browns then came in. Mrs. Brown I had met before. And when I saw Mr. Brown, I realized that he was the contractor who had built our rock terrace two summers before, and had made an excellent job of it. I reminded him of that project, and he informed me that our recommendation had got him a bigger job for our neighbors across the street. He spoke of himself, deprecatingly, as a "fourth-grade scholar," meaning that the fourth grade was the limit of his schooling. I could see that Minnijean's occasional defensive responses might be a rejection of this side of her family in favor of her mother's greater polish, though I had also seen that she loved her father dearly, as he loved her.

Mr. Blossom asked me to speak of Minnijean's school problems. I did, very frankly, prefacing my remarks with the assurance that I liked Minnijean and felt that her problems were not unusual for a girl of her age, but that her behavior was unacceptable because of our unusual situation. Both Mr. and Mrs. Brown seemed cooperative. I got the impression that they had not realized how much Minnijean had contributed to her own troubles. In fact, until the previous conference with Mr. Blossom, they had thought the chili-dropping an accident. Minnijean had admitted to them, when Mr. Blossom had pressed her, that it was deliberate. That news had been quite a shock to them.

Mr. Blossom also said that since his last conference with the Browns he had heard of some of Minnijean's talking out of turn to the guards, even calling one of them an obscenity. Minnijean still denied the words. He put it straight to Minnijean that she must stop deceiving her parents and that she must start behaving properly. He set the date when Minnijean could return at one week from this conference.

The next morning, Tuesday, January 7, J. O. told me that he had learned from Gloria and Carlotta that the car in which they were riding home had been hit by an iron pipe wielded by two boys on a motor scooter, who had exchanged words with the driver of the car, Chris Mercer. The girls didn't know the boys, but Jefferson Thomas, who was also in the car, did. When Jefferson came into my office at noon, I asked him about them. They were in his gym class, he said, and he told me the names the other boys called them. When I reported these names to J. O., his comment was, "A couple of tenth grade punks."

Since the early days of our desegregation when there was so much absence for our attendance clerk to record, I had assumed the daily chore of counting the number of absentees from the attendance office chart, reporting that number to the superintendent's secretary, who in turn, was to call it in to the FBI. On this Tuesday, as I scanned the list, I became aware of what seemed to be an unusually large number of our hard-core segregationists absent from school. My suspicions were further aroused when Margaret Reiman told me that one such girl from her homeroom had been around in the hall before school but was missing at homeroom time. She also said that two boys, also segregationists, not from her homeroom, had been seen before school but were missing now. Later in the morning Imogene Brown, homeroom teacher of the girl who had protested being barred from school programs, reported that the girl was absent, but that her mother thought she was in school. The homeroom teacher and the mother made several calls back and forth, and the mother even called the attendance office to see whether her daughter could be in the health room, so sure was she that her daughter was in school. At midafternoon the girl, herself, called me to say that she was at home, that she had developed a toothache after she came to school, and that she had gone to her dentist and had the tooth pulled. She said that her mother now understood the situation and would send a note excusing her. She brought the note the next day, but I charged her with leaving school without permission and assigned her the usual penalty for this infraction, five days in early study hall.

Margaret Reiman was not able to talk with the mother of her homeroom girl. Each time she called during the evening, the girl said her mother was not at home. Finally, the girl gave Mrs. Reiman a number where she said her mother could be reached. Mrs. Reiman did not call; but a half hour later a person who said she was the mother called Mrs. Reiman. Margaret Reiman was not fooled. By Wednesday I had learned where the girl's mother worked and called her there. She had not been aware of her daughter's absence; an assignment to early study hall for truancy for the daughter, the result.

One of the boys who had been seen at school, then disappeared, brought an excuse from his sister-in-law that he had been ill on Tuesday. He lived in such a mixed-up family situation that he could not be charged with truancy, having produced this feeble verification. But J. O. noted that the illness had been transitory enough for him to appear on Steve Stephens' teen-age program on TV that afternoon. The other boy was truant and was given the usual ten-days-in-early-study-hall penalty.

Besides these four absentees on January 7, fifteen other pupils absent on that day were ones whose names had become familiar in reports of disturbances. These absences caused me to wonder a few days later whether any or all of these boys and girls had met on January 7 to plan the campaign of harassment that was certainly stepped up afterward.

But except for puzzling over the truancies and their implications, Wednesday was not a particularly bad day. J. O. told me of a romance that had come to light between one of the married National Guardsmen and a girl in our school, reported to him by Captain Stumbaugh. Apparently a serious affair had not developed before the girl's parents became aware of it, and that guardsman was never assigned to the school again for duty. The wonder to me was that more of these affairs did not develop between some of our more aggressive girls and the young men separated from their wives.

Gloria Ray came in on that Wednesday to ask whether she might apply for membership in the Beta Club, the national honorary society, which required a B average and good citizenship. Our school bulletin had announced that tenth graders who qualified might apply; and certainly Gloria qualified. I told her that I would ask Mr. Matthews; and that if his answer was no, it would not be because either he or I thought that answer was right, but because it was necessary if we were to operate the school.

On Thursday, incidents began to happen. At 10:15, Melba Pattillo came to my office with a pass from Room 201. "I don't want to be a pessimist, Mrs. Huckaby," she said, "but I dropped a book as I was walking down the hall. There was no one near me, and I stooped down to pick it up. The next thing I knew, I was on the floor. I didn't lose my balance; I was pushed from behind. I don't know whether it was an accident or not."

I asked Melba whether she had recognized any student in the vicinity, and she named the girl who had protested being ruled off programs for the semester. "I don't think she would do that, do you?" I asked. "No, I don't," said Melba. She said there were guards nearby who saw her after the accident, but probably not the accident itself. She said the same of a man teacher, outside whose door the incident happened. I recognized the room as Pat Aydelott's. I talked with him, learning that he had seen two girls run down the hall after Melba was knocked down.

J. O. brought the two guards to my office. They had not seen the incident as it happened, but they had seen the two girls who were responsible leave the scene. One they described as dressed in a blue and white dress with a full skirt, the other as a blond with a pony tail. The girls had gone into Room 208 or 209, typing classes. I went down the hall and looked into those rooms. The two who fitted the guard's description were in 208: the blond whom Melba had recognized and a small brunette who had been on my list of suspicious absentees on Tuesday.

I sent for the two girls. The blond girl vowed that knocking down Melba was accidental. The blond and brunette were walking down the hall, the blond slightly ahead. She turned to say something to her friend, who accidentally ran into her, knocking her into Melba, who had stooped over to get her book. The blond declared that she had then said, "Oh, pardon me," and she and her friend had walked on to class.

The brunette's story followed the leader's closely, except that she wanted to describe the "mean look" Melba gave them when she got up. I discouraged this description of anyone's expression after she had been knocked down and pointed out that Mr. Aydelott's report of their speed down the hall did not agree with theirs, but told them that I was willing to accept their report that the incident was accidental—or at least not premeditated. I sternly criticized their manners in leaving a person whom they had knocked down without offering an apology and help, no matter who that person was. I even talked about noblesse oblige, a term—and an idea—that these girls had never heard of. I realized that I was not making any impression on them.

"But I said, 'Pardon me,' and I certainly am not going to pick up her books for her," said the blond. "Mrs. Huckaby, you know I've never lied to you," she insisted. I did not present any of the evidence I might have to the contrary but dismissed the girls to their classes.

After school, Melba came by to say she guessed she would have to take the pessimistic view after all about being knocked over that morning; someone had bragged about it at lunch and the word had spread. Since Melba and the blond girl were in the same homeroom, I told their homeroom teacher of the happening.

That evening Mrs. Pattillo called me to talk about the incident. I told her that I had had to accept the explanation that the incident was accidental, though the best I could really report was that the circumstances indicated that it was not premeditated. Mrs. Pattillo's attitude was friendly and not in the least contentious. I assured her that the school shared her concern for the safety and welfare of her child.

Carlotta Walls, too, had some difficulties that day. Two boys, one of whom she had mentioned to me before Christmas as being threatening to her in classes, had harassed her. One had tried to trip her as she left her biology class and then had followed her briefly to step on her heels. The other boy, the one she had mentioned to me once before, had come up to her as he sharpened his pencil near her desk and muttered a threat to kill her or one of the other Nine.

Loreen Lee, Latin teacher, had told me on Thursday after school of a demonstration that had escaped my attention: a good many girls were dressing all in black. Since black and gold are the school colors, almost all the girls had black skirts and sweaters; so this costume was not unique. But Mrs. Lee said that since only certain girls who were known segregationists had appeared in black, all in one day, she was sure it was intended to be symbolic. During the next few days I watched, too, and I was sure she was correct. The demonstration persisted through January, never too widespread or too obvious, and sometimes participated in by girls who just thought that all-black had become a teen-age fashion. One day three teachers who dropped by during class break for cokes in the conference room were astonished to learn that they were right in the segregationist fashion, and I teased them about it. Other demonstrations, equally unnoticed by the faculty, happened from time to time throughout January. Sybil Hefley informed me that Thursday, January 30, was "stare day." Friday, the 31st, was "black day," again. As typical as such fads are among teen-agers, it was sad that they should be directed so cruelly against other boys and girls in their school.

On Friday, January 10, Melba Pattillo came in at Period 3 to report that there seemed to be a campaign to step on her heels, led by the blond pony-tailed girl and her best friend. Melba said she had tried to break up their game by stepping into a classroom and letting them pass, but they waited for her to come out and resumed their harassment.

I told Captain Stumbaugh of Melba's report so that he could alert the guards. Then I checked the schedules of the three girls and noted that their paths were not due to cross again during the day; so I looked up Shirley Stancil, the small girl's homeroom teacher, to ask her to talk with her pupil before school tomorrow morning. That child's attitude toward me had been so belligerent since the clothes-switching incident that I was sure that if I spoke to her she would say I was "threatening" her. My precautions were not enough.

At 2:35 a guard escorted this girl and Elizabeth Eckford into my office. The guard pointed to the small girl and said, "This girl pushed this girl [Elizabeth] down the stairs." "Is that what happened?" I asked the small blond, calling her by name. She nodded. I sent Elizabeth on to class and took the white girl to Jess's office. He, also, asked her whether she had pushed Elizabeth on the stairs. "No," she said, "but I shoved her. I took my books and shoved her," illustrating with her stack of books. "I wouldn't *touch* her myself—or any of them." No, Elizabeth had never done anything to her, but she had to her friends. She had scratched one of them and had "smarted off."

J. O. Powell stayed with the girl in another office while Jess and I conferred. I recommended her suspension. Jess had me bring her back to his office. He reminded her of his previous conference with her and her mother during which they had agreed that she would stay entirely clear of the black pupils. Since she had violated that agreement and had committed an unprovoked act of hostility toward one of the girls, he told her that she was suspended from school; that the minimum length of any suspension was three days; but that she and her mother would have to apply to the superintendent for readmittance. I asked her whether she wanted to call her mother. She said no, that her best friend had already called her.

I walked with the girl to her locker on the first floor, where she got her books and wraps. She was indignant that she was being suspended when other kids who had pushed the blacks had not been. I reminded her of her previous warning and of her promise. She said she thought that the reason that her friend (she of the pony-tail) had not been suspended was that Mr. Matthews was afraid of her. She asked whether she could sit in the car and wait for the kids she rode to school with; and since school dismissal was only minutes away, I agreed. But I told her she must not be on the school grounds during the period of her suspension, and I reminded her that she and her mother would have to see the superintendent. "She's been wanting to see him, anyway," the girl said, in a threatening manner.

After school a guard brought the pony-tailed blond, the brunette who had been in on knocking Melba down, and that girl's brother to my office. The three had approached him belligerently and called him names for getting the small blond suspended. Jess talked with the group, pointing out the accumulating blots on their school records. I talked with the boy, particularly, since I had been his English teacher last year and knew him personally. I spoke about his beautiful voice and the acceptance it had won him in school. His membership in the a cappella choir was not something he should risk by getting into trouble. The three students had called the guard "nigger lover"; and I assured them that the name— corrected for pronunciation—fitted me as well, for I loved all human beings and accepted them. Their faces were stony. Jess sent the pupils on their way.

As a sequel: On the following Monday the boy involved stopped me in the hall. "I've had a talk with my sister," he said. "I told her to let [the blond] get into these things but to stay out of them herself." He declared that he was going to stay out of them, too. But he didn't.

From J. O.'s reports of what happened that Friday, I learned that this boy had been reported for what Ernest called insignificant matters in the gym class: steaming up the shower room while Ernest was showering, and for throwing wet towels at him.

Terrence Roberts had had some trouble that day, too. One of the boys suspended last October for kicking the black boys and knocking the books from their arms, the incident I had intervened in, had challenged Terrence to a fight, alleging that Terrence had called him an s.o.b. When J. O. called in the white boy, he reported that Terrence did not answer him in any way in response to his challenge, but that he kept his hands in his pockets all the time the white boy was talking to him. "That nigger's got more nerve than anybody I ever saw," said the challenger.

The *Gazette* on Saturday morning quoted the suspended girl's mother as saying that her daughter had shoved the black girl when she "got in her way." The afternoon paper, the *Democrat*, in a different version, quoted the mother as saying her daughter had "just brushed past" Elizabeth Eckford "as students do all of the time" and that Elizabeth "started to hit" her daughter. In both stories the mother was quoted as protesting the fact that Elizabeth had not been suspended, too, and as saying that she would confer with Mr. Matthews and Mr. Blossom on Monday.

Sunday's *Democrat* carried a news picture of a group of our biology students touring the University Medical Center's biochemistry department on Saturday. In the picture I was glad to see Gloria Ray and Jefferson Thomas. I was glad, that is, until Maude Reid, their teacher, told me how avidly the photographers had maneuvered to get the black students into every shot; and until I learned later that parents of the white students pictured with them had been subjected to the usual obnoxious phone calls from anonymous hecklers.

Having been delayed after school on Friday by the guard and his hecklers, I hurried off for the last weekend duck hunt of the season without stopping to write up the girl's suspension. Since suspensions were for a minimum of three school days, there would be time enough on Monday morning to get it done. But on Monday, I found that matters would not wait. Mr. Blossom phoned for a copy of the suspension notice and sent the office custodian out to pick it up. The girl's mother was already in his office. When Jess got back to school from the regular Monday morning meeting of principals with Mr. Blossom, he reported that the mother had left Mr. Blossom's office with the announced intention of consulting her lawyer. Her daughter had been put out of school unjustly, merely because of an unintentional accident.

The suspension of this girl was only one of the causes of the tension that was almost palpable in school this Monday morning, January 13. It was the day set for Minnijean to return to school after her suspension for dumping the chili. She came by my office before school to get her official readmittance slip. She looked nice in a new pink felt skirt and a white blouse. I complimented her on her ladylike appearance and said I hoped she would act as she looked. She was a little scared, she said. Wilma Means, the substitute teacher for my classes, who was in my office, told Minnijean that she must pray for strength and courage. "I have prayed," said Minnijean. In her demeanor there was nothing of the show-off or braggart that had alienated many in September and October. My teacher's heart ached for her, and I wished her good luck. She thanked me and left to face a day that I was sure would be hard for her. But all her days had been hard. I heard nothing during the day to indicate trouble for Minnijean. Only later did I learn that someone had ruined her pretty skirt at noon by squirting ink on it.

On Tuesday morning Elizabeth Eckford came in, crying softly. She had been knocked "flat down" as she came up the stairs at the north end of the building. I asked whether she knew who did it. She didn't; but she said it was a girl in a gray coat. I asked whether she noticed anyone nearby who might have seen the incident, and she mentioned a girl who might have seen it. It would be a touchy matter to involve the girl she named by questioning her; for this was the girl whose father had written Jess demanding that if Mrs. Bates was ever to be allowed to question his daughter at school, he be allowed to be present at the questioning. Mrs. Bates was not at school, but I did not think it good to call this girl to my office to ask whether she could give us a clue to the culprit in this shoving incident. Instead, I asked Christine Poindexter, her homeroom teacher, to question her, and Miss Poindexter reported that the girl said she had seen nothing. We continued to look for "the girl in the gray coat."

On Tuesday, January 14, shortly after nine, I had a call from a male voice (clearly too young) that purported to be the father of the girl recently pushed into Elizabeth. He asked that she be excused to come home, since he had come in from work, ill. He asked how he could get his daughter out of school, and I told him that he would have to come for her in person. As soon as the caller hung up, I dialed the girl's home phone number, but there was no reply. I hunted for the girl and found her lying down in the health room. She said she was not asking to be excused from school because she didn't want to miss her exams. Her father was out of town, she said, and her mother was away from home, looking after an aunt. I told her that someone was trying to get her out of school.

The caller was persistent. An hour later, Jeanne McDermott, who handled the switchboard, notified me of a call that had come in for the girl, the caller still identifying himself as her father. He left a number for her to call back. By using the cross index, Mrs. McDermott had found that that number belonged to our blond suspended girl. Surmising that the caller was a boy, absent from school, who was a frequent companion of the small blond, we did not deliver the message.

The papers reported a big Citizens' Council rally on Tuesday evening, and on Wednesday there were repercussions around school. Cards stamped "Remember Little Rock," that slogan encircling the design of the soldier holding a bayonet in the back of two girls, appeared, pinned to some blouses and shirts. Some teachers ignored the signs; some approved them, I suppose. But many teachers required, as I did, that the signs be removed while the student was under school supervision.

Melba came in shortly after noon to tell me of some continuing harassment during the last few days. She showed me the back of her skirt, which had been splattered with ink, and she said that Thelma and Minnijean had also had clothes spoiled in that way in the last day or two. Melba did not know for sure when her skirt had been ruined; but she had a good idea. When she had dressed after gym, the skirt was all right; but in the cafeteria, as she passed a table where the suspended girl's boy friend and her pony-tailed girl friend were lunching with others, she heard them call out something about having "got one of them" and saw them point at her skirt, which she then found to be covered with ink splotches. She hadn't seen the ink squirted, naturally. Melba and Minnijean came in after school to show me ink-splattered blouses. My journal for the day ends: "We'll have to get rid of the ring-leaders," and I named the boy and the girl Melba had mentioned.

Thursday, January 16, was rather peaceful during the morning, and I was glad that it started that way. Jess always attended Rotary Club at noon on Thursdays, and I preferred to have him at school when things got rough. The peace of the morning was deceptive. About midway through the first lunch period, J. O. called me to ask whether the suspended blond had been reinstated since her suspension for pushing Elizabeth on the stairs. I told him that she hadn't. Captain Stumbaugh had reported to J. O. that the girl was having lunch in the cafeteria. I told J. O. that I wanted to see for myself, and he said he and Captain Stumbaugh would come, too.

When they got to my office door, the small blond was with them. She looked petulant, as usual. I unpinned the Remember Little Rock sign from her baby blue sweater blouse as I asked her why she was violating her suspension by coming to school. She said we hadn't sent a copy of her suspension to her home and she had come to get it. I reminded her that she had been told not to come on school property while she was suspended, and I added that she was to leave at once. She said that she would have to tell the Reverend Pruden first, and asked for the Remember Little Rock card back. I did not return it and told her that displaying it was still another violation of school regulations. After she walked away, I called the superintendent's office to tell him at once of this violation of the girl's suspension, forgetting that he was a Rotarian, too. I then called the hotel where the Rotarians were lunching to ask them to have Jess call me back. He called; and I ended my account by telling him that Captain Stumbaugh was keeping the girl under observation. Jess called again in fifteen minutes. This time I could tell him that Captain Stumbaugh had brought word that the girl had left the school grounds.

I breathed easier. But I shouldn't have. Near the end of the second lunch period I looked up from my desk to see Minnijean, followed by a guard, enter the door. I saw at once that her shoulders had been doused with soup. She was half laughing, half crying. As I brought her into my inner office, she said, "May I call my mother?" and I said, "Yes, but not until you tell me what happened." So she told me.

"I got my lunch and was sitting talking with Elizabeth when I felt this bowl or tray fall on my back and the hot soup on my neck and back. The bowl hit the floor and broke. I looked around and this boy said, 'Oh, excuse me,' and walked on. I said to Elizabeth, 'Oh, well, they got even with me.' The guard came and took me out. I managed to keep a pleasant look on the way out. I know what the boy looks like."

I found a clean blouse and skirt in my clothes closet and asked Minnijean to take off her soupy outer clothing so I could wipe the soup from her back and arms. Then, hearing an increase of noise in the halls, I left her in my inner office with the door closed and walked out into the corridor and stood at my door. In my outer office, I noticed Elizabeth sitting at the table. The hall was full of excited kids. Guards were walking slowly through the mass, saying and doing nothing, but being there. The greatest excitement was in front of the main office, where most of the two or three hundred youngsters seemed to be drawn to the disturbance. A large group of them set up a cheer, "Fifteen for ———," and they called the name of the suspended girl's boyfriend, the one who had souped Minnijean.

Since it was almost time for the warning bell for the next class, I called Jeanne McDermott in the main office to suggest that she ring it now to keep the crowd from building up and to start the pupils on to class. I told Elizabeth to stay where she was for a few minutes. The halls began to clear; and when I saw that black youngsters were moving through the halls without undue attention, I sent Elizabeth on to class.

Back in the inner office again, I had Miss Carpenter check Minnijean for burns from the hot soup, and the nurse found no injury. By 3:00 Jess Matthews had returned and talked to Minnijean, expressing his regret, and her mother had come to take her home to bathe and wash her clothes.

Meanwhile, J. O. and Margaret Reiman had been dealing with

the boy who had thrown the soup. The boy said he did it because Minnijean called him "white trash." "So you had to prove it," was Mrs. Reiman's reply.

The boy repeated the "white trash" charge to J. O. but said the soup-spilling was accidental, that he tripped over Minnijean's chair. The guard said this explanation was not possible. The boy's father came for a conference. In a general review of the boy's school record, which included truancies and forgeries of teachers' names to passes, the boy justified these matters by saying, "Oh, you've got to lie to somebody to get to do anything around here, unless you're a nigger." He was suspended.

Friday morning's *Gazette* reported that a platoon of soldiers had been sent to the school at 8:15 Thursday evening after telephoned bomb threats. No bombs were found. This was the third bomb threat, the *Gazette* reported. They had missed a few.

On Friday, students did not report to school, this being a day for the teachers to complete their semester records and assign and record grades. As usual on this midterm report day, the PTA served a sandwich lunch to teachers. I was amazed that there were enough brave mothers to carry out the project. And so the first semester was over.

On Saturday morning when I answered the phone, no one replied, though the line was open. I hung up. The next time this happened, I outlasted the silence of the caller by *my* silence. Finally, there was a keen whistle, meant to be ear-piercing; but I was not holding the receiver near my ear. I still kept the line open till my caller gave up. I did not answer the phone again on Saturday. Late Sunday morning the telephone harassment began again. We checked occasionally with my parents to be sure they weren't calling us, but we did not answer the phone all day.

Monday, January 20, the first day of the new semester, was a disturbing one. The Mothers' League had announced a meeting for Monday night to hear the Reverend Wesley Pruden discuss "What the Race-Mixers Are Planning for Us," with a special invitation to Central High students. One hundred ninety-six students, many of them "hard core," were absent from school that day, and I wondered what they were up to. When I told Jess of the absences, he issued a special bulletin asking each homeroom teacher to use particular care in checking and reporting as soon as possible the reasons for all absences. Minnijean, Melba, and Terrence were absent.

About 9:30 there came to the switchboard another telephoned bomb threat. As usual, Assistant Police Chief Gene Smith, the FBI, and the military were alerted and came out immediately; and, as usual, a search was begun under the direction of O. W. Romine, maintenance supervisor for the schools. But this time they found dynamite—only one stick, without fuse or cap, but still dynamite— in an unused locker. Jess took a tranquilizer and missed lunch. I had a headache, but I ate lunch.

The lunch period produced an incident which J. O. investigated and reported. Two boys, both involved in racial incidents from the beginning of school, had tried to trip Carlotta, Ernest reported, as they were on their way to lunch. The second boy then hit Ernest in the face with his fist. Ernest had chased his attacker, who had tried to escape through a cafeteria door that was fastened, giving Ernest time to alert a guard, who stopped the boy. The boy admitted hitting Ernest, but he declared it was in retaliation for Ernest's having tried to trip the boy with him. J. O. recommended that the white boys be suspended. He was getting plenty angry at the situation that made it impossible for us to do what was just. We knew which students were telling the truth. But with the current temper of Little Rock, where would we get, suspending white children on the unsupported word of black children? If we did, we would have to suspend the blacks on the unsupported testimony of the whites. It would not have taken a day to get all the black pupils suspended, that way. It was cruel and unfair; but we were stuck with it.

During the afternoon a guard reported that he had seen two girls going through the lower hall, inking a stamp on a pad and stamping "Remember Little Rock" signs on walls and bannisters. He showed me the signs and pointed out the girls in the journalism room, both known to me for being on the fringe of "incidents." I called in the girl who had done the actual stamping and told her to take the stamp home and never bring it to school again. She worked as an office monitor in the main office before school and at Period 7, and I should have asked Jeanne McDermott to remove her from these jobs. But I was still trying to treat students as learners and not as a part of an adult-directed plot. Of course I was wrong—again.

At home, after dinner, Ray Mosley of the *Arkansas Gazette* called to ask me my given name and Mr. Powell's initials. J. O. and I, said Mr. Mosley, had been called on by the Citizens' Council to resign, along with Mr. Blossom and Mr. Matthews. The United Press called, too, with the same cheerful information.

To calm my thoughts, I got out my grammar and reviewed for tomorrow night's final examination in the University of Arkansas extension course I was taking. It settled my mind so that I slept—some. But I was conscious of a cold wind that came up and blew all night.

I felt better Tuesday morning. The story of the dynamite found at school had kept my name off page one of the morning paper, anyhow. It was buried on page two, in a quote from the Reverend Mr. Pruden. A few teachers met me with humorous congratulations on getting my name on the blacklist. I told them that I really would have preferred an orchid on this twenty-eighth anniversary of my coming to Central, but perhaps the blacklist was all right as a substitute.

There was a determined effort to get us to close school on that Tuesday. Shortly before 11 o'clock, I began to get calls from mothers who said that the radio was reporting bomb threats at Central. I told the callers that any parents who wished to do so could come to school in person and take their children out. One mother protested that inconvenience as much as the imagined danger to her child. A member of the Mothers' League came in to demand her two children. I sent for them immediately to sign out, but I pointed out to the mother that the hourly threats we were under probably were from people who would like to have us close the school. One anonymous threat that morning had already been checked out as false. The mother was incensed that Mr. Matthews had ignored her letter to send her children home any time there was a bomb threat. I assured her that I knew nothing of any such request, and I told her that we had no intention of closing school every time an anonymous threat was received, for there seemed to be plenty of people willing to call in every hour to achieve that end. I told her, further, that the superintendent, the principal, and several teachers had children in our school; and that certainly they would not keep their children here if they really believed a bomb was about to explode. Two unidentified mothers who were listening left, evidently satisfied to leave their children in school.

The son and the daughter of the Mothers' League mother came to the office and checked out. The mother asked her daughter whether she had delivered the letter she had sent to Mr. Matthews, and she said she had. (Jess found it in his office mailbox later in the day.) The mother, still angry, left with her children, but her son checked back into school an hour later. A student told me that she had seen the daughter the night before, as a part of a TV news report on the Citizens' Council meeting, singing a duet, "I'm Dreaming of a White Central." The other singer was the girl who had once pushed her friend into Elizabeth with the result that the friend, to quote her mother, got "scratched and clawed"—as the paper reported.

Other parents called or came. One father said his son had called him, crying, to say a bomb was due to go off at 2:30. Most parents who called were easily identifiable as Mothers' League members or their sympathizers.

No bomb went off at school, at 2:30 or later. If it had, the Little Rock assistant police chief and members of the FBI would have gone up with the rest of us, for they were in the halls to observe. Absent from school all day, and probably busy at telephones, I guessed, were our two suspended pupils, the small girl and her boyfriend; and others, including the pony-tailed blond.

But there were still too many with segregationist views who were in school. Carlotta reported more difficulty in biology class from three boys and a girl. And the boy who struck Ernest was involved in shoving another boy into Gloria. A pure accident, he said. Just scuffling. No adult witnesses.

After school on Tuesday I went by my parents' apartment to show Mother and Father that I was still alive, then home for a quick supper before Sybil Hefley picked me up to take me to the Graduate Center for the examination in advanced grammar. I was back at home by 8:40. My day on the integration front was not quite over. Mr. Blossom called to ask me to be at the hearing before the school board at 5:15 on Wednesday, the hearing requested by the mother of the suspended blond—and her lawyer.

The *Gazette* on Wednesday morning reported the bomb threats at Central on Tuesday and Mr. Blossom's explanation that a few people seemed to be trying to force the closing of the school. Under Ray Mosley's by-line, the story went on to quote Amis Guthridge, attorney for the Capital Citizens' Council, as challenging Mr. Blossom's remarks: "We think perhaps this might be an inside job to discredit the people opposed to race-mixing. We think the whole thing is a hoax."

Mr. Guthridge also had an affidavit signed by the mother who had removed her son and daughter from school for the afternoon, quoting her discussion with me and saying, "She assured me beyond doubt that the report (of a bomb in school) was false. She was so calm I had to believe she was sincere. This worried me. How did she know it was false? Is it reasonable to assume that they (school officials) know who planted the report? Are they trying to create conditions to force the closing of the school so they can blame it on segregationists?" I took a little good-natured ribbing at school for my darkly suspicious calmness.

Minnijean's semester failure in American history made it advisable to reduce her program so that she could have a study hall. Ordinarily, a student with her program would have been advised to drop glee club. But I advocated to Miss Hensley, her counselor, that she be left in that class, in which she was so successful, and that she drop speech. That change would have a corollary advantage. If she dropped speech at Period 5, she could be placed in study hall at Period 6 and have lunch at Period 5, a different lunch time, where the kids had not witnessed or been involved in either food-dumping incident. The changes were made.

There were minor disturbing reports. Minnijean reported that, as she walked into her English class, a girl said, under her breath, "Here comes that nigger." Melba came by to say that she thought some ink-throwing was being planned by a group in her typing class. She was vague about details and about how she knew of the plan. And Mrs. Means, who had been helping the coaches supervise the lunchroom since the chili dumping, reported that our suspended blond had appeared there again for lunch.

Elizabeth Eckford came in just as Period 7 started and with a catch in her voice told me a girl had spit on her. She held out her left hand as if I could see the mark of discourtesy it had received. I asked her whether she knew the girl. She didn't, but she could describe her. "Even if we knew, that wouldn't help us much, would it?" I asked, and sent her into the lavatory with directions to wash her hand hard with soap and water before going to class.

Jess, J. O., and I were about equally exhausted by the end of the day and left school promptly to go home and rest a while before our appearance before the board on the small girl's suspension. I stretched out for a few minutes, took a bath, and drank a glass of milk. I got to the boardroom at 5:15.

As I opened the door and walked into the lobby at Eighth and Louisiana streets, I was aghast at the number of people gathered there. I didn't realize who they were until·I saw four students who had recently been involved in incidents, including our pony-tailed leader. The adults, men and women, were an awful-looking crew. It wasn't that they were shabby, for they weren't. But their faces were full of hate, and they seemed to murmur as I passed through on my way to the boardroom. It was a feeling that was new to me, and terrifying. Upstairs in the boardroom, I spoke to the members of the board individually; and I said to one of them, Harold Engstrom, who had been in one of my English classes when he was a boy, "Now I know how the early martyrs felt when they were thrown to the lions."

I spoke to Archie House, school board lawyer, and told him my name. He remembered me from a fraternity lawsuit a few years back. "That was just a skirmish compared to this," he remarked.

By this time Mr. Blossom and Dr. William Cooper, president of the board, had come in, and Amis Guthridge of the Citizens' Council, who was the lawyer for the suspended girl's mother who had demanded this hearing. Mr. Guthridge spoke to the board, requesting that the people gathered downstairs be admitted to the meeting. "I don't know why they are here except that they must be interested. But if you refuse to admit them, you may hear from them; and then, of course, the papers will have something to say—they always do," he said. No one believed what he had said; but no one called him a liar, either.

Some members of the board seemed to feel that it would be best to admit the crowd; but after Mr. Blossom pointed out that all hearings on personnel are private; that the mother had asked only for a hearing for herself, her daughter, and her lawyer; and that Mr. Guthridge had added the request for Mr. Matthews, Mr. Powell, and me—and some student witnesses for the girl, Dr. Cooper went down and informed the group that they could not sit in. After a few minutes, Dr. Cooper, Amis Guthridge, the mother and daughter, the four student witnesses (all involved in other incidents, and led by the pony-tailed blond), and the pony-tailed girl's father came in.

We rearranged ourselves in a circle, and I could hear the children murmuring among themselves. The pony-tailed leader's voice was recognizable: "She's scared." And I was; I am frightened by hate.

Dr. Cooper began by reading from the account of the pushing incident that I had written for the superintendent. Mr. Blossom had had it mimeographed for each member of the board. "Who wrote that?" Mr. Guthridge asked. "Mrs. Huckaby," Dr. Cooper replied. "I haven't seen that statement," Mr. Guthridge said. "May I have it?" My heart faltered as Dr. Cooper handed it over. It had been written as a confidential report to the superintendent, not as a document to be put into the hands of the lawyer for the Capital Citizens' Council.

Amis Guthridge began to read aloud, very sarcastically at times, my account of the morning annoyances of Melba, my knowledge of the suspended girl's strong feelings about "niggers." "You have kindly strong feelings, too, don't you, Mrs. Huckaby?" he smirked. I couldn't resist his rural vernacular use of *kindly*. "*Kindly*?" I said. "You don't think I've been at Central for twenty-eight years without feeling kindly toward children, do you? Of course I feel kindly." It was ridiculous of me to pull linguistic rank on him, for he didn't get the point. Dr. Cooper shushed me and said we were off the subject.

As Mr. Guthridge read on, he came to some reference to Mr. Powell. "Mr. Powell," he simpered. "And is Mr. Powell here?" From slightly behind Amis and a little to his right, J. O. boomed out, "*Right here!*" Mr. Guthridge started, and several of us smiled.

When he read in my report that I had not questioned Elizabeth about being pushed, he wanted to press the point of why. Mr. House, sitting beside me, murmured, "I wouldn't answer that."

When Mr. Guthridge, in his reading, got to the end of the interview with the girl in Mr. Matthews's office, Dr. Cooper said, "Now, Amis, that's all about this incident. Please give the paper back to me." Mr. Guthridge hesitated, perceptibly. J. O. reached out his hand as if to take the paper. Amis jerked it back, but got up and handed it reluctantly to Dr. Cooper. Mr. Guthridge asked the girl to come forward, sit down, and give her account of the incident. She was just on her way to class, she said, and had to go back for her notebook. She was coming down the stairs, talking to her best friend over her shoulder and didn't see anyone in front of her when she accidentally brushed into this "nigger girl," who turned, gave her the meanest look she ever saw, and drew back her arm to strike her. The guard, she said, took Elizabeth's arm, then grabbed her (the narrator) and said, "Come on to the office." She had not denied that she shoved Elizabeth intentionally when we questioned her, she said, because we kept her so confused, hurrying her from one office to the next, that she couldn't think.

Mr. Guthridge then asked the girl to testify to some of my actions, such as jerking the "Remember Little Rock" sign from her sweater, but Dr. Cooper brought him back to the subject before the board, the girl's suspension.

Mr. Guthridge called the girl's best friend, the pony-tailed segregationist leader, to the witness chair. Her story, again, was of an unforeseen and inadvertent accident. She said that she and the other three friends here to testify were standing on the first floor, telling their friend to hurry. She added drama to the story by telling of the guard's method of apprehending her friend. "You see how little she is. Well, he just grabbed her so hard it just lifted her off the floor!"

Harold Engstrom had noted the discrepancy in the testimony of the two girls, the suspended girl saying she had been looking back at her best friend as she went down the stairs, the best friend saying that she was at the foot of the stairs, telling her friend to hurry. "How do those stairs go?" he asked the pony-tail. "How do those stairs go? How do *any* stairs go?" she said, testily. "Why, *up. Up* from the first floor to the second, *up* from the second floor to the third!" "Then, if your friend was on the stairs, she couldn't have been looking back at you on the first floor," Harold said, calmly. Mr. Guthridge conceded the point. But he wanted the testifying friend to get in a few verbal licks at me. "I just want to know," she said, "why I am a member of the speech activities class and Mr. Matthews and Mrs. Huckaby wouldn't let me do *anything* on a program." Dr. Cooper ruled that the subject of the hearing was being lost again, and asked whether the other witnesses had any other facts to bring out about the incident. Mr. Guthridge asked each in turn whether the witness's account was correct. Each agreed, in turn.

No rebuttal was called for, and all of us except the board members left the room. At the top of the stairs, I spoke to the suspended girl's mother and said that of course I thought her daughter needed to be in school, but that she needed to attend peaceably. "I'm glad to hear you say that," said Amis. I did not reply, since I had not addressed him. Some of the crowd were still downstairs. "Isn't she the cutest thing," someone murmured as the young people went out the door. I didn't know which girl they referred to, but I shuddered.

We had a bomb call by 8:00 A.M. on Thursday, a second threat later in the morning, and a firecracker "bomb" was found in a locker. The cigarette attached to it had been lighted, but it had gone out. At noon, a fire was discovered and extinguished in another locker. And school went on.

Loreen Lee and Christine Poindexter, standing in the hall as classes passed, saw a boy spit on Minnijean as she started down the stairs. They didn't know the boy, but Miss Poindexter followed him to his class and asked his teacher his name. He was an orphan, living in a foster home. That his foster parent was connected with the administration of the schools would have made quite a scandal, if it had become known. I told Jess, and he spoke with the foster parent, who said he would get the boy straightened out. He did.

During the morning I had a call from one of the officers of the Mothers' League, one who had been in the crowd outside Central in the early fall but who had no children here. She just wanted to know, she said, whether the suspended girl would be permitted to take the final exams she had missed when she returned on Monday. It was none of the caller's business, of course; and knowing the girl's lack of scholastic ability, I imagined that taking the exams would not help her record. But I didn't say this to my caller, who went on to complain that everyone was giving her the runaround on her question. I gave her more of the same.

J. O. had an unusual experience with a boy who had been brought in by a guard for deliberately following Ernest Green and stepping on his heels. During the conference the boy, as well as J. O., took notes; and at the end of the conference he asked to see what J. O. had written. When J. O. asked why the boy was taking notes, he said they were for his father. We were to hear from him later.

After school, Jess, J. O., and I went by Mr. Blossom's office for a conference, the gist of which was that General Walker was getting pretty upset over our situation, particularly about our pony-tailed segregationist leader who, he felt, should be put out of school. I was sure that the general was no more distressed than we were. But, as he should have known by now, putting a segregationist pupil out of school was not a simple matter.

The March of Dimes assembly on Friday brought to school one Robert Shaw, a polio victim from babyhood, who had never been able to attend school but who had "attended" by telephone for his high school courses. This was his first physical contact with his schoolmates. Minnijean was afraid to attend assembly, she said; so I let her sit in my office. I beckoned her out into the hall when the a cappella choir sang, for I knew that one of her dreams was to become a member of that group.

About noon, J. O. and I were in Jess's office trying to think of some constructive changes in our method of handling our problems. Another bomb threat came in to the switchboard. That broke up the conference, for the routine called for Jess to notify the police chief, the superintendent, the FBI, and General Walker's office. Then the premises had to be searched, and J. O. was involved in that. I went back to my office.

Jennie Perkins came in to tell me that when she had called about the absence of one of her pupils, the girl said she had stayed home because she had heard there was going to be trouble at school. I called the girl herself to ask what kind of trouble she expected. She had heard, she said, that she was to be called into my office for wearing black to school. I assured her that she could wear any color dress she wanted to. So ended the first week of the second semester.

On Monday, both the boy who had souped Minnijean and the girl whose mother had demanded the board hearing were readmitted to school after their suspensions. Peculiarly enough, Monday and Tuesday passed with relative quiet. The boy who had verbally harassed the guard for reporting the small girl who had shoved Elizabeth and who had later appeared as a witness for her at the board hearing was reported by a guard for addressing Minnijean as a "nigger-looking bitch." The guard had difficulty in persuading the boy to go to the office. When I saw the boy square off at the guard, I went up to him. He listened to me, his last year's teacher, and went on to see J. O., to whom he declared that his remark was made to a friend in a humorous manner. Jess asked the boy's father to come for a conference, and the father vowed that his son would give no further trouble.

The guards were always conscious of the blond pony-tailed girl and her activities. On Monday one guard reported seeing her show three girls and a boy in a group a card—probably "Remember Little Rock"—pinned under the hem of her skirt. On Tuesday, another guard saw her go in and out of the cafeteria several times. On her last trip she was carrying several soft drinks. As she passed the guard, she commented, "You can leave, now. I'm not going to eat in the cafeteria today, but I will tomorrow."

On Wednesday, January 29, school attendance was excellent: only 82 of our 1800 students absent. The Key Club Capers, which almost everyone wanted to see, and given on school time at a nominal fee, was almost certainly the reason for the upsurge of good health. I knew this from experience in previous years. Almost everyone bought tickets for the show, which lasted half the morning. The hundred or so who didn't buy tickets were provided study halls. Elizabeth reported to me later that in the study hall she had been pelleted by spitballs.

At noon, both Carol Carter and Sissi Brandon told me that a boy who had been suspended for an accumulation of truancies had announced that he was going to "get" Minnijean after school. This boy's annoyances had been one of Minnijean's reasons for dropping French class in the fall. The teachers who gave me the report of the threat didn't know what the boy planned to do; but we alerted the guards and J. O. Sure enough Susie West and Sissi Brandon approached the Fourteenth Street exit just in time to see this boy kick Minnijean's rear as she walked toward her mother's car. One-hundred-pound Sissi was hauling the protesting boy back to the building when J. O. arrived and took over. In the office, the boy first said that another boy had dared him to kick Minnijean. Later he admitted that he had said earlier that he would "get" her, and so make the most of his suspension. Since the boy was already suspended, the most J. O. could do was to warn him to stay away from school and to add this occurrence as a bar to his readmittance.

Only after the boy had left did the guard who always observed the exit of the black pupils report to J. O. that he had seen what looked like a knife in the boy's hand during the attack on Minnijean. J. O. was upset that he hadn't thought to check the boy's pockets while he was in the office.

So Minnijean, vulnerable for those very extrovert qualities that make other teenagers popular, was becoming the prime target of the mob. The suspended boy was not the only one who would get her.

On Thursday, Minnijean was not able to come to school, too badly bruised, her mother said. I was sure that not all the bruises were physical. I got statements from all the adults who had knowledge of the kicking so that Jess could make a full report to the superintendent. Later in the day we learned that Mrs. Brown and Minnijean had been to the prosecuting attorney's office to get a warrant for the boy's arrest for assault. Prosecutor J. Frank Holt refused the request.

The father of the boy who had taken notes during his conference with J. O. came to school by request. Margaret Reiman had confiscated from his son some printed cards, the bayonet-in-the-back type, but these with the caption "Brotherhood by Bayonet," which the boy was distributing. In the ensuing conference, both the father and the son agreed that the boy would stop distributing such materials and stay clear of the black students.

Melba Pattillo's locker had been tampered with. I got one of the custodians to straighten the catch so that she could open it.

I had not seen the Key Club Capers matinee, so I went to the evening performance. By our agreement with the girl segregationist leader, she had been barred from performing publicly on the stage only for the first semester. So there she was on stage, in her white evening dress, her own idea of a southern belle. Believing as I did that she was the ringleader of much of the harassment of the Nine, I could hardly stomach the show. At home, Glen reported that I had had one anonymous phone call.

Thursday (it had been "stare day") had not been a good day. Friday ("black day") was no better. The Nine were more frightened—who could blame them?—and their parents were more critical of our "lack of firmness." And we, "in charge," were operating with the support of the superintendent, five of the six board members, and a few guards. The "moderate" leadership of the city was paralyzed. Federal officials were evidently not going to prosecute and punish those who were obstructing and opposing federal court orders. And there was constant indication that the state government was actually assisting in, if not directing, the harassment. We could only try to outlast them: to run school for our 1800 boys and girls, black and white, meanwhile trying to protect the Nine from physical injury.

Our Friday absentee list, including those who signed out to leave school during the day on excuses from parents, seemed to indicate some further planning session of the segregationists. It was hard to tell, really, for it might be merely typical of the poor adjustment to school that many of this group displayed, anyway. Several of those who had been in trouble, including the small girl who had returned only this week from her suspension, were missing. And her boyfriend who had been suspended for souping Minnijean reported to the health room in late morning and asked to sign out.

Melba's locker was broken again. Again the custodian repaired it. Gloria Ray's locker handle was twisted so that she couldn't open it. The custodian straightened the catch. We were to have a pep assembly at 1:15 for the basketball team. Melba, Thelma, and Elizabeth asked if they could sit in my office. I let them.

Immediately after assembly, the upper quarter, scholastically, of the junior class stayed in the auditorium to hear Joan Rule, former Central student, talk about the Rotary International Youth Seminar in which she had recently taken part. As I listened to Joan from the back of the auditorium, Miss Carpenter, the school nurse, came for me to tell me that Elizabeth Eckford had told her she was going home and wouldn't say why. I found Elizabeth in my office with her coat on, and with a note of permission to see me from Mrs. Wheeler, her gym teacher. She was standing dejectedly, looking out the front window; and when she turned, I saw that she had been crying. She said she wanted to see her doctor. I asked her whether she had been hurt. She said no, but that she had taken all she could take in gym class and wanted a doctor's permit to take hygiene, instead. I asked what had happened today, and she spoke of a ball being thrown at her. I asked her whether there were any particular girls who made trouble for her, and she named a girl who had tried to pick a fight with her. I said I thought we could handle that girl, for she had already been suspended once for a fight (with a white girl) and would be expelled if she fought again. Were there any others who caused her trouble? All the girls in her line "said things" to her except two, she said, but she mentioned no actions.

I tried to persuade Elizabeth to stay in school for her last class, speech, but she said she had already called her grandfather and he was coming for her. So while she was signing out at 2:30, I called the lieutenant in charge of the guard to tell him that she was leaving early and that I was seeing her out. Joan Rule, who had finished her talk, came in, and the three of us walked to the Fourteenth Street exit. As we stood waiting, Jess and Mr. Eckford joined us. Mr. Eckford, a middle-aged, rotund man, was very much disturbed. He had made it to school in three minutes, he said, having got the impression from Elizabeth's call that some attack had been made on her such as that on Minnijean a couple of days before. He chided Jess and me, "Can't you keep order and discipline?" "No," I said. "Not the same kind in gym classes where there are a hundred students to a teacher and the pupils move about freely that we can in a regular class—and certainly not without community backing."

"You mean the guards and teachers can't keep order?" "The guards don't go to girls' gym classes, of course," said Jess, "and it's impossible for the teacher to follow one pupil around and still conduct a gym class for ninety to a hundred pupils."

Captain Stumbaugh and J. O. were present by this time. I reassured them that there had been no incident. Mr. Eckford continued to talk about the length of time he had lived in Little Rock, about no member of his family having ever been in trouble, and about his having many white friends, some of his friends "also friends of Mr. Matthews." All of these facts I was sure were true; but I knew from my own experience that none of them had any bearing in the Little Rock we lived in now. By this time, Elizabeth had gone out to her grandfather's car to wait for him. I went back to my office.

After school I went to the gym office to ask Mary Wheeler whether she had observed anything out of the way in Elizabeth's class. She said she hadn't. When she missed Elizabeth she went to the dressing room to see if she was sick, "Not physically," was Elizabeth's reply. Mrs. Wheeler asked if anything had happened, since a student was due to ask permission before leaving a class. Elizabeth did not report any incident or any person, but just said she wanted to "see Mrs. Huckaby." So Mrs. Wheeler gave her a pass to my office.

Mrs. Wheeler also reported that in gym class on Thursday the group Elizabeth was assigned to in building a pyramid accepted her well and worked well with her. This group was not the "line" Elizabeth had mentioned to me.

At home, I had a call from L. C. Bates, husband of Daisy Bates of the NAACP and editor of a black newspaper. He said he wanted to "confirm" something. I thought it probably was my statement about not being able to maintain discipline (without the qualifications I had made to that statement). I told him that I was not free to discuss matters with the press. He said he was not asking for publication; but I still refused to discuss anything about school, telling him that he must get his information as usual from the administration.

My evening at home was spent writing up incidents for that office. But another week and another month were past. Tomorrow would be February. As January ended, we were reading of the proposal of Chancellor Pilkington of Hope, Arkansas, to solve our problems at Central: the Nine were to go back to Horace Mann High School, the school board was to resign, and the community to vote for or against integration—a plan heartily approved by the governor, you may be sure. One of the "reliable sources of information" at Central had sent the *Democrat* a picture of one of the unused lockers at Central bolted shut, a move that had been made necessary to reduce the chances of finding dynamite in one. The only good news in the evening paper was that Gene Smith had been named police chief (he had been acting in that capacity for months) despite the protests of several members of the Central High School Mothers' League because of his actions against the mob on September 23.

The proposed plan to relax the guard at Central on Monday, February 3, was not put into effect, since the times did not suggest relaxation. Minnijean, back at school after her two-day absence because of the kicking on Wednesday, was frightened and asked for a guard to follow her. The guard reported that some small objects, probably candies—Tootsie Rolls—were thrown at her as she left the cafeteria. The papers reported that Governor Faubus was speeding up his decision on whether to run for a third term. Representative Brooks Hays was in town, seeking conferences with state and local authorities.

On Tuesday, Mary Wheeler came in to talk further about her gym class and Elizabeth; and Elizabeth herself reported another incident of one girl's shoving another into her, this time in her speech class.

At Mr. Blossom's request, I had another conference with Minnijean. An anonymous caller had predicted that Minnijean was planning to run through the halls at Central screaming that she had been raped. She was as amazed at that prediction as Mr. Blossom and I had been and said she would be careful not to do anything that could be interpreted as suggesting that. Minnijean wanted assurance about her behavior after her return from suspension, and I assured her that no one had reported anything unbecoming in her actions. I complimented her on her behavior, in spite of all the things that had happened to her. Recalling Melba's experience when she had leaned over to pick up her books, I suggested that she not pick up anything tossed in her direction.

J. O. had some reports of trouble from Terrence Roberts. His locker had been tampered with and the lock stolen. Terrence reported, too, that two boys from his last period study hall had kicked him as he went to his locker after school. And he had seen one of the boys kick Jefferson Thomas last week. But no teacher or guard witnessed either attack.

J. O. did not agree with Jess's policy of not suspending pupils for racial incidents that were not authenticated by adult witnesses. From now on, all his reports to the superintendent recommended permanent suspension for those students reported by the Nine for repeated harassment.

Three boys (including the soup spiller) and three girls (including the pony-tailed leader) who had been involved in racial incidents were absent on Tuesday. Were they plotting further incidents? Were they reporting to the representative of the governor? These possibilities always entered our minds. The governor had charged, in a speech before the Lions' Club at Forrest City, that National Guardsmen were "tailing" certain white students about the building and grounds of Central because Superintendent Blossom had listed them as potential troublemakers. I am sure those troublemakers felt watched, for the guards knew them as well as we did.

The three boys absent on Tuesday were still absent on Wednesday. Except for paper balls thrown at Carlotta by the usual boys in her biology class, no incidents were reported. Captain Stumbaugh told us that the next phase of the National Guard withdrawal was to begin on Thursday, with no guards in evidence except before school, at noon, and after school. He thought that the withdrawal would not be noted or commented on till Friday. That day was to be College Day, sponsored by the Beta Club. The excitement of having visitors from colleges all over the state could be counted on to lessen integration pressures.

The *Democrat* on Wednesday evening reported that the Little Rock crisis was having its effect: five states had passed "Little Rock" bills, to close schools rather than to integrate. Faubus was described as "cool" toward any meeting with Representative Brooks Hays.

Margaret Reiman called me on Wednesday evening. She had been walking down the hall that morning and had passed two or three black students being followed by two or three white students. Only after she had passed both groups did she realize that one of the white girls had been saying, "Nigger! Nigger!" Margaret didn't know the white pupils. But she told me what corridor to watch, and I made a mental note to be there in the morning. But at the time I should have been in the hall Thursday morning, I was in my office talking with a girl whose homeroom teacher had sent her to me for truancy on Wednesday. The bell for beginning school had not yet rung when a guard brought in two very angry girls, a white girl and Minnijean. I dismissed the guard, sent the truant on to her homeroom, and heard the girls' stories.

"We decided we would follow Minnijean to the south end of the building," the white girl said. "We told the guard, jokingly, to keep an eye on us. I turned to say something to a friend, Minnijean stopped, and I ran into her. She laughed at me. I said, 'You think you're smart, don't you.' When she got to her homeroom door, she said to me, 'Goodbye, paddy. White trash!' She turned to go in her homeroom, and I threw my purse and hit her with it. Then the guard came and said, 'Let's go to the office.' Minnijean picked up my purse from the floor and threw it to my feet. I went with the guard."

Minnijean's report was different. She said that the white girl, with other boys and girls, had made a practice for several days of following her, murmuring, "Nigger, nigger, nigger." That morning, Minnijean continued, this girl had followed her again, with the same refrain. Minnijean stopped, and the girl ran into her. The white girl then said, "If you stop again, I'll kick you like that boy did," adding a vulgar statement that would naturally conclude such a threat. She continued to call names till Minnijean got to her homeroom. There Minnijean turned and said, "Will you please stop talking to me, white trash?" Then the white girl threw her purse at her and hit her in the head with it.

I took both girls to Jess's office and we reviewed the problem.

He pointed out to them that they were both wrong in their name-calling back and forth, and that the only way they could handle the situation was for them to admit the wrong and agree to have nothing to do with each other and to stay out of one another's way. Minnijean agreed to this, but the white girl would only reply, "I don't know."

Minnijean was sent on to her class. The white girl was asked whether she needed more time to think the matter over. She said she guessed she did. She was reminded that, after she withdrew from Central at the time of our desegregation to attend a county school and then decided to come back here, her father had come with her and had written out a statement that she would live peaceably in our integrated school.

Jess suggested that she might like to go home, talk with her parents, and take a little time to think the matter over, emphasizing the fact that we were not suspending her, yet. This we were anxious not to have to do, for that would force us to suspend Minnijean again, since both girls had been involved in name-calling and purse-throwing.

The white girl agreed and dialed her home, but she asked me to do the talking for her. After I told the mother what had happened she remarked that "that Negro had been causing a lot of trouble" for her daughter, a comment that did not encourage me about the kind of counseling she might get at home. The mother said that her husband would come for their daughter.

When the father came, he said he thought he had better withdraw his daughter from school and send her elsewhere. I read him his daughter's account of the incident, since I would incorporate it in my report, along with Minnijean's. The father did not express criticism of school officials, merely of integration, which he predicted would eventually result in injury to some child, white or colored. I gave the father the girl's report card and returned the fees she had paid for the semester. She collected her gym clothes and her books from her locker and was gone by 10:15. I wrote out her withdrawal.

But the problems of this day had just begun. At 11:00, after classes had changed between third and fourth periods, I saw a small group of girls talking excitedly in the hall. Two of them, the segregationist leader and the small girl recently returned from her suspension, went into the attendance office. Since Bonnie Brietz was not at her desk at the moment and the girls were talking with a student monitor, I asked what they wanted. Both said they were sick, though neither looked so. The leader said she had already talked with her mother (from the phone booth in the hall, I supposed), and she was going home. I asked whether they had got excused from their classes to come to the health room; and since they hadn't, sent them back for passes. I asked Mrs. Brietz, now back in her office, to ask Marion Carpenter to come from her study hall to check the health of the girls. Meanwhile I talked with Jess. He thought it best, if the girls' mothers so directed, to excuse them from school.

When Miss Carpenter checked with the girls, the small girl agreed to take an aspirin and see whether she would feel like staying in school after resting an hour. But the segregationist leader insisted that she must leave. I had her get her mother on the phone, and I told the mother that I understood that she wanted her daughter to come home. She had heard on the radio that there was another bomb scare and she wanted her home. I said her daughter had told me she wanted to leave because she was sick, that I didn't think she was sick; the building was quiet, but if she wished, I would send her. The girl signed out at 11:17. Donna Wells, a teacher, saw her in the hall later, in close conference with the boy who had been a witness for the small girl at the board hearing. Zinta Hopkins, the girl leader's counselor, told me of a forty-minute conference she had had with this girl the day before, during which she had professed that she was staying out of integration troubles at school, but that after school hours she had plenty of segregation business to attend to. She also boasted to Mrs. Hopkins that many times in recent months she had sat across the desk from Governor Faubus and talked to him.

Questions came to my mind by the end of the day. Did this girl want to leave school to investigate the withdrawal of the white girl who had got into the dispute with Minnijean? Or to report the affair to someone? Did she leave to organize the telephone calls we soon became aware of? Or did she leave to avoid being implicated in the noon-hour incident, knowing that one was being planned?

At 11:45, Mrs. Roberts, Terrence's mother, appeared at the main office, very much upset. She had had a call from a man who identified himself as Mr. Matthews, saying that Terrence had been injured in a fight. Jess had already left for Rotary Club; but of course he had not called, and no fight or injury had been reported. J. O. took Mrs. Roberts to Terrence's class so she could see him through the door. Satisfied that her son was all right, Mrs. Roberts left.

Other calls were going to other parents, or they were listening to radio news, in some cases. Eight or ten parents came for their sons or daughters. One white girl's mother had had a call that her daughter was in serious difficulty at school. I called the girl to the phone to assure her mother that she was in no trouble. The mother told me that the caller had asked her how she felt about integration.

But these were only minor disturbances of the day. At 11:55, I went to the lunchroom to be there when the pupils came in for the first lunch period. I stayed till Mrs. Means could get there from her English class. She came at 12:05. As I left, J. O. and I got word of an incident involving a black girl and white boys; so I went to the main office. Carlotta was there. She told me that as she went toward the cafeteria, two boys had met her on the stair landing, and one of them had kicked her. She did not know the boys; but she pointed them out to a guard, who directed them to the office. The boys' story, all innocence, was that they were peacefully walking toward the cafeteria when a guard stopped them and sent them to the office. Both had been involved previously.

As I walked on toward my office, I found Minnijean standing in the hall, trembling and wanting to go home because she couldn't keep from crying. I took her into my inner office and told her to go ahead and cry, if she felt like it, and then tell me what had happened. She cried only briefly and then said that a group of girls in her glee club class had gathered behind her and said things to her. She mentioned the names of three girls. They were charging her with having caused the white girl to get put out of school this morning. One girl had asked another whether the blond segregation leader had heard of the incident so that she could report it. When Minnijean seemed to be feeling better, I asked her whether she felt like going to lunch, and she went.

Ten minutes later, as I was standing at my office door watching the first pupils come upstairs from lunch, Minnijean came running up the steps, crying loudly. A guard was following her. As she went into my office, I saw the soup on her back. Since few students had seen her come in, I hurriedly closed her in my inner office and went into the outer hall, closing the outer door, too. Most of the pack had followed the boy who had souped Minnijean and were beginning to raise a commotion. A girl began to scream wildly. Some teachers, Opie, and some officers of the guard came out into the hall to try to calm the confusion. Several of our better students hurriedly removed themselves from that area, shaking their heads as they walked off. Some fifty or sixty boys and girls remained in the huddle, a few contending for a turn at the phone booth. I asked Bonnie Brietz to call the office and ask for an early class bell. After it rang, I walked down the center of the hall, urging the laggards to go on to class. One of the girls trying to make a call from the phone booth was the one who had been screaming, a guard said. (I remembered that this same girl had run through the halls on September 23, urging others to leave after the Nine came in. I had often been aware of her presence in the second-floor hall before school in the morning, in conference with other boys and girls who had caused us concern. The guard told me that this girl had approached him this morning, twenty minutes *before* we had had a bomb threat call, asking whether the bomb had been found.)

When the halls were clear, I went back to my office. Minnijean had already talked with her mother on my phone. Again I had her change clothes; again I asked Miss Carpenter to examine her shoulders for burns; and I suggested that she needed to leave before the next lunch period, while the halls were still clear. She collected her things from her locker and left school by the front door to meet her mother on Park Street.

J. O. had interviewed the soup-thrower, a boy frequently involved in incidents, the last time for striking Ernest Green. The boy justified his act only by saying, "I remembered that she had poured soup on some white boys and went over and dumped some on her." He was expelled.

Meanwhile, the small blond girl had stayed her hour in the health room without improvement in her health, she said. She was insistent on going home. I told Miss Carpenter to let her go, if she could reach her mother and the nurse did talk directly to the mother. By that time, Minnijean was in my office, waiting for her mother to pick her up. I asked Miss Carpenter to delay the other girl's departure till Minnijean was gone, and to instruct her to go straight home.

At the second lunch period, Mrs. Means, who had witnessed the soup-throwing incident, was too "shook up," she said, to go back to the cafeteria. So I took her place. Early in the period, I saw the small blond come in, look around, and make for her boyfriend, the one who had doused Minnijean the first time, in the cafeteria line. I asked her whether she hadn't checked out of school, sick; and when she said she had, I asked her to leave. "But my mother said I could eat lunch at school before I left," she said. "But I am telling you that if you have signed out of school, you are not to eat lunch here," I replied. She turned and ran out of the cafeteria.

I watched her boyfriend in the line. He had approached the line by a devious route that took him past the table where Terrence Roberts was seated. In line, he did not stay put, finally managing to get immediately in front of Jefferson Thomas. After he selected his food, he went to a table in the northeast corner of the cafeteria. It was crowded with girls—no boys, though boys dropped by for a hilarious word now and then. He kept up a continual yelping sound, as he ate and visited. After he finished eating, he took his tray to the far side of the room, where I was standing near the blacks' table. He simpered at me, "Watching something?" He broke a dish as he emptied his tray and strolled by me again, watching me all the while. "Is the show over?" I asked. His group left, still hilarious.

One of the boys of whom Carlotta had complained late this morning was in the lunchroom. He had been suspended earlier in the year for racial harassment; and since I hadn't heard what disposition had been made of the morning affair, I asked him whether he was still in school. He said he was, and that he hadn't done anything. After he finished his lunch, he, two other boys, and a bunch of girls whom I didn't know came and sat at a table just next to the one where Jefferson, Elizabeth, and Melba were sitting. The white boys and girls just sat there, obviously waiting. I waited, too, having signaled the black students not to leave. They had nowhere to go, with security, till they could be in their classes, with teachers in charge. Only when the black children rose as the bell rang, did this boy and his harassing group rise. I placed myself between the two groups, at the door made a slight delaying action against the whites, and motioned for a guard to follow the blacks. The boy's manner had been directly challenging and disrespectful of my authority. The segregationist youths were getting bolder with their successes.

When Jess got back from Rotary and heard our accounts of the past two hours, he said he would have to suspend Minnijean, not, of course, for getting souped again, but for violating her probation by calling the girl names and getting involved in the exchange of purse throwing. The truth, of course, was that we could no longer run the school if Minnijean was there. There were plenty of marginal youngsters who would be glad to be put out of school to gain the approval of their group by souping Minnijean week after week—or even day after day. Their target had been selected. Or, perhaps, she had selected herself. After all, she had dumped the chili first.

Jess asked me to call Mrs. Brown to let her know his decision. I could not, for she had not given me her new, unlisted phone number. But I wrote out the suspension notice, addressed it to Mr. and Mrs. Brown, and gave it to Carlotta Walls for delivery. She said Thelma Mothershed would take it to the Browns.

So, in spite of the best we could do, the segregationists had won this battle. Minnijean Brown would not be back at Central High School.

Now there were Eight.

Eight To Go

So Minnijean was out. It was an admission of defeat on our part, I felt. But I was sure that Minnijean's continued presence in Central High would have been a hazard to the other Eight. Her suspension, dated February 6, read: "Reinstated on probation January 13, 1958, with the agreement that she would not retaliate verbally or physically to any harassment but would leave the matter to authorities to handle. After provocation of a girl student, she called the girl 'white trash', after which the girl threw her purse at Minnijean." Certainly this was hardly a harsh enough indictment for an expulsion. It was not volatile, natural Minnijean that was our difficulty. It was just that she and our impossible situation would not mix.

What would be the effect of this ouster on the behavior of the segregationists? Would this triumph make them more confident? Could the Eight—could the school withstand their assaults?

The *Arkansas Gazette* on Friday, February 7, carried our difficulties on page one: BOMB THREATS, INCIDENTS STIR CENTRAL HIGH. On the first page of Section B was the story of a ninety-minute conference on Thursday between Congressman Brooks Hays and Governor Faubus, with Forrest Rozzell, executive director of the Arkansas Education Association, also present.

At school on Friday morning the halls were an incongruous mixture of Beta Club honor students who were hosts for our College Day visitors and of our usual segregationist stir. Before school

I had visitors, two angry men who charged that the "occupation troops" had stolen books from their daughters' lockers during the bomb search the day before. One of the men was a member of Governor Faubus' official statehouse family, and he refused to believe Jess's statement that no student lockers had been opened in that search. He was not, apparently, angry with me. (He had played golf with my husband a few times.) But he was obviously mad at the school, its officials, and the "feds." The girls later found their books where they had left them.

After the lunch hours, Mrs. Means came by to report the same group waiting for the blacks as on Thursday in the cafeteria. And a guard reported that the girl who had on one occasion pushed her friend into Elizabeth Eckford was calling out, "I smell a guard," as she went into the cafeteria with her boyfriend. J. O. was recommending the suspension of Carlotta's kicker, on the basis of his involvement in previous incidents; but Jess still insisted that some overt incident, to which a teacher or a guard was a witness, must be the cause of any suspension.

Friday afternoon brought the welcome weekend respite from school disturbances, but it produced more evidence of the sickness of the community. Sunday's *Democrat* noted: SPECTACULAR FOUR-ALARM FIRE DESTROYS NEGRO COLLEGE GYM at Arkansas Baptist College. Under that headline was a second: TWO CALLERS TAKE CREDIT FOR BLAZE. The Reverend J. Hodge Alves of Christ Episcopal Church, who had taken a great deal of verbal abuse as an outspoken opponent of the segregationists, announced to his congregation that he had accepted a church appointment in Virginia.

On Monday more of the Eight's lockers were tampered with, obscenities written on them, names called, and authority defied. The first soup spiller, having been back in school only briefly, was suspended again, not for his segregationist activities but for cutting study hall! As he left school after his suspension, he took childish vengeance on some teachers. He stopped at the door of Micky McGalin, our young speech teacher, and having got the attention of her class, spat on the floor. Upstairs, he paused at Miss Browning's door and said, dramatically, "I *hate* you." As he passed my office, he stopped to address me: "You bitch!" And so he left.

As they departed the cafeteria at noon, we asked the pack of troublemakers to go to the office, where the principal warned them to stop their harassments. All asserted they had a right to stay in the cafeteria till the bell rang. But the father of the boy whose long list of involvement in incidents stretched from October to the reported kicking of Carlotta only the week before, came to school the next day to assure the principal that he would control his son.

It was faculty meeting day. Jess had an important message for us from the superintendent. The Arkansas Legislative Council had decided to conduct a probe of the affairs at Central High School. Many of us would be questioned; and, since we could be subpoenaed if we did not testify willingly, the superintendent advised us to talk with the questioners. The fact that the state police were to be used as interrogators seemed to many of us a crude attempt at intimidation. We would be called, Jess said, and interviews arranged at times we agreed to. After the faculty meeting, Jess told J. O. and me that the board would provide a court reporter to be present at our interviews and his, since it was quite important that what we might say not be distorted in the report. The whole sickening investigation sounded like what might go on in a police state.

The afternoon paper did not do much to cheer me. The "Our Readers' Views" column had a letter from Mrs. Clyde Thomason, who identified herself as recording secretary of the Mothers' League, and whose letter was captioned, "Be Proud of Arkansas." She wrote, in part, "Integration can never be successful. Governor Faubus is the defender of the Constitution. People would stand behind their school boards if their school boards would stay with the majority of the people." Another letter, signed T. D., was about "Central High Incidents" and quoted Thurgood Marshall as saying he didn't know how much more unpleasant treatment blacks could take at Central High. T. D. asked whether anyone outside the school office had a reliable list of the number of incidents. "It seems to me there is at least one a week," he wrote, "reported in the papers, and if we judge by rumors there must have been a good deal more." T. D. was right.

The state policeman whose daughter had asked me about testifying about me to the Mothers' League was at school with his wife to enquire why his daughter had been dismissed from her post as an attendance office monitor. Bonnie Brietz, the attendance office clerk, was frank in telling them that, although she had shifted their daughter's time for working in the office so that she would not lunch at the same time as the girl segregationist leader, each time that girl came into the adjoining health room, the couple's daughter had left her post to confer with her. This, Mrs. Brietz would not tolerate. The couple then talked with each of their daughter's teachers. Although the state policeman was not in uniform, we were wary. We all knew that he was an officer in Mr. Faubus' state police.

Evidently, some sort of subversive planning was going on among the segregationist students. Two were fifteen minutes tardy, though they had been seen around school before the tardy bell. Miss Carpenter reported seeing one of them in conference with the girl leader, teacher passes in hand, after which the tardy girl came into the attendance office while Mrs. Brietz was out and started looking through the card file of student schedules. I stopped her unauthorized search to ask what she was looking for. She said she had a boy's car keys and she wanted to find him and return the keys. I offered to send them to the boy if she would tell me whose they were, but she refused and left the office. Two other pupils arrived late. One said he had had trouble opening his locker; another said he had been detained by business. Still another of our regular harassers was absent. His note the next day had his mother's name forged to it and said he had been to the dentist. He could not remember the dentist's name.

At noon on Tuesday, Coach Allen Howard, supervising in the cafeteria, sent a boy to the office for hitting Terrence Roberts in the back. This boy, after withdrawing from Central on October 18, had been attending school in Benton, Arkansas, and had only recently reentered our school. His version of the cafeteria affair was that he was about to sit down after getting himself a coke when "a nigger bumped into me and then I hit him with an elbow in the back." Terrence, when he was asked about the incident, made nothing of it, though he said the group of boys at the table where this boy ate had been troublesome in the past with minor annoyances.

My journal for Tuesday noted, "The military withdrawing more each day. Now around only before school, at noon, and after school. Not to be here at all on Friday."

Things went well Wednesday morning, possibly because the girl leader was absent, along with several of her followers. The absence of one of these, the girl who had charged that Elizabeth had "scratched and clawed" her, was explained later in the day when agents of the FBI came to see whether I could give them any help in identifying the handwriting on an obscene letter received by this girl. They did not show me the letter but asked to see samples of several handwritings. The letter was reported to have threatened the girl's life. I never learned the outcome—except that there was no murder.

After lunch came a girl to make a most preposterous charge— that Thelma Mothershed had kicked her! Thelma was the one whose heart condition had concerned us so that her schedule had been rearranged to preclude her climbing stairs unnecessarily. She had had almost no individual hazing, partly because she was small, mild-mannered, quiet, and not in the least assertive; and partly because of the respect most teen-agers show for those with physical handicaps. The thought of Thelma kicking anyone, even in retaliation, was too much for me to believe. But the complaining girl said that as she and a friend were coming up the stairs from lunch, walking behind Thelma and Elizabeth Eckford, Thelma kicked her, and then Elizabeth laughed at her.

I sent for Thelma. She did not know that she had touched anyone with her foot. She and Elizabeth were playing with each other as they walked up the stairs, but she had not intentionally, or, so far as she knew, unintentionally, kicked the girl. I sent for the girl's friend, who claimed to have observed the incident. The friend thought the kick could have been accidental, for she said Thelma was walking with "big steps." After we had talked for a while, the friend asked whether she and the girl who had made the accusation could talk privately for a few minutes. They went out into the hall; and when they came back, the accusing girl said she was ready to accept Thelma's explanation. Experienced as I had become with the varying reactions of parents, I suggested that she get her mother on the phone. Her mother was at work as a nurse's

These are typical of the cards that were passed among white segregationists in Little Rock during the 1957–58 session at Central High School. One Down Eight To Go was circulated after Minnijean Brown was expelled.

Minnijean Brown and her mother leaving Virgil Blossom's office after being refused a hearing on her expulsion, February 18, 1958.
ARKANSAS DEMOCRAT

Minnijean bids an affectionate goodbye to her friends, Elizabeth Eckford, Ernest Green, Thelma Mothershed, Jefferson Thomas, Gloria Ray, Terrence Roberts, Melba Pattillo, and Carlotta Walls.

ARKANSAS DEMOCRAT

One of many anonymously telephoned bomb scares precipitated a "fire drill." While the students were outside the building the 101st, with the help of Jess Matthews and staff, made a search for a bomb but never found one.

ARKANSAS DEMOCRAT

Captain Leon Stumbaugh, federalized National Guard, bids official farewell to Jess Matthews, principal, on May 28, 1958.

ARKANSAS DEMOCRAT

Ernest Green receives his diploma from Jess Matthews, principal, Little Rock Central High School, May 27, 1958.

ARKANSAS DEMOCRAT

Ernest Green, now assistant to the secretary of labor for employment and training in President Carter's administration, addresses the twentieth anniversary of desegregation assembly at Central, September, 1977.
ARKANSAS GAZETTE

aide at the state hospital, but we reached her. I explained what had happened and told her that her daughter was willing to accept Thelma's explanation. But when the mother understood that Thelma was black, *she* lashed out, "You mean a nigger girl kicked my daughter? I'm getting a lawyer."

Being wary of claims of dire injury by now, I asked Miss Carpenter to look at the girl's knee. She found no abrasion or bruise, nor did the girl claim any injury. The nurse, having known Thelma well all year, expressed doubt that she intentionally kicked anyone.

I told all three girls that the less they discussed the matter with other students, the better (wasted words). The accusing girl's friend suggested that she would go home with her friend and try to dissuade the mother from making an issue of the matter. The two white girls went on to class. I called Thelma's mother to let her know what had happened, let Thelma talk with her, too, and then sent her to her class. During the interviews I had depleted my Kleenex supply considerably, about equally to the accuser and the accused.

At the PTA meeting after school I was presented with a life membership pin. I was pleased; but I wondered whether Jess had to twist any arms for me to be the teacher so honored this year. I was a controversial figure, and I knew it.

The afternoon paper had headlined: EXPULSION OF NEGRO STUDIED. Minnijean was out for good, I knew. STUDENT THREATENED IN LETTER. The mother whose daughter had received the letter had provided that news. The FBI had "no comment." STATE AGENTS QUESTION MORE THAN 50 IN CHS INTEGRATION TROUBLES. Some teachers had told the reporter that they had been questioned. A "source" estimated that fifty or sixty people had been questioned, including students and parents—Mothers' League people for the most part, I surmised. Governor Faubus was quoted as saying that about six weeks before, in a conference with State Representative Paul Van Dalsen of Perry County (one of the state's least populated counties, but with the most powerful representative, since he was chairman of the Legislative Council), and with the state police director, Herman Lindsey, he had arranged to provide the council with state police investigators. The council committee conducting the investigation of Central High had already had several closed-door meetings, but the governor said none of the "evidence" they had gathered had been discussed with him.

The *Arkansas Gazette* on Thursday morning carried the reported kicking by Thelma Mothershed. It quoted the white girl, accurately, I'm sure, as saying, "Another girl and I laughed and I guess Thelma thought we were laughing at she and another girl so she turned around and laughed at me"—not what she had told me at all. The article further quoted the girl as saying that she then called Thelma "something I shouldn't have." The next morning the girl came to tell me that she and her mother were not doing anything about the kicking and were considering the matter settled.

Joan Rule, who had been at school two weeks before to talk to juniors and had been concerned when Elizabeth Eckford had come into my office upset, came to school to meet with a committee from one of our service clubs of which she had been a member in her high school days. She was greatly concerned about her school. She suggested to me the formation of a group of alumni to serve as Friends of Central High School. I sent her to talk with Emma Scott, the editor of the *Journal of Arkansas Education*, whose ideas were always constructive. I hoped such a group could do something for us. We certainly needed friends.

At the superintendent's request, I compiled an interim report on the small girl who had returned on January 27 after the board hearing. I found that she had failed all the makeup tests for the first semester and had failing semester marks in all subjects. But she seemed to be trying to fulfill current assignments in her classes. She had asked to be excused from her typing class once when the girl who had had the set-to with Minnijean appeared at the classroom door after her withdrawal. Her attitude toward school authority remained defiant. When a firecracker had been set off in front of the main office on February 10, she and the segregationist leader, who had been observed handing something to a boy, were the only ones who did not appear startled by the noise but had "died laughing," according to a guard. There were absences—"to see the dentist"—when some of her friends were also absent.

As I wrote these matters into the report, I wondered whether some of these youngsters had been busy giving testimony to the state police. Or was it some plotting of the incidents that had been occurring since the group absences? Or could it be just the usual truancy of a bunch of kids not really interested in school?

There were more immediate problems than such speculations. One result of having fewer guards within the building was the increase in locker tampering—Ernest Green's now. Helen Conrad reported hearing a girl laughingly remark, "Everything's gone but that book under his locker." Helen Conrad felt that the girl knew who had broken it open and stolen the books, but the girl denied that when I asked for her help. Four boys were seen frequently in that vicinity, all of them peripherally involved in racial incidents. Although Margaret Reiman and Mrs. Conrad, whose classrooms were across the hall from Ernest's locker, tried to watch closely, the locker was tampered with while they were busy in their rooms or at lunch.

The girl segregationist leader and the small girl were the center of a noisy group in the upper hall on Thursday at the lunch hour. Just after lunch, Doris Glenn brought a boy to the office for spitting on Terrence Roberts and Jefferson Thomas as they walked down the hall. Mrs. Glenn was particularly amazed that the boy would do such a thing in the presence of a teacher. When she asked his name, the boy gave it to her without hesitation. The segregationists were getting bolder—with the assured backing of state authority.

Two obscene letters claimed my attention. The FBI was still investigating one of them. And one white girl brought a letter from another white girl, both segregationist by persuasion, to complain about. The vocabularies of some of these girls amazed me.

The afternoon paper had an article by AP writer Sy Ramsey, headlined: THEY BOTHER YOU ALL THE TIME, OUSTED NEGRO STUDENT CONTENDS. It quoted Minnijean as saying that once she had several white acquaintances but now had only one, a girl. "Make that half a friend—when she's with me, she's my friend, when she's with the white students, she acts differently." Mr. Ramsey described Minnijean as partly bitter, partly resigned, and quoted her further: "They throw rocks, they spill ink on your clothes, they call you 'nigger', they just keep bothering you every five minutes." What she said was a fair report.

Friday, Valentine's Day, the ground was covered with snow. The very rarity of snow in Little Rock makes driving hazardous, for the city is not equipped to clear the streets, cars are not fitted with snow tires, and motorists have not developed the techniques for driving over snowy streets. Glen, who was a better driver than I, took me to school. I saw no guards in the halls, though there were one or two at observation points, as I learned from Captain Stumbaugh's report of the hard snowballing the black students got as they entered school. The guard said Thelma was crying.

Carlotta reported that her locker had been broken open and the only book she had left there overnight had been stolen. Micky McGalin reported hearing a boy, in company with two others, use abusive and obscene language to Carlotta in the hall before school. The boy denied the language when J. O. charged him with it. After the snowballing, Melba was afraid to go to her homeroom.

Jess put in a request for the return of the guards. The "brass" descended on his office, protesting that they were not police. Well, neither were we; but we were having to act like policemen.

Ernest's locker was broken open at noon, again, and his books stolen. I was able to replace his lost books from my cabinet of books furnished by the PTA for pupils in need of them. The FBI agents were out for the third day in a row on the obscene letter matter. I had no idea whether they were learning anything, and of course I still hadn't seen the letter. I talked with a girl about a report that she had bumped Carlotta deliberately. I had talked with her in November about a similar incident. She admitted bumping Carlotta, but she said Carlotta bumped her, first.

Jess read my report to the superintendent about the small girl who had returned to school after the board hearing and added a note of his own: "Shortly after this girl returned to school from her recent suspension, she showed a couple of teachers a little book she had in her purse and told them she was putting the name of anyone she did not like in the book and that they would have to answer to the Legislature. This girl is absent today, February 14. About 9:15 this morning the switchboard had a call for a boy. Caller identified herself as mother and said, 'Emergency and please have him call back.' The number given was this girl's."

The parents of the boy who spit on Terrence and Jefferson came to school to confer with Jess about Thursday's incident. They seemed most cooperative and assured the principals that they appreciated the opportunity to work with the school in an effort to prevent their son's further involvement in incidents.

While I waited for Glen to pick me up after school, Susie West came in. Susie was a brilliant young English teacher, tall and very slender, with a pixie's face. She was dressed for the outside cold, her coat buttoned and a scarf tied over her short, dark hair. Tears were running down her cheeks. At the north exit she had just seen a vicious, hard snowball attack on the black students by a gang of boys. A black father had left his car to try to intervene, but he was attacked, too. Many students had laughed at the assault, and so had one or two teachers. "How can people be like that, Elizabeth?" Susie wailed. Her face was no longer pixie-ish; in its compassion it was the beautiful face of the Madonna.

The black students had escaped to cars as J. O. and Captain Stumbaugh arrived. J. O. was furious. "It was the worst damn thing I ever saw," he said. "The police were there, but they did nothing." Captain Stumbaugh and his men, too, were visibly shaken. J. O.'s written account of the snowballing gave the names of nine boys he had identified, including the boy whose parents had just conferred with Jess on the spitting incident. Most of the others had previously been involved in racial incidents. For them, J. O. recommended suspension. Included also in J. O.'s list was the name of the boy who, on the first day the Nine attended, had offered to help Jefferson Thomas in my English class. His attitude had been molded and hardened since September 23.

Glen took me home. The afternoon paper had a picture of the morning snowballing of the guard's jeep; a story of a bomb found at the home of the Lorch family (Mrs. Lorch was the white woman who had befriended Elizabeth Eckford when she faced the crowd alone on the day the Faubus-directed National Guard turned back the Nine); a reference to the February 22 date of the upcoming meeting of the Legislative Council to hear the report of the state police interrogations; and a vigorous denial by Governor Faubus of the charge of W. F. (Billy) Rector, Little Rock businessman, that Faubus' policy in the matter of integration of Central High had caused the city to lose a probable $10 million shopping center. The governor charged Mr. Rector with being an integrationist—as well as a Republican!

My brother Bill called Friday evening. The New York *Times* had carried the story of Minnijean's suspension and he was concerned for me. I assured him I was all right. I could not say the same for the school.

On Sunday, February 16, both papers printed a statement of policy by the board of directors of the Little Rock School District. It was a welcomed statement. It commended most of the students for their behavior but warned those whose conduct was interfering with the education of themselves and others that the board would take any action necessary to protect education. It stated that each student would be judged individually and that his attitude toward integration would not be considered. It further stated that any student whose conduct was unsatisfactory would be expelled. It appealed to all students to maintain good conduct and to all adults to refrain from encouraging students to unsatisfactory behavior. It was signed by all six of the directors.

Mr. Blossom had asked Jess, J. O., and me to meet with him and the parents of black pupils at the school administration building at two o'clock that Sunday. One parent, father or mother, of each student except Melba Pattillo was present. Mr. Thomas, Jefferson's father, was the spokesman. He urged us to call an assembly of all students and "lay down the law" to them. We vetoed that project— most of our students didn't need scolding, and the others probably would have caused a demonstration. We discussed the problem of locker vandalism without coming to a solution. Mr. Thomas read a list of names of boys and girls harassing the students. We knew those names, too. Mr. Thomas said he had called and talked with some of their parents and had gotten cooperation from some of them. He thought that the cafeteria situation had improved. We suggested to the parents that a varying pattern of the arrival and departure of their youngsters might help; both time of arrival and the entrance or exit used should be changed from time to time.

As we left the meeting, Jess told me that someone had thrown a rock through Susie West's apartment window, with a paper tied to it bearing the words *Nigger-loving bitch*. She had moved in with friends, temporarily. Her father had come down from Russellvile and wanted her to resign her teaching job and come home. FBI agents were investigating. Jess had word, too, from one of the military officers that our segregationist girl leader was reporting regularly to a certain officer of the state police, whose name he told me. I did not doubt the truth of that.

On Monday, February 17, with the board's policy now firmly in support of us, we got tough. Sergeant Roy Blackwood reported that he had seen the girl leader stop another girl on the stairs and ask her whether she wanted a card to wear. Then she handed her a small white card, bearing in bold black type the words ONE DOWN— EIGHT To Go. At the top of the stairs, Sergeant Blackwood saw the girl distribute two more of the cards.

As Jess and I discussed this report, we agreed that this action of the girl was an overt threat to the school and some of its students. The evident reference to the expulsion of Minnijean and the intention of causing the eight remaining black pupils to leave was subversive of school policy and of federal court orders. I suggested, and Jess agreed, that we not call the girl on the carpet until the last period of the day to avoid as much school disturbance as possible and to avoid, also, having the story in the noon edition of the *Arkansas Democrat*.

At the end of the second lunch period, Dorothy Lenggenhager, a history teacher, saw a boy, without provocation of any kind, deliberately push Gloria Ray as she was going down the stairs. Gloria caught the railing and did not fall. Mrs. Lenggenhager was horrified. She took the boy to the office, where J. O. described him as "congenial and happy over his accomplishment." The boy told the principal that he pushed Gloria because "She's a nigger." Jess suspended him. In the hall, Jess saw a boy who had been twice counseled about his segregationist activities at school and whose father had promised to keep him under control, wearing a ONE DOWN— EIGHT To Go badge. Jess suspended him. He still had to deal with the girl who had distributed the cards.

I sent for her, and she came in happily. Jess told her that he was suspending her for distributing signs. She was astonished. She had only given away a few of the signs, which had been given to her. She had given them only to those who had asked for them. She had a right to her opinions. We had no right to put her out of school because we didn't like her opinions about integration. She cried. She sobbed. And then she shouted and bawled.

She left the office. In a very few minutes her father came in. He was fully as angry and almost as noisy as his daughter. I finally left Jess with him. The people in the outer office were trying to look as if they hadn't heard anything, as people might if they had overheard a family fight. I was red-faced and exhausted by the scene.

Details of this girl's activities were appended to the copy of the formal suspension notice that went to the superintendent. They summarized our difficulties with her since September 23, the first day her anti-integration activities had come to our attention.

On Tuesday I saw no ONE DOWN—EIGHT TO GO signs, but others did. Abby Foster, who saw a boy passing out the cards before school, followed him to his homeroom and pointed him out to his teacher. Geneva Howerton gave his name and those of three other boys she had seen wearing the cards to J. O. In view of the fact that none had been previously identified with incidents, J. O. did not recommend their suspension, after he got their promises not to take any further part in such activities.

Dorothy Lenggenhager reported that she had had a phone call Monday night from a caller, supposedly the mother of the boy suspended for pushing Gloria on the stairs. The caller scolded Dorothy for taking the boy to the office after the incident. Dorothy asked the caller what she thought a teacher should have done in such a case. "Look the other way," was the reply.

Elizabeth Eckford came to my office, crying, at noon, to report that a "fat boy with glasses" had deliberately knocked her books from her arms. The boy, from Elizabeth's description, was probably the same one who had told J. O. that he had been "fighting niggers since he was five years old." Elizabeth said this boy had, earlier, spoken obscenely to her and made obscene gestures.

Ernest Green reported to J. O. that three boys, whom he named, had thrown wadded up soaking wet towels at him after Coach Clyde Hart had left their gym class. That wouldn't have been more than a prank if Ernest could have thrown the towels back—without starting a riot.

The *Gazette* had reported our suspensions in its Tuesday morning edition. The *Democrat* that afternoon had a lengthy quotation from the suspended girl, who contended she had been "singled out ever since I left school the first day the Negro students entered. I left the building by a window and the police put me in a wagon and took me to headquarters." Her father was also quoted: "I asked Mr. Matthews and Mrs. Huckaby if they thought children were really getting an education when they're suspending them every few days this way." Pictured in the same paper were Mrs. Brown and Minnijean leaving the school board office after her permanent suspension had been confirmed. A further story about Central High was headlined: CHS HALL PATROLS ELIMINATED. GUARDSMEN, STILL IN BUILDING, MAKE PERIODIC CHECKS. It quoted "reliable information" as the source of this news, without confirmation by the military district. Mentioned, too, was a railroad flare, which looked something like a big firecracker but was not explosive, that had been found in the school and brought to the office by a senior boy, Bill Hicks.

On Wednesday, February 19, Mr. Blossom was quite tied up in hearings on our suspensions, Jess reported. He asked me to make a complete list of the suspended girl's various involvements in anti-integration matters at school for Mr. Blossom's reference. When I completed the list, it covered three typewritten pages.

One of the boys who had bothered Gloria in her homeroom earlier in the year, came to the attendance office to try to check out as ill. Miss Carpenter was teaching a hygiene class, and Mrs. Brietz was on a coffee break; so I had the boy lie down in the boys' health room. He had thrown his black leather jacket on a chair. I picked it up to hang it more neatly over the back of the chair. What could this boy have in his pockets to make his coat so heavy? I pictured at least a Colt .45 in each pocket, but I was not going to investigate without a witness, so I got J. O. The pockets were filled with new nuts and bolts and screws the boy had "picked up" in the woodwork class from which he had come to the office. I was almost as much relieved as I was disgusted by his pilfering.

Helen Marshall, who had taught art at Central for several years but was teaching in college, now, came by to see how we were getting along, since all she knew about us was what she read in the papers. She hugged Jess when she saw him. She not only hugged me, but she paid me a compliment. "Liz," she said, looking at me with critical attention, "I don't think you look as *haggard* as you did last October." Perhaps I was adjusting to living in crisis.

On Thursday, Pauline Dunn, biology teacher, got on the segregationists' blacklist, if she was not already there. She had twin brothers in her tenth grade homeroom, both already "called to preach." Miss Dunn had always had members of her homeroom who were willing to do so to read a few verses of the Bible each day, as state law required. The twin boys reported at home that, after their turns at Bible reading, Carlotta Walls would be next, alphabetically, a situation that they didn't like. Their mother had called Miss Dunn the night before, she reported, begging her not to let Carlotta take a turn at reading the Bible to the homeroom. Miss Dunn, flabbergasted at the request, had no intention of honoring it. Carlotta took her turn at Bible reading.

A new girl in school, not "hep" to the current interpretation of southern hospitality, came in to tell me that she had been kicked and called names because she had expressed antisegregation feelings. I offered sympathy—and action, if she would furnish me the names, or even the descriptions, of her hecklers. Since I heard nothing further from her, I suppose she learned to "adjust."

We ignored a bomb threat phoned in to the office at noon. More alarming to Jess was the sight of a state police car that stopped in front of the school. He watched the officer, in uniform, enter a first-floor door. When Jess went to investigate, he found that one of the teachers had arranged for her "interrogation" to be held at this time and place as most convenient to her. The principal questioned the propriety of her decision, and the policeman left without the interview.

During gym class that afternoon, Terrence Roberts' school clothes were tossed under the shower. Since my closet supplies were only for girls, he was allowed to go home. That made him miss his final class of the day.

In the afternoon paper I read of a citizens' group asking the school board to petition the federal court for relief from integration. Walter Guy, the spokesman, claimed the support of black leaders. Daisy Bates, however, was quoted as denying that the NAACP would support any plan for sending the black children back to Horace Mann High School. I was against that, too. I certainly didn't want to go through this sort of year again, and I never doubted that total desegregation was both right and inevitable.

As I sat comfortably at home, I was glad that I didn't have to be at the school board meeting, hearing the cases of the girl leader and one of the suspended boys. Amis Guthridge had been quoted as saying that if his clients were not reinstated immediately, he would charge the members with misfeasance and malfeasance in office. Whatever that meant, I didn't want to be hearing him make that statement.

On Friday, February 21, I dressed in my red suit and my better shoes. The Southernaires were having their annual Martha Washington tea for the teachers and I wanted to look as well as I could for the party. I was glad I had made that effort, for Jess and I were called to the school administration office twice on the matter of the suspended girl, and TV cameras and news photographers took our pictures as we entered the building. Waiting downstairs were Amis Guthridge and the usual Mothers' Leaguers. On our first trip to the boardrooms, I was not called to talk with that body. On the second trip, the board wanted to ask me specifically whether I thought the girl leader should be permitted to return to school. As a long-time teacher, I am always hopeful of young people. There is always a chance—a slim chance, sometimes—that education can change them. I have seen it happen. So I said yes, I thought she should return, but only if she would agree to stay out of all anti-integration activities at school or directed toward the school.

Back at school I saw signs pinned on almost every blouse and shirt, but these were legitimate signs, provided by the student council, urging the basketball team to "Beat Fort Smith." There were other signs, too, being shown surreptitiously. Shirley Stancil had taken one from a boy that read, in black print on an orange background:

> Daisy is a bloom
> Virgil is a Blossom
> Daisy is a coon
> Virgil is a possum

It was neither good wit nor good verse, but it satisfied some name-calling desire and sought to link Virgil Blossom, the superintendent of schools, with Daisy Bates, the president of the Arkansas NAACP, as integrationists. The boy told Mrs. Stancil that the signs came from "the print shop." They were probably not from Central High School's print shop; but they could have been.

Under the BEAT FORT SMITH card on one girl's blouse I saw a telltale orange corner. I asked her to remove the card and give it to me. It read: ONE BLACK WAS BROWN/BUT/SHE'S NOT AROUN'. The apostrophe to protect the rhyme was too sophisticated for the boys in our print shop, I thought. These signs, though certainly not acceptable at school, were not actually subversive. Unlike the ONE DOWN card, they threatened no action against the school or our students.

The afternoon paper had a four-column headline: SCHOOL BOARD CITES INABILITY TO ENFORCE COMPLIANCE; ASKS U.S. COURT TO HALT INTEGRATION. Another front-page story was headlined: U.S. WON'T GET INTO CHS CASE, quoting Attorney General William Rogers as authority. A third story, headed CHS JUNIOR SUSPENDED TWO WEEKS, quoted Amis Guthridge as telling the board that he thought it was malfeasance to exclude the suspended girl's attorney from the hearing, as they had.

Saturday morning's *Gazette* quoted from a speech by its editor, Harry Ashmore, in Cambridge, Massachusetts, in which he criticized the federal government's decision to leave to the Little Rock School Board the entire burden of carrying out the court order to integrate "against impossible odds." He also criticized the president, saying, "At no time did Mr. Eisenhower attempt to use the great moral force of his office to persuade Southerners of the justice of the course the Supreme Court required of them." I concurred with his quoted remarks, except that I would have included the teachers, the federalized guardsmen, and the black students as also bearing some of the burden.

I had been happy earlier in the week to read that Minnijean Brown had been given a scholarship to Lincoln School in New York. Now she wouldn't miss her chance for a high school education. Governor Faubus had been quoted as saying that she should not have been expelled from school, merely sent back to the all-

Negro high school, Horace Mann. The Saturday afternoon *Democrat* pictured Minnijean at the airport, leaving for New York, though a bomb threat had delayed the takeoff of her flight.

On Monday two teachers who had children in Central brought me copies of a letter that had evidently been mailed to all parents. The letter was a copy of an "editorial" entitled: "Shall the School Board Deprive Children of an Education Because They Opposed Race-Mixing?" Here is about one-fourth of the letter:

> Now that all is chaos and confusion at Central High, the above-named gentlemen [the school board] say it's really the children's fault. The children, they say, should be good sports, and accept the outrage the school board has placed on their backs.
>
> Furthermore, the School Board threatens stern measures. They strongly intimate that wholesale and permanent dismissals will be visited on all those children who do not cease to resist race-mixing.
>
> What an hour we have come to—and what outrage confronts us and our children. Our children have been reared to believe in a segregated society. It has been and is the only code of life they have ever known. Now they are under bayonets and rifles of the U.S. Army whose booted soldiers occupy their classrooms and are forcing on them a way of life foreign to their training, contrary to their convictions and nauseating to their esthetic being.
>
> The Little Rock School Board now publicly joins Virgil Blossom and smiling Jess Matthews in telling the children of Central High School that if they don't go along with this ugly spectacle and be nice about it that they will deprive them of their right to an education.
>
> The ultimatum has been served. The crackdown on our children has started. The school board gives us only one choice—*Submit*.
> And that's a terrible word for a red blooded American.

At the end of the piece was the statement, "This editorial published as a Public Service by the Capital Citizens' Council, 1110 West Capitol Ave. Little Rock-P.O. Box 1997." The envelopes in which these editorials had been mailed bore on the outside the Brotherhood by Bayonet seal.

But except for the shudder this letter gave me, Monday and Tuesday, February 24 and 25, were the kind of beautiful early spring days we often have late in February, sunny and warm. We were so peaceful at school that I got more desk work done in a couple of days than I had accomplished in months. The Monday afternoon paper pictured Amis Guthridge failing to get Prosecutor Frank Holt to file a charge of misfeasance and malfeasance against the board and Mr. Blossom. In the background of the picture, standing beside Margaret Jackson, I recognized the suspended girl and the boy who had kicked Minnijean, both wearing ONE DOWN badges. But at least they were not at school. And the peace at school was priceless. I even enjoyed the repetitious and long drawn-out (till 5:30 P.M.) tryouts by a hundred sophomore and junior girls for cheerleader. J. O. insisted that this lull was only temporary. But I was going to enjoy it and the beautiful weather while they lasted.

Wednesday morning was still warm, but rainy. There were tornado warnings during the day and the barometer was low. But it was calm at school. At noon, Marguerite Warr, Mr. Blossom's secretary, called to tell me that a conference had been set up with the suspended girl and her parents for 7:30 P.M. at Mr. Blossom's office and that he wanted Jess Matthews and me there. The subject of the conference was to be the change in the girl's attitude toward school which the board had decided must be established before she could return to school on Monday, March 3.

It was still drizzling at 7:15 when Jess picked me up, so I wore my raincoat and picked up my umbrella as I left. When we walked into Mr. Blossom's office, having left our rain gear as we entered, we found that the girl and her parents were already there. We six were the only ones in the building. The girl was dressed in a white wool dress, mouton jacket, high heels. She did not look like a schoolgirl. I imagined this was how she was dressed as she went about the state making speeches to Citizens' Councils, an activity that had been reported in the *Arkansas Democrat* recently. The girl introduced her mother, whose face was strained and twitching; in fact, her whole body seemed to twitch nervously. Jess and I had met the father before.

From the beginning, the conference was wholly unsatisfactory. The girl took charge. She told Mr. Blossom, Jess, and me what she thought of our persecution of her; she declared we had no right to keep her from doing what she had been doing—out of school, she said. She cited her perfect school record. Mr. Blossom tried to bring the conference to the subject we were supposed to be considering, an improvement in her attitude toward the school and its problems.

He told the parents that I had told the board of their daughter's good qualities and had said that she would be an acceptable school citizen if she would discontinue those activities that we considered undesirable. But the girl refused to admit that any change was needed, except in Jess and me, of whom both she and her mother expressed extreme hatred because of our persecution. Their eyes flashed in anger as they looked at me. When Mr. Blossom tried to get some promise from the girl about her future behavior, the only agreement she would make was that she would "not distribute another card—*period*!"

When Mr. Blossom saw that what was supposed to be a conference had deteriorated into a harangue, he dismissed Jess and me but asked the girl and her parents to stay. I collected my raincoat and umbrella, Jess got his top coat and hat, and we walked out through the secretary's office and down the long corridor toward the lobby and the exit. As we passed the school mailboxes, Jess stopped to collect the mail for Central High School. I went to the lobby and put on my raincoat.

Almost immediately, I heard the high-heeled tapping of women running behind me. My first thought was that the girl wanted to agree to our terms and she and her mother wanted us to come back. I turned, smiling, but when I saw the faces of mother and daughter, I knew I had been mistaken. They have run out on Mr. Blossom, I thought.

I didn't have much time for further thinking. As the girl snatched the umbrella from my hand, her mother reached out and took off my glasses, saying, "I'm going to hit you for what you have done to my daughter." Jess, following closely behind them, called to the mother, "Here, you can't hit a lady," and pushed between us. "Don't you dare touch my mother," screamed the girl, waving my umbrella at us. Seeing a path of retreat open to me, I hurried back down the corridor where I met Mr. Blossom. "You may need the police," I told him.

I took sanctuary in the superintendent's offices and closed the door. I could hear the screaming mother and girl, but I did not understand all they were saying. I did hear the mother call out, "Two hundred women have called me and said they would pay my fine if I'd hit her!" The father was shouting, too, apparently trying to get

172 *Crisis at Central High*

his wife and daughter out of the office. I heard the girl shriek at him, "You've turned against me, too!"

After a few minutes, the noise subsided and I knew that the family had left. And when Jess and Mr. Blossom opened the door and came into the secretary's office, I was relieved to see that the superintendent had my glasses in his hand.

Mr. Blossom felt that the matter needed to be reported to the police. I protested that I had no intention of filing charges against anyone, but he said that wasn't the point. The fact that the attack had been made needed to be on the police record to protect me in the future. He called the police.

When officers Cox and Halcumb came in, I told them what had happened, and Mr. Blossom and Jess added details. Mr. Blossom feared the family, or their friends, might be waiting for us outside and asked the police to follow Jess's car home, which they did.

My seeming calmness during the attack and afterward, I attribute to two things: inexperience; and a sort of congenital slowness to react—that same slowness that always kept me from being a good quail hunter. The covey would be up and gone before I got ready to fire my shotgun. But I was not really calm. Glen and I were both sleepless most of the night. The teaching profession had never been such a hazardous one before in our lifetimes of experience.

Thursday, on Jess's suggestion, I wrote out the account of the evening fully; Lovey Pettyjohn, who typed it for me, and J. O. Powell, the only other person to read it, were aghast. The day turned out to be calm and peaceful, but I was tired. The evening, however, was restful, at dinner with friends at Lillian and Wallace Wills's, while Glen attended a meeting of Smoke Hole Hunting Club. I didn't mention to my friends the excitement of the evening before.

After a good night's sleep, I felt better on Friday. Cap and gown measurements were being taken for seniors; and there were preparations to make for next week: Rotary Conference selections on Monday; Girls' State selections on Tuesday; and Pentangle Clubs selections on Wednesday. It felt good to work at something constructive, for a change. There had been no major incident at school since the girl leader's suspension. Besides that disciplinary action, the conferences Jess had been having with several parents of children who had been involved in incidents could have been a cause for the lull.

Wilma Means, who was helping Bonnie Brietz in the attendance office with the school census cards, brought me the first word of the "attack" on me. It was an inaccurate account that had been related to her by one of the men teachers who had segregationist friends. It had doubtless originated with the girl involved, for, according to the story, she had hit me and chased me with my umbrella. I assured Mrs. Means that it was not a true story.

At 6:30 that evening, J. O., who had been watching the news on TV, called me to report that the board had expelled the suspended girl, but that her father said he would put her back in school on Monday, with the governor's protection. A reporter from the *Gazette* called. He had had an anonymous caller who had related the umbrella story. I had no comment.

On Saturday I was bothered by reporters who had heard garbled accounts of the attack. One read me the story as it was carried in the Memphis *Commercial Appeal*. I had no comment. But I was relieved to see that the *Democrat* that afternoon carried no story of the incident. I didn't want my parents to read of it in the papers; but I was not going to alarm them by telling them the story unless I had to. The *Democrat* did quote the father's statement of his determination to take his daughter to school and of his claim that "she has been crucified by three people who are determined to beat into submission all opposition" to court-ordered integration. He identified the three people as Mr. Blossom, Mr. Matthews, and Mrs. Huckaby. The story reported, also, that neither school officials nor the girl's family would comment on a reported meeting on Wednesday in which some heated words were reported to have been exchanged.

Glen and I went to Smoke Hole Club on Sunday to relax, taking the papers along. By now, the father was quoted in the *Gazette*: "Due to physical and emotional condition of my daughter I have decided against the probability of subjecting her to humiliation and further callous treatment by school officials and armed troops." He would not bring her to school on Monday. I was glad to hear it.

Still, I was uneasy Monday, March 3. I feared that the expelled girl's friends, upset by the weekend stories, would feel they needed to demonstrate their sympathy for her, even though she was not attempting to attend school. The boy who had been suspended for distributing ONE DOWN signs was back in school. Judging from the extra security precautions that were evident, I was not the only uneasy one.

Just before school started, something was thrown at Melba Pattillo and Thelma Mothershed as they came in the north entrance. They weren't sure what it was, but after homeroom period I went to the north entrance and found an egg broken against the door of Room 152. The egg undoubtedly missed its target.

The *Arkansas Gazette*, having supported the schools in their efforts to follow the orders of the courts in integration, carried none of the segregationists' advertisements. But the *Arkansas Democrat* on March 3 carried an ad, paid for by something called the Freedom Fund and signed Julian Miller, which announced in large, black letters: EXPELLED FROM CENTRAL HIGH SCHOOL and invited the public to see and hear the expelled girl on Channel 7 on Tuesday at 8:30 P.M. The girl, it promised, would "reveal the shocking conditions existing in Central High School." It further stated that she "will tell the sinister reasons which led to her expulsion by the Little Rock School Board."

On Tuesday morning, the small blond friend of the expelled girl, the friend whose return to school had followed the board hearing with her lawyer, Amis Guthridge, came in to ask about withdrawing from school. She left without starting the procedure. There was the usual all-day stir as report cards were being circulated and grades recorded on them. There was also the this-year-only kind of stir—bomb calls to the switchboard, necessitating the notification of the police, the military, the FBI, and the school administration. New cards were being circulated: a girl, wielding an umbrella, was pictured chasing a teacher who was dropping a book as she ran. The title under the picture was "Communism on the Run." I found one of the cards in my box in the office, the student with the umbrella labeled in handwriting with the expelled girl's name, the teacher labeled "Huckaby."

Jess brought me a typed list of the questions and answers that would be on the Channel 7 interview with the expelled girl. After she had identified herself as a young person being persecuted for her beliefs, her mother was to testify to her daughter's good school record and to the fact that she had caused her parents no concern. In the matter of the distribution of the cards, One Down—Eight To Go, the girl was to charge that she had been singled out, although a large proportion of the students in Central were distributing the cards. She was to be given a chance to recount the brutality of the police who picked her up on September 23 when she escaped from Central through a window when the blacks first entered. She was to charge that her fan mail, addressed in care of the school, was either being withheld or mutilated before it was sent on to her. And last, she was to place the blame for her expulsion on Mr. Blossom, Jess, and me—all integrationists.

After school a honking group of cars formed in front of the school on Park Street, decorated with signs in support of the ousted girl. The procession circled the school a few times, then headed downtown. After it was gone, I left school to check on mother and father. As I crossed Main Street on my way home, I could still hear the honking, advertising the evening telecast.

Not having a TV set, we were spared the broadcast. But we knew it was over when the crank calls began. We just took the telephone off the hook for the rest of the evening. It was so quiet, we heard the first geese go over on their migration north to their nesting grounds. They were starting early this year, and we hoped that was a sign that spring would be early, too.

On Wednesday morning the *Gazette* quoted a school board statement issued after the broadcast giving as the reason for the girl's expulsion the fact that she and her mother had "physically attacked a woman staff member." Glen declared that he was taking me to school. At school, Jess Matthews passed on Mr. Blossom's warning to be careful crossing streets and walking near parked cars; an "accident" might happen to me. My teacher friends asked me no questions, but many were solicitous. From the teachers' lounge that was frequented by the smokers among the women teachers came a whimsical paper with twenty-two signatures under the heading Elizabeth Huckleby Fan Club. "Huckleby" was the way the girl had pronounced my name Tuesday night, and "Fan Club" was in imitation of the one formed by her supporters. Two Hearts and a "We luv U" decorated the sheet, with a notation that a copy was to be sent to Amis Guthridge, the spelling of whose name was distorted with unteacherly vulgarity.

I called Mother and Father to assure them that I was all right, that the attack mentioned was last week, and that I had not been hurt. The New York *Times* carried the story and evidently mentioned my name, for a telegram came from Bill, speaking of my "moral and physical courage" as "inspiring." Bill had me sounding like Joan of Arc.

After supper that evening I heard Glen go to his gun cabinet in the back room and unload and reload his shotgun. I wondered what new hunting regulation was making him change shells in his gun. After supper, as I was reading the *Democrat*, I realized what he had been doing. He pointed to a headline on page 2: PROTECTION ASKED FOR EDUCATORS. Mr. Blossom had asked that Jess Matthews' home and ours be watched by police for possible violence. "Glasscock [assistant police chief] said the regular patrol cars in the vicinity had been told to watch the houses but that no special officers had been put on duty. He said this was the same procedure that had been followed when Mrs. Daisy Bates, state NAACP president, had asked protection of her Little Rock home." That protection, as everyone knew, had not been effective. Glen thought it might be up to him, so he had loaded his gun with buckshot.

As for the expelled girl's broadcast, it must not have been too effective. Oscar Alagood, of Channel 7, was quoted as saying that 85 percent of the three hundred calls to the station after the program were critical of the broadcast. Assistant Chief R. E. Glasscock refuted the girl's charges of being seized and roughed up as she (a mere bystander, as she told it) was taken to the police station on September 23. He was quoted as saying that he was the officer who arrested the girl after she broke through the police lines around the school for the fourth time, and he denied that she was manhandled or thrown to the ground, as she had charged.

But more significant news than expelled students or attacks on educators was in the March 5, 1958, newspapers: CONFIDENT FAUBUS FILES FOR THIRD TERM was the headline.

Again on Thursday, Glen took me to school and brought me

home. It was a busy, normal day. Alberta Harris directed an excellent senior talent assembly with the theme "Outer Space." At noon, the six hundred students who had bought tickets were permitted to attend the Little Rock-Jonesboro basketball game in the state tournament. There were no racial incidents reported. Of the Eight, only Thelma was absent.

In the late afternoon, at home, Emma Scott came by with a gift for me, a red nylon petticoat "for courage," she said. She had been out of town, but radio reports she had heard as she drove over the state on business for the Education Association had disturbed her. I let her read the factual account I had written about the attack so that she would have the whole story.

I had heard from other people: Helen Marshall; Olga and Carl Frick, both former pupils. But there weren't many who wrote me. Some dear friends outside the school system, although they talked with me often, never mentioned the integration crisis or my part in it. Although other former students let me hear from them at other times during the year, of the thousands who had sat in my classes, I heard from fewer than twenty-five. I felt that I must have been a total failure as a teacher to have inspired so little confidence. Perhaps I expected too much from a culture in which noninvolvement is an ideal.

But I heard from the other side. There was one letter, evidently from an elderly woman in neighboring Pine Bluff. At least she signed her name. Without salutation (perhaps she could not bring herself to address me as *Dear*) she wrote: "I am going to tell you what I think of eny teacher that mistreat a white in it own school in favor of a negro isn't as good as a negro. The negro belongs in his school and if you think so much of them why don't you apply for a job at woodrow mann school—I say one kicked out and eight to go and three teachers."

From Shreveport, Louisiana, unsigned, here is another excerpt:

> You go right on entertaining Mrs. Daisy Bates in your home with dinner parties which we hear that you do. Also keep inviting the nine little negro's to your home for candy makings.—Keep going and I'm sure you will make a name for yourself as a real negro lover as that's what we hear you are anyway.

From a mother who would hate to have you as a teacher of her children, what could you expect of people in Arkansas anyway. People laugh when that name is mentioned because of the ignorants in that state.

Another, from rural Georgia, was written on the business stationery of his gasoline station, and signed:

My dear Mrs. Huckaby: Why don't you and the teachers go home and stay there until things are in satisfactory order in the High School? The real White People in this country cant understand how it is that White Teachers will continue to defy the councils of their own folks as you are doing. That situation cannot happen in Georgia because we are all willing to standup and be counted. Quit your work go home and stay until order is fully restored. Stop your hypocracy.

By Friday morning, since nothing untoward had happened, I drove my own car to and from school. But that was almost the only usual thing about the day.

Someone on the first floor hit Elizabeth Eckford in the back with an egg, splashing it mostly on her coat and books. She had wiped most of it off, but there were still traces on her blouse. She told me, too, that the lock on her locker had been broken off overnight. But she had lost nothing, since she had taken all her books home to study. She was on her way to gym, now. (Her gym class had been shifted from that difficult 7th period.) Before the gym class was over, I sent her a clean blouse from my clothes closet.

State Police headquarters called me to set up an appointment for my interrogation. I set Monday evening at seven in my home, then called Mr. Blossom's secretary so that a court reporter could be secured for that time to record the questions and answers.

Vaughn Munroe, in Little Rock to assist in the annual Red Cross drive, was to speak and sing at a student assembly after lunch. Before he sang, he was to be interviewed by reporters from all the student newspapers in high schools in Little Rock, North Little Rock, and Pulaski County—white high schools. The interview was to take place in the conference room next to my office, so I moved the teachers' coffee pots from there into my office. I was down on my knees trying to find the electric outlet behind the bookcase when Clark G. Ponder, from the drugstore on the corner,

appeared at my door, grinning, and handed me a subpoena to answer, with other defendants, the complaint of the expelled girl,
"a minor, by her father, natural guardian and next friend. Upon
failure to answer, the complaint will be taken for confesse," etc. I
put the paper on my desk and went on with the business of setting
up the coffee.

I did not attend the assembly. Near the end of the program, I
looked up from my desk to see two ambulance attendants wheeling
a stretcher down the corridor. They stopped to ask directions to the
injured person. Neither Miss Carpenter nor I knew of any injury,
and we knew the call must have been a hoax. Since the attendants
did not have time to get out of the building before the halls would
be full of boys and girls pouring out of the assembly, we ushered
the men and their stretchers into my office, closed the door, and
pulled down the shade. There they stayed till the halls were clear.
By that time Miss Carpenter had arranged with them a way to
check with us before responding to any more calls to Central.

As I moved the coffeemaking equipment back into its usual
place in the conference room, I found a blue envelope stuck on the
bulletin board. Addressed to me in schoolboy handwriting, it was
from a "Knight of the *Old South.*" Inside the envelope was a new
printed card:

> Rockabye Huckaby, betray your own race,
> Get an umbrella smack in your face;
> When white folks discover all that takes place
> You'll leave Central High in total disgrace.

If Friday had been active, Monday was full. It was a cloudy, cool,
and rather dreary day. As soon as I got to school, Jess Matthews told
me that we were due to have a conference with Mr. Blossom and
the school board lawyers at 2:00 P.M. At 11:00 I went home to get
my copy of the notes about the expelled girl for Mr. Blossom, a list I
had felt I should not leave at school, available for theft. In the
morning mail at home I found a typed card, signed "Listener":
"Why don't you get transfered to Horace Mann? You must feel
mighty proud of yourself—if you could hear what lots of the students, teachers and neighbors think of you, you would transfer out
of the state. Washington, D.C. or New York City would be good

places for your kind." It was the word *neighbors* that got to me. I had lived in the same house since I married, twenty-five years before. To think that my neighbors hated me was hard, indeed.

Jess and I picked up Mr. Blossom and met Archie House and his young assistant, John Haley, in the law firm's office. We went over the case. Although in normal times the community and the courts in Little Rock would have backed any school board in expelling a student for an attack on a teacher, these times were not normal. The vocal element of the community, led by a lawyer and a preacher, neither of whom had been a molder of public thought in our city before now, were in charge, supported by the silence of the many who were normally our community leaders. Judge Mitchell Cockrill, whose court would ordinarily hear the case, had disqualified himself on the grounds that he had a daughter in Central High School. Chancellor Ford Smith of Woodruff County would preside; and the segregationist feeling in that east Arkansas area was overwhelming. It looked as if we were outnumbered. The only witnesses to the attack were the participants. Mr. House was pessimistic about the case. Mr. Blossom told us that a mediator had appeared and that negotiations were underway for an out-of-court settlement, with the girl to sign a statement regretting her attack on me before she returned to school. The mediator was Wesley Wood, who had been employed by the same company as the girl's father, and knew him there, but who was now a lawyer in private practice. Mr. Blossom said the outcome of the negotiations was uncertain and we must be prepared to go into court on Wednesday if they were unsuccessful. Mr. House suggested, and we agreed, that Dick Butler be called in to help in the presentation of our case in court.

As we left Mr. House's office, one of the young men in the outer office showed us in the afternoon *Democrat* a story of an Arkansas Supreme Court decision upholding the testimony of a man who charged he had been falsely arrested last summer and whose testimony had been corroborated by "Mrs. Elizabeth Huckaby, assistant principal of Central High School, who said that she had tried to intervene and was threatened with arrest." The Elizabeth Huckaby who had intervened was a clerk in Pfeifers Department Store. I recalled reading the account the summer before and being mildly shocked to note that some unknown person shared my name. This false identification would do nothing to help me, picturing, as it seemed to, a teacher stepping into something that was none of her business.

When I got home at 5:30, told Glen of the afternoon conference, and explained the incorrect identification in the afternoon paper, he lost his equanimity for the first time. He was going to "get" Amis Guthridge and all his crew if they didn't leave me alone, etc., etc. It was my turn to do the calming, as we fixed and ate a hurried meal. The state police were due at seven. I called the city editor of the *Democrat* to protest the incorrect identification of Mrs. Elizabeth Huckaby. He promised to print a correction next day.

The court reporter came at 6:55. He was Scrivener Mizell, whom I hadn't seen since he was a pupil in my class about twenty years earlier. I was glad to see him and to have someone who knew me record the interview. When the two state police came at 7:05, here was my former pupil again, Lawrence Gwyn, still rather embarrassed and protesting that he hadn't been a good English student. Sergeant Chesley Slayton, a chunky officer, was the other interrogator. I sat on the sofa, with Glen, his arms folded, sitting rigidly beside me. The three others sat separately about our small living room.

Before the questioning could begin, we were interrupted by our neighbor, Mrs. David Ray, who found she could not back out of our shared driveway because the state police car was blocking it. "Why, Lawrence, I thought you knew better than that!" I said, and opened the door for him to go move his car. The incident left him even more ill-at-ease.

Sergeant Gwyn made a preliminary statement, saying that this was just a talk, not questions; that the purpose was to find out what mistakes we had made at Central (he got a bit confused here, correcting his implication that his former English teacher could have made any mistakes) for the purpose of passing legislation that would keep people from making the same mistakes when "the problem" got into south and east Arkansas. He tried to be folksy about the Legislative Council, asking whether I had taught Joel Ledbetter or Max Howell (I hadn't). Then came the questions.

In general, the interrogators asked whether education was progressing at Central (Yes, it was); whether discipline, "excluding the extremist group out there which for all practical purposes are segregationists" was greater than usual (No); whether the troops, the 101st and the federalized National Guard, had interfered with teachers or students (No, the troops, including the National Guard, the 101st, and the federalized National Guard, had been uniformly courteous and had left the educational processes to the teachers). Specifically, Sergeant Gwyn asked whether an obscene letter had been pushed under my door (I hadn't seen one); whether a male student had called me a bad name (Yes); and about the girl segregationist we had suspended (It would be unethical and unwise to discuss a matter to come up in court this week). Prompted by Sergeant Slayton, Sergeant Gwyn asked about the educational progress of the black pupils (Normal); about the bomb scares (I objected to the word *scares*, since all had been hoaxes). Sergeant Slayton wanted to know about the percentage of suspensions, exclusive of those from the "big walkout" (Four girls for the year—about normal). Sergeant Gwyn wanted to know about the big cheering group rushing the office after incidents (I admitted the cheering group—small, out of 1800 students—but not the "rushing the office" part.); whether I had had to give up teaching (Yes, no secret); and finally, what suggestions I could make to the Legislative Council (None; I could speak only on education, not on lawmaking.).

Claiming, piously, that the purpose of the state police was to "ask Mr. Powell, yourself, Mr. Matthews, and Mr. Blossom if there is anything that we can do to help you in any way," the state police left at 7:20. Having established that he and Glen shared an interest in hunting, Scrivener stayed for Glen to show him his hunting guns.

There was no word on Tuesday morning about the progress of negotiations for the suspended girl's return to school. J. O. reported that there had been more locker trouble at school on Monday: Ernest's locker, again. His lock, three textbooks, and an eleven-dollar slide rule had been stolen. Guards who were watching that area, across from Room 312, said that the break-in occurred during the approximately seven minutes of the first lunch period when they were not there. As always, someone was watching the watchers.

J. O. reported a find in one of the unused lockers on the first floor, a box of .22 rifle shorts. Such a find is not unusual in a school attended by almost a thousand teen-aged boys. In our circumstances, however, it had to be considered a threat.

At noon on Tuesday, one of the black-jacketed boys who had been hanging around Ernest's locker made a direct hit with a tomato on Carlotta's blouse. I supplied her with a clean one. The boy was not identified.

At home after school, facing as I was an appearance in court as a defendant on Wednesday, I did what any woman would do: I washed my hair. At midevening, Mr. Blossom called me to say that the board had accepted a much-modified and watered-down version of the statement they had proposed for the girl to sign. The statement contained no acknowledgment of error on her part and no reference to her attack on me; but she did promise to obey the rules of the school. Mr. Blossom was apologetic; he hoped I wouldn't feel that he and the board had not supported me. I was merely relieved. I didn't care whether we had won or lost—as long as the girl had agreed to obey the rules of the school. I was just glad not to have to face that Amis Guthridge again. Mr. Blossom suggested that I not have any future contact with the girl when she returned but ask the teacher in whose class she was most successful, to counsel with her if need arose. After Mr. Blossom hung up, I tried to call Jess, but his line was tied up all evening. Finally, I telephoned the teacher; but she was noncommittal. The girl had been perfect in her class, and she did not want to become involved. Knowing what being involved could mean, I understood that.

The letter the girl had signed read, merely, "If you will reinstate me, I promise in the future to conform to the rules. I understand that if I violate the promises contained in this letter, the order expelling me from Central High School will be reinstated." It was good enough, as far as I was concerned.

I dressed in my best suit on Wednesday, partly to boost my morale and partly because we were to have a PTA meeting. A number of teachers came by my office, incensed at the expelled girl's having been returned on her own terms. At 8:30, one of the business education teachers came in, interrupting the meeting I was having with the Pentangle Board, and urging me to look out the front window with her. The returning student, in her mouton jacket, and with her father was being interviewed by a TV reporter near the street in front of the school. I was sure that the teacher who had called me to the window was more interested in seeing how I would react than in expressing support of me, so I went back to my meeting, leaving her to look out my window by herself.

After school had started, Jess came in to report on the girl's readmittance. She had received some "we don't want you here" calls from students as she came up the front steps, he said. She had told Jess that Mr. Blossom had said she didn't have to carry a readmittance slip to her classes—as all returning students, even those absent for personal illness, are required to do. (Later Mr. Blossom denied that he had told her this.)

It poured rain all day. By noon, I was conscious that I was very tired. Micky McGalin came in to joke about the bomb searchers having raided her personal supplies in her unlocked locker in the teachers' rest room. Shirley Stancil came in to say she had slapped a pupil; she just thought she ought to let someone know. A boy had buzzed her with an electric device that she had taken away from another pupil. Her action, she said, was unprofessional, but automatic. Susie West reported a mysterious visitor, a man who came by taxi, peered about into classrooms, then left by taxi—probably a curious tourist. I took the visits of these three young teachers to be their way of showing their support and affection. It helped.

On Thursday, some teachers reported that the readmitted girl was telling other students how the school board had begged her to come back to school and had promised her that she didn't have to be responsible to Mrs. Huckaby. She swished through the upper hall as usual, but she did not look my way. Both newspapers had identified the mediator by name and had given factual accounts of his mediation. His statement, "The peace and tranquillity which was exemplified in Central High School yesterday proves the success of the undertaking," was only slightly inaccurate.

The *Gazette* reported that the Reverend Wesley Pruden had spoken at the meeting of the Junction City, Louisiana, Citizens' Council as a substitute for the reinstated girl. "She was jumping to come down here," Mr. Pruden was quoted as saying, "but her parents and others thought it would be best if she did not, in view of her recent reinstatement."

Had we won or lost in our ONE DOWN—EIGHT To Go case? I did not know. The girl segregationist leader was still with us, still a threat. But she was under a peace bond, of a kind. Her TV appearance and interview had revealed her as having some characteristics most parents would not want their daughters to imitate.

We had been ONE DOWN since February 6. It was now Friday, March 14, and we still had our EIGHT. And we had only nine more weeks of school.

CHAPTER VIII

March 13–May 13

Peace and Tranquillity at Central High School

The predicted peace and tranquillity in Central High was, by mid-March of 1958, not even a cease-fire. Although the in-school leadership of the segregationists had been put under an interdiction of sorts, the black students could not be relaxed, nor could those of us who wished them and Central well. Verbal abuse and sneak physical assaults remained all too common.

The chief means of harassing the Eight was by breaking open their lockers and stealing their books. It was easy and quick to put a screwdriver or small iron rod through the hasp of the lock, give it a twist—and there was the open locker. The dissident group worked hard at this. It gave me a wry satisfaction to replace the stolen books from the store of books I kept on hand, bought with funds provided to the PTA by the Community Chest for youngsters who could not afford to buy books. Certainly the blacks could not afford to buy new books to replace those stolen so regularly.

On March 13, two girls hurried into my office before school to report that they had seen a boy run into the boys' lavatory next to Room 234 with a gym satchel, Ernest Green's, they thought, since he was the only boy who carried one. (Ernest found it necessary to take his gym equipment with him to prevent its being stolen from his gym locker.) By the time I called J. O., Ernest had reported his loss. J. O. checked the lavatory and found, in the commodes, all Ernest's gym equipment except one shoe, which apparently had already gone down the drain, since the lavatory floor was flooded by a stoppage.

By the middle of March, J. O. and Captain Stumbaugh had concentrated all the lockers of the black students near the bookstore in the second-floor corridor. A federalized guard checked them from time to time; but the thieves used lookouts to prevent their apprehension. On one occasion the guard had just passed by and removed a sign, THE NIGGER'S LOCKER from Locker No. 1649 and returned to find a boy with a screwdriver in hand, his three lookouts having failed him. By the time the guard got the boy to the office, he had divested himself of the screwdriver. His mother was called in for a conference.

In a March 26 report J. O. wrote:

> Interviewed by Captain Stumbaugh and the undersigned this date, Ernest Green and Terrence Roberts concurred in their statements that physical harassment and abuse have decreased markedly during the previous several weeks. They stated that they are now able to walk through the halls during congested traffic intervals without molestation, and that the few who continue to employ verbal abuse are the same ones who have been doing the same thing since last September. Asked specifically how many students were involved, Ernest indicated five, and Terrence limited his "regular" hecklers to two. They said, further, that incidents in the gym shower and locker rooms have decreased, and that heckling and abuse in the cafeteria had practically stopped. Ernest added that their main current problem was that of keeping locks, lockers, and books in lockers.

We expected some concentration of attacks on one of the Eight, as there had been on Minnijean among the Nine. For a while, I thought the target might be Melba Pattillo. She was conspicuous because she was tall and anything but *meek*—that characteristic most approved for blacks by traditionalists. She had sometimes been mistaken for Minnijean because they were similar in size. It was hard to pin down Melba's reports of difficulties. Ernest's and Carlotta's by contrast, were always specific. Melba had reported that one boy frequently heckled her in homeroom. Jess counseled with the boy. On March 18 Melba reported that a slender blond boy had blocked her path and Ernest's on the stairs. Ernest, she said, had just walked around the boy. Ernest did not report this as an incident. After school on the same day, Melba reported that a slender, dark-haired boy who had once been in a study hall with her had either hit her or started to hit her with a book. She had just looked at him, though she said she might have warned him not to touch her. She could not identify either of these boys.

Even little Thelma Mothershed reported trouble on that same day. A group of boys had begun waiting for her, she said, between third and fourth floors. With the help of Alice Ann Coffman, the secretary to the band director, whose office was on the fourth floor, the boys were identified as coming from Anne Nunnally's home-room. Miss Nunnally began to watch these boys; Thelma was advised to delay her trip to the fourth floor for a minute or two; and the situation cleared.

But Melba's problems remained. On Tuesday, April 8, she came in after school. She wanted to report that a boy in her English class had used some very insulting language in making a report on *Huckleberry Finn*. I asked for specifics. She said that the boy kept saying, "and the nigger did this or the nigger did that." I mentioned that Mark Twain calls one of the main characters in that story Nigger Jim, making it hard to talk about that novel without using the offensive term. Melba said it was the boy's way of looking at her as he said it that insulted her. She said that the teacher was not to blame, that the boy was not always polite to her either. I agreed that, from Melba's report, the boy's manners were open to criticism.

I was sure Melba was still meeting some discourtesy around school but asked her whether she didn't agree that physical assaults had vanished. She did not agree entirely but said they were only occasional and by unknown persons, "like the boy who bopped Ernest in the face on the stairs" the other day. She said Ernest didn't report it, for he didn't know the boy's name and that we couldn't do anything about such unidentified pupils. But Melba did not relate any specific things that had happened to her.

The next day Melba was back. She had been spat on, "the fourth time by the same boy." He generally stood near 215 or 213 at this passing period, Melba said, and if he did it again, she would certainly grab him. I advised her against this course and suggested that she grab the nearest teacher and point out the boy.

It soon became apparent, however, that it was Ernest Green, the only senior among the Eight, who had been singled out as the next one to go. If he could be prevented from graduating, that would represent a real victory for the Capital Citizens' Council and the Mothers' League, and for segregationists in general. They would like to boast that no Negro had ever graduated from Central High School.

One special annoyance since midyear had been the small printed cards, most of them merely name-calling or just in poor taste, about black leaders or school administrators. For a while, I was naïve enough to think that the Intelligence group represented by Mr. Pryor (so secret we never found out his given name) in the back office, or the FBI, perhaps, might be interested in finding the source of these cards and seeking to enjoin their distribution, since the ONE DOWN—EIGHT TO GO card, at least, had been subversive of court orders. But Bonnie Brietz's husband, who was a printer, told her that any printer could tell the kind of press, type, and ink being used and trace the cards to the printer—if authorities really wanted to find him. After the suspensions for the distribution of the ONE DOWN signs, not so many cards were in evidence at school. But a teacher whose daughter was in high school reported that distribution of the cards continued among students who went to the public library to study at night.

Shirley Stancil had told me in March that a magazine salesman had volunteered the information to her that the cards were being printed by an eccentric who had a press and a bookshop in the Arcade Building, next to the public library. The salesman also thought that Shirley would like to know that Ernest Green would be the next black student to be driven off from Central High School. I had passed Shirley's report on to J. O., who passed it on to Mr. Pryor. I imagine the information was filed. That seemed to be the fate of all information turned in to that office.

One of the cards in circulation in early April read:

> LITTLE NIGGER AT CENTRAL HIGH
> HAS GOT MIGHTY FREE WITH HIS EYE
> WINKS AT WHITE GIRLS,
> GRABS THEIR BLOND CURLS:
> LITTLE NIGGER SURE IS ANXIOUS TO DIE.

Significantly, it was printed in green ink.

On April 10 a plot began to materialize. The father of the reinstated girl called Jess to say that something was going to have to be done about Ernest Green's winking at his daughter around school. He also asserted that when his daughter and an adult woman cousin were in Pfeifers Department Store on Saturday, Ernest was there and brushed against her with a familiar remark. He further stated that his daughter had been practicing cheerleading in her yard when Ernest passed in a car and called a greeting to her. Jess told the father that he found the accusation hard to believe, since this was the first such report he had ever had about Ernest. As for things that happened away from school, Jess suggested that the father contact Mrs. Green, who was a teacher in the public schools and a very sensible woman. The father said he thought Ernest was attempting to get his daughter put out of school.

Jess talked with Ernest, who said that the only place he and the girl crossed paths was in the cafeteria and that he never spoke to her or even looked at her. He said he and his mother were in Pfeifers on Saturday, but that he did not see, come near, or speak to the girl. Jess advised Ernest to continue avoiding her.

After the first lunch period, Wilma Means, who had just come upstairs from supervising the first lunch period but who knew nothing of Jess's conference with Ernest, spoke to me in the teachers' lounge. "You should have seen [the girl's name] in the cafeteria today. She paraded to and fro past Ernest Green *four* times, staring hard at him each of the eight times she passed his table. Ernest never raised his eyes." Ernest, blessed with a friendly disposition, with no tendency toward either aggression or retreat, and with unusually good judgment for a sixteen-year-old boy, would not be as easy a target as Minnijean.

On the next day, a boy who had withdrawn from Central and had threatened to come back to "make trouble" blocked Ernest's way as he was leaving gym. But Ernest side-stepped the boy, and there was no incident. Jefferson Thomas was still having rocks thrown at him and getting bumped and kicked. The peace and tranquillity were not perfect.

But that part of my life not primarily concerned with integration improved, both in school and out, after the expulsion crisis. At school, I noted on Friday, March 14, that I was working on student aid reports, on Pentangle girls' club matters, and that I even had time to fit and give to a student some much-needed school clothes. On Saturday I went with Glen on a predawn scouting trip for wild turkeys around Nall's Lake, sixty miles away. My journal for that day notes, also, that I had had the best night's sleep in two weeks.

Saturday afternoon's *Democrat* reported a speech by Jess Matthews to principals attending a Beta Club meeting at Raleigh, North Carolina. The paper headlined the story: PRINCIPAL OF CHS 'CONFIDENT,' and quoted what he had said—and what was true: that most teachers and students "have gone about their regular school program without the knowledge of any incidents until they read about them in the newspapers or saw and heard them on radio or TV.—No child has been physically injured, no persons in town have been killed or seriously hurt, and no teacher has resigned his or her position. There has been no mob violence on the campus or within the school." So there were some successes to report, though no cause for excessive self-congratulation.

Glen felt easy enough, now, about my safety at home to make his annual turkey-hunting trip to Alabama. He left at 3:45 A.M. on Friday, March 21. Jess was leaving, too, and had asked me to help him write a letter, a sort of position paper for presentation to his associates at the North Central Association of Schools and Colleges, meeting in Chicago. As Jess returned from Chicago, I was to leave for the National Association of Women Deans and Counselors' meeting in St. Louis on Wednesday, March 26. Then J. O. Powell was to take a few days off for fishing. Mr. Blossom felt that each of us needed a break from the constant tension. Meanwhile, Harry Carter, formerly vice-principal of Central and now athletic director for the stadium, was to be brought into the office to help as each of us took our turn away from school.

Ruth Owens of Hall High School in Little Rock (not yet desegregated) and I attended the NAWDC convention together. One of the section meetings I attended had school integration for the topic. Many participants in the discussion expressed firm convictions about desegregation, citing Central High School as a horrible example of bigotry, but showing a massive lack of understanding of what our particular problems had been. I said nothing until the meeting was being concluded. Then I introduced myself and gave the audience some of the same facts Jess had told the principals at Raleigh and Chicago. I added that neither the school nor the town, and certainly not the school administration or the teachers, should be the objects of their scorn and resentment. We had been caught in a political contest: first in state politics, then in a struggle between state and national politics. Furthermore, many of our teachers and townspeople were morally and philosophically committed to the fact that desegregation was right and desirable.

After the concluding banquet of the association, Claire Fulcher, from Bridgeport, Connecticut, whom I had met in the discussion group, told me that Jeanne Noble of City College of New York wanted to meet me. Since Ruth Owens and I had invited all the Arkansas deans to our room after the dinner, we asked Claire and Jeanne to join us. Jeanne, a brilliant and beautiful young black woman, told me that she had been in Little Rock in the fall and had driven past Central with Daisy Bates. She had seen and talked with Minnijean Brown in New York since she had entered the Lincoln school. Jeanne's report of Minnijean's remark after her first visit to a nightclub: "I didn't know *fat* people went to a nightclub!" sounded just like Minnijean. Claire Fulcher, Jeanne Noble, Bernice Smith of Henderson State, Ella Merle Shanks of Hendrix, Eleanor Tyler and Grace Vineyard of the University of Arkansas, Olive Ferguson of Arkansas State Teachers' College, Marjorie Harrod of Southern State College, Ruth, and I talked on into the night, mostly about Central High School and its problems, since everyone was both curious and concerned about us.

When I got back to school on Monday morning, I was glad to see that Jess looked rested after his North Central Association trip. Both he and his report had been well received, he said. After the public and private abuse he had taken in Little Rock and Arkansas, some acceptance by his professional friends was cheering.

On April 1, I was a guest at a buffet supper at Emma Scott's for a visiting lady from Norway, a member of parliament. Among other guests were Forrest Rozzell, executive secretary of the Arkansas Education Association; the executive secretary of the Council on Human Relations; and the Reverend Colbert Cartwright, pastor of the Pulaski Heights Christian Church and one of Little Rock's most outspoken supporters of integration. All these, their wives, Emma, and I tried to help the Norwegian visitor understand what had happened in Little Rock. Very likely we were also trying to help ourselves understand it, as well.

An Easter holiday gave me four days in the woods with Glen, on the last day of which he bagged his annual Arkansas wild turkey, which we dressed and put in cold storage for Christmas dinner. Meanwhile, as I was enjoying some personal life again, there had been activity in the community and state during March, everyone professing to be helpful in solving the problems of Central High School and the town, each according to his own light.

The Arkansas Supreme Court dismissed the case against the man arrested on September 25, with the ruling that a civilian did not have to obey an army officer. The man's lawyer, Kenneth Coffelt, was disappointed that the court had not ruled that the use of federal troops was unconstitutional.

Jim Johnson, unsuccessful segregationist opponent of Governor Faubus in the last election, was the main speaker at the meeting of the Mothers' League at the Skyway of the Lafayette Hotel on the evening of March 20. He urged the signing of a petition for a constitutional amendment to provide for segregated schools in Arkansas. Full-page forms for securing thousands of signatures were carried subsequently in the *Arkansas Democrat*. Margaret Jackson was cheered loudly, the paper reported, when she said that Pine Bluff, influenced by Little Rock's difficulties, had delayed segregation of schools. The papers also reported that the expelled and returned Central High girl and her father had attended this meeting.

Walter Guy told a Young Business Men's Association in mid-March that, although the school board had ruled out his proposal last fall to petition the federal court to remove the black students from Central High, the board had, on February 20, petitioned the court for a delay of integration for next year.

The Reverend Wesley Pruden predicted on March 18 to the Yazoo City, Mississippi, Citizens' Council that Arkansas would crush integration, which was Communist inspired. The means? Petitions to recall integrationist school boards.

On March 21 the Capital Citizens' Council, meeting in the Hotel Marion ballroom, had as its speaker Senator Sam Engelhardt of Alabama. Senator Engelhardt urged his hearers to curb Negro voters, citing as a model the gerrymandering of Tuskegee, Alabama. Our girl leader, according to the newspaper, had asked the senator whether there were any teen-age "moderates" in Alabama. Only one, Senator Engelhardt told her; and since that one had made a "moderate" speech in Chicago, he hadn't had an unbroken window in his house.

On March 24 and 25, Sara McCorkle, director of women's activities of the Association of Citizens' Councils of Mississippi, was in Little Rock conferring with officers of the local Citizens' Council and the Mothers' League. Her picture, that of an elderly, handsome woman, appeared above a listing of her background recommendations: past state president of the Mississippi American Legion Auxiliary; past officer of the Eight and Forty; past grand matron of the Order of the Eastern Star; state parliamentarian of the Mississippi Business and Professional Women; and a Christian education worker in the Episcopal church.

The NAACP published, late in March, a letter to Secretary of the Army Wilber M. Brucker criticizing the "do nothing" guards at Central, who just stood by when incidents occurred. It cited forty-two incidents. (I could list seventy-two by the end of January.) Secretary Brucker replied that guards were under orders to take action, and did so. Secretary Roy Wilkins of the NAACP then called for "sterner action" by CHS troops.

Governor Faubus was verbally attacking the "Communists" who were behind the integration of Central High School, citing Mr. and Mrs. Lee Lorch as Communists in his public speeches. (Mrs. Lorch had befriended Elizabeth Eckford on September 23.)

Unhelpful public statements continued into April. On the eighteenth, State Representative Frank Ross of Desha County, manager of the McGehee Chamber of Commerce, proposed to the Legislative Council that the slogan of Little Rock be changed from City of Roses to City of Daisy Blossom. The resolution passed, amid great hilarity. Of the three Little Rock members of the council, only Representative J. H. Cottrell objected. Representative Glenn F. Walther made a joke about the slogan. Senator Max Howell had no comment.

On April 19 Judge Lee Ward of Paragould announced to oppose Governor Faubus in the Democratic primary, declaring that integration was not the issue but that he proposed to restore dignity and integrity to the office of governor.

During the first week of April the most independent attempt to solve the Central High School problem came in a proposal by Herbert Thomas, a respected businessman and philanthropist of Little Rock and Arkansas. He was not aligned with or against any political group. His proposal, the withdrawal of blacks from Central High School and a new start at gradual desegregation after study by a commission, had been made after long study and from great social concern, he said. His proposal was, from the first, unpopular with both sides: the Mothers' League and the Citizens' Council and segregationists in general opposed all integration; the NAACP and the Council on Human Relations felt that withdrawal of the blacks would be a step backward. So did I.

One evening late in April, Mrs. D. D. Terry called me. Mrs. Terry was a remarkable woman, one of the great ones of our town for her intelligence, her vision, her courage, and her persistence. She was one of the few white persons who had maintained continuous contacts with black leaders during the crisis. She was almost unique in being unassailable, personally. Her husband, a former congressman and a lawyer, was in his seventies and no longer active in practice. She had sufficient wealth not to be vulnerable economically. And her place on the social scale, though she was not a "society woman," was secure. Her family, the Fletchers, were among the oldest in Little Rock and on the neighboring large farms. Her brother was John Gould Fletcher, the poet. A cousin was Bishop Albert Fletcher of the Little Rock diocese of the Roman Catholic Church, though Mrs. Terry, herself, was an Episcopalian. She lived in the old Fletcher family home, originally built by Albert Pike, a beautiful antebellum, white-columned house on a tree-shaded block downtown. So in Little Rock she was a personage; but she was also a real person.

Mrs. Terry told me that she was disturbed that Mr. Thomas' plan called for the removal of the black children from Central. She thought I would agree with her on that. I told her that I did, that I wanted them to stay at Central, and that I had worked all year to keep them there. Mrs. Terry felt that I might be able to tell Mr. Thomas about the eight children and help him to see the importance of their staying at Central. Would I talk with him if she could arrange for us to see him? Of course I would. The next day she called again to say that Mr. Thomas would see us in his home early Friday evening.

The Thomas home, set back among pine trees off Highway 10 in the western edge of Little Rock, was lovely in the soft spring evening. I remember the white azaleas and dogwood, not massed, but airy and dainty against the other shrubs, beautiful in the late twilight. Inside the house were sprays of cut azaleas in big vases. The Thomases, friendly and informal, recalled meeting me through PTA activities. At Mrs. Terry's suggestion, I talked about the Eight individually, their problems and their successes, their abilities and their vulnerabilities. Mrs. Thomas knew Terrence Roberts; his mother had occasionally helped her serve parties. She spoke of Terrence's mother as a fine woman, but she thought she would be happier to have Terrence out of the dangerous situation he was in. Mr. Thomas felt that the students must be "given up" for next year, if Faubus remained as governor. He said his hope for a defeat of Faubus had risen during the last few days, with Judge Ward's announcement of his candidacy.

When the Terrys and I left, I was convinced of Mr. Thomas' sincerity, but I saw little chance for success for his plan. Nor did I want it to succeed. Hard as the school year had been, I could see that we had made some real gains toward desegregation in school. I did not want us to retreat, even for a year. A retreat would not make things easier, but harder, after the hiatus.

We were still having our ups and downs at school. On April 10 one of our students had a fight with a black girl at the bus stop on the drugstore corner. The black girl was not one of ours. The police took the fighters to court, accompanied by several volunteer "witnesses" for the white girl involved. I recognized the names of all, from their former truancies as well as their segregationist involvements.

One girl who came in voluntarily on April 17 cheered me considerably with what she had to say. She had been in the walkout in the fall; but she came to tell me that she had changed her attitude toward integration completely since then. She now felt that the black students had a right to be at Central. I was curious to know what had changed her attitude. Dr. W. O. Vaught, the pastor of her church (Immanuel Baptist) was the person who had influenced her, she said.

On Thursday, April 24, the military tried an experiment: they were not on duty at school. Jess called me in early to tell me about their absence and to give me a number to call in case of trouble. He was to be in conference with Mr. Blossom most of the morning and at Rotary Club at noon. I told him I thought we would be all right, till the news got out, at least. At noon he came by for a few minutes to tell us that the outside jeep patrol was still on guard. We had no trouble reported.

There was plenty of normal school activity that Thursday. Elections were held before school and during homeroom. The local science fair was set up in the Field House. Gloria Ray and Robin Woods came by to tell me that their exhibits had won honorable mention. The science teachers reported later, with disgust, that vandals among the viewers had either broken the exhibits or stolen the award ribbons from all the blacks' entries.

A former Communist party member lectured at an after-lunch assembly. Many students and a few teachers thought the message inspiring. It was interesting to note how many of these were persons who were opposed to integration.

On Friday morning the state science fair was held in our Field House. Those Central students who had won awards in our local fair were officially excused from all classes to stay by their projects and explain them. Gloria Ray's name was listed among the winners in our daily bulletin. But Gloria's day did not start smoothly.

Just before nine she came to my office to leave her books, the lock having been twisted off her locker a few days before. She told me that as she ran back to her father's car to get a part of her exhibit she was hit on the leg by a rock thrown by a boy who then darted around the Field House. She didn't feel she needed to see the nurse—just a bruise, she said—and she was anxious to get back to her exhibit.

After school that day, Gloria brought to my office two friends she had made at the fair, a blond girl and a boy she had been taking on a tour of her school. These youngsters were from Harrison, Arkansas, in the northern part of the state. It was interesting to see young people who had not been infected by the local affliction—fear of association with blacks.

In this connection, Captain Stumbaugh told me of a boy who had moved from Springfield, Missouri, to Little Rock, and who had talked in a friendly way with Ernest Green. Immediately he began to have telephoned threats. His car was damaged by vandals, who left a note: "This is what happens to nigger lovers."

Our national notoriety brought visitors, not all of them merely the curious. The last Saturday in April, Anna Halton of Fisk University in Nashville visited with me at my home for a couple of hours. She was making a sociological study of school integration for the National Council of Churches, she told me. We talked about happenings and attitudes at Central, though she asked me nothing that had not already been well publicized, including my opinion.

The following Monday, Jess brought to my office a visitor whom he did not have the time or the patience to listen to. She was an elderly woman, a Mrs. Crowder, I believe she said, who had once been a teacher and who was on her way, with a daughter and her family, perhaps, to vacation in Hot Springs. Mrs. Crowder wanted to tell me the story of her girlhood, and I let her. It turned out to be a fascinating story to me; and before I ushered her out of the building at 4:40 (the doors were chained shut every afternoon at 4:45) I wished she could write her story, or let someone write it for her. Briefly, it was this:

She had been born a Calhoun of Kentucky. Her grandmother, fiercely southern, taught her to honor the Confederacy and hate the Yankee Union. But her father, a minister, was sent by his church to study at Harvard and took his family with him to Cambridge. The best school for his little daughter, his associates told him, was the Agassiz School; and after a great deal of soul searching, he sent her there, in spite of the fact that the principal of the school was Maria Baldwin, a black woman who had grown up in the home of Henry Wadsworth Longfellow and been educated by him. The little Calhoun girl was very resistant to Miss Baldwin because she was a Negro; she hated her, even while knowing that she was a wonderful teacher and always fair in her decisions. There was some sort of emotional climax, some series of events that included the awarding of a spelling medal to the little girl, that ended in her acceptance of Miss Baldwin and love for her. And there was still a greater climax on the occasion of her father's taking her to hear Edward Everett Hale read his "The Man Without a Country." She understood, then, that the United States, not the Confederate states, deserved her loyalty.

I think Mrs. Crowder came to Central with her story under the misapprehension that we in charge of the school were living with some of the illusions she had had as a child. Some people in Little Rock were, of course, though she was not talking with one of them. But I loved her story.

The following day I listed in my journal as a "normal day at school." The next sentence, "Lock broken off 1643 again," shows what I was accepting as normal. The next day, another lock having been broken off, Carlotta came to leave her wraps in my office. She reported an incident that she hadn't realized had happened till she got home the day before and found the back of her dress splattered with ink. Then she remembered that, as her Spanish class was watching a film in the darkened room, she had felt something wet on her back and had turned to see two girls giggling behind her.

Melba continued to get verbal abuse and be blocked on the stairs. Terrence reported being kicked and being slapped on the head from behind with a rolled-up magazine. Both Terrence and Jefferson again had locks twisted off their lockers. So the tranquillity continued.

I had a sympathy caller on Friday, May 2. Through the pouring rain came Dr. Margaret Quale, who knew something of what we were experiencing at Central because she was teaching psychology at the University of Alabama during its desegregation by Autherine Lucy. Dr. Quale had once taught in Little Rock, she told me, and was now retired. She expressed her sympathy and support, donned her rain gear, and left. It was cheerful to meet a survivor from a similar adventure.

The school yearbook, the *Pix*, was distributed the first week in May. Little else could be accomplished at school on the day of its distribution, since student mores demanded that one's yearbook be circulated to all one's friends, to be decorated with their autographs under flattering statements about the owner of the book. Carlotta and Gloria both reported some nice things written in their books by white classmates, Carlotta's mostly by those in her Spanish class, Gloria's by her English classmates. Piety, not friendship, seemed to be the theme of the tributes these girls showed me. Billye Jean Spotts, an intelligent, humorous girl who was one of my office monitors, commented to me that "the meanest kids often wrote the most pious sentiments" in one's book.

The publication of the *Pix* brought a visitor to school whose presence dramatized how sensitive we still were to outside pressures. The devil himself could not have been more abhorred by the segregationists than Daisy Bates. Her visit to Central in the fall had reverberated through the propaganda of the Mothers' League and the Citizens' Council for months. Her husband, L. C. Bates, now came to school to buy a *Pix*, having been told when he called the downtown administrative office (without their asking him to identify himself) that Central was where he could get one. When he was recognized at school, he was given a reprimand by the journalism teacher—for coming to school without a press permit!

During late April and early May some events occurred, not at Central but concerning it, that had a bearing on our school situation. The Eighth Circuit Court of Appeals in St. Louis refused the appeal of Governor Faubus to dissolve the injunction against his interference with the integration of Central High School. In refusing the appeal, the court censured the governor. The Arkansas State Board of Education side-stepped any discussion of the Thomas plan. Judge Harry J. Lemley, of Hope, Arkansas, was named to hear the Little Rock School Board's case asking delay of the integration case, the hearing set for June 3, in federal court. The *Arkansas Gazette* and its editor and publisher were named Pulitzer Prize winners for their editorials on the desegregation of Central High School and for their constructive support of the schools in this crisis. And President Eisenhower announced that the federalized troops would leave Central High School at the end of the term, May 29.

The peace at Central continued as usual. On Thursday, May 8, a rock fight developed between a group of Dunbar Junior High boys (black), walking past Central on their way to a track meet at the stadium, and a group of Central boys, out for the lunch hour, on the school grounds adjacent to the street. Better planning, which would have routed the Dunbar students down the street on the other side of the school, or would have sent them past the school twenty minutes earlier or later, when no one would have been outdoors at Central, could have prevented the clash. But that is hindsight. The fact that a black student teacher waved a pistol out a car window while the fracas was in progress did nothing to help matters. It was a starter's pistol, loaded with blanks. But who could tell that from seeing it in the hand of a man in a car? Calm was finally restored by the two sergeants and the captain on duty at school, along with two jeep loads of reserves called up.

On Tuesday, May 13, late in the morning, I was startled by a series of loud explosions from the first floor, down the stairs from my office, near the nursery-school rooms. I walked down the stairs and met a girl and a boy who had seen some boys light the firecrackers and run. Teachers outside the building who saw the boys and their car reported the license number. A check of the suspension list at nearby West Side Junior High School and some research on the license number gave Jess the names of two junior high boys and the older brother of one, a former Central student, to turn over to juvenile court.

The newspapers had reported that Melba Pattillo's mother's contract to teach with the North Little Rock Schools, a separate school district from Little Rock, had not been renewed for next year. The reason? Apparently the fact that she was letting Melba attend a "white" school. Since Melba had checked out of school ill on Friday, the most recent date that a locker had been broken open, I called her in to ask what she had lost. She had missed two textbooks, a zipper notebook, and an umbrella. The books I replaced. The other possessions were just gone.

As I walked down the hall with Melba, she said to me, "I'll bet you'll be glad when this year is over. I hope you can get some rest this summer."

"I'll bet you'll be glad, too," I said.

She heaved a humorous sigh. "Leave us crawl into caves," she said. "The only person I want to see this summer is my psychiatrist."

CHAPTER IX

May 14–June 3

Commencement, or Conclusion?

Would Ernest Green graduate from Central High School? Like the last question in a soap opera episode, this was the problem that hung in our thoughts during the last weeks of school. Ridiculous, trite as the question sounded, it had a tragic, serious meaning to us at Central, and to Ernest and his family and friends, I am sure. First, there was no way to guarantee that he would pass the courses necessary for graduation. His grades were poor, in some courses, whether because of inadequate previous schooling; his youth (at sixteen he was almost two years younger than most of our seniors); the prejudices of some—though not all—of his teachers; or the disturbance and physical and emotional harassment connected with his attendance at Central High School, no one knew. We could only hope—in English and physics, particularly.

Besides having all these natural and unnatural hazards to contend with, Ernest was faced with massive outside opposition to his graduation. Captain Stumbaugh furnished me with a copy of a letter Ernest had received, signed "A worried senior":

> I am one of over six hundred graduating seniors at Central High School. As you know, graduation night is quickly approaching. It will be an evening which I and my other classmates shall never forget.
> At present there is a great deal of conversation among Centralites over the trouble that will most probably arise if you should decide to be present to receive your diploma. Naturally you deserve your

sheepskin as much as anyone else, and I would not stop you from getting it. However, there are, as you well know, many who would gladly do so. Therefore, I am asking you, Ernest, to please refrain from attending these exercises. It will be a time that I and hundreds of others do not wish to have marred. For the sake of your classmates and good common sense, please give your utmost consideration to this.

I hope that you will let your unselfishness and good judgement dominate your decision.

No one who read the letter thought that it had been written by a member of the graduating class. It was an adult composition. The sentences beginning with the qualifying words and phrases: *As you know*, *At present*, *Naturally*, *However*, *Therefore* sounded rather like a lawyer or a preacher. The first-person pronoun preceding the third-person pronoun in a compound subject: *I and my many classmates*, *I and hundreds of others*, is not characteristic of the writing of a high school student. *Sheepskin* is not a term currently used for diploma, though an older generation used it. But whoever wrote it, the letter was a cruelly selfish plea for Ernest to be unselfish. The attitude was the familiar one: I love you; but keep out of my way, and stay in your place. The threat of what might happen if he did not was implicit.

Ernest had no intention of acceding to the request of "worried senior," whoever he was, nor did the school administration want him to be absent. It was almost as important to us as to Ernest and his race for him to graduate. Maybe it was more important to us. But we also knew that the occasion could be dangerous for him.

Ernest and his graduation could not be our only concern in those final days of the school year. The tempo of harassment of all the Eight increased as end-of-the-year events occurred. On May 14, after the usual interminable but well-prepared Recognition Assembly, staged by the student council, in which awards for service to the school were presented, Jess and I went to the PTA Council tea. When I got back to school, Miss Carpenter told me that Terrence Roberts had been in the health room. Someone had hit him on the head with a large rock as he passed between the Field House and the main building. The blow had raised a big knot on his head, but he did not want to go home. Terrence was like that.

The late spring days had turned warm, and I used my office window airconditioner on Thursday and Friday. But using it forced me to close the door between my office and the hall, an invitation to mischief in the hall on these last, critical days at school. So I used the airconditioner only occasionally, and I always stood outside my door while classes passed. So did many of the other teachers, and where they did, incidents seldom occurred. It was stretches of corridors where there were no classrooms or where teachers were not at their doors that were the danger spots. Those—and outside the building.

Maude Reid came in to tell me that Gloria Ray had asked to take her biology final test early so that she wouldn't have to come to school on Monday, the 26th. I talked with Gloria, who, though she had shown remarkable courage all year, now seemed really frightened. The war of nerves—and physical knocks—was getting to her. Of course we couldn't give the black students special privileges we didn't give others—and stay in business. But I told Gloria that we would work out a plan for her and the others during exam time. During our conference, she mentioned one of our regular harassers who waited daily at the north end of the building to block the entrance. I passed this word on to the guard.

Gloria got a brief reprieve from facing harassment on Friday. She got sent home, along with twenty-six white pupils, all of them broken out with three-day measles. The ailment had hit other youngsters, and even three teachers, earlier in the week.

I called in Carlotta Walls, whose appraisals were always calm and factual, to ask her about increased tensions around school. She said that the black students were all receiving verbal threats to "get" them on the last day of classes, May 26. By then, the threatening students seemed to feel, their school credits would be established and school authorities could not punish them.

Monday, the 19th, was rainy. An *Arkansas Democrat* reporter called. Jess Matthews was in a meeting and not available, so I took the call. The reporter was checking a rumor that we did not plan to have commencement exercises.

K. N. M. Pillai of Bombay, India, a newsman, was brought in to talk with me a while about desegregation at Central. Mr. Pillai was a pleasant, competent reporter, considerably hampered by his local escort, a man who did most of the talking in an effort, apparently, to preserve (or restore) the good name of Little Rock.

Tuesday, Senior Class Day, was not a satisfactory one at school. The seniors, most of them, enjoyed it, I'm sure: a holiday from school, during which they were supposed to go to War Memorial Park for a program and a picnic lunch. About half of them went. The others either went briefly, or not at all, then picnicked farther afield. This day always leaves the school understaffed, for senior homeroom teachers as senior sponsors are expected to attend the festivities at the park. That leaves their tenth and eleventh grade classes to be cared for by the remaining teachers, who have their own responsibilities, as well. The heckling of the black youngsters increased. Melba's locker was broken into again and her possessions stolen once more. But for some, Senior Class Day was a triumph. The black senior volunteered to stay at home and not come to school or go to the picnic at all.

Mrs. John Reid called me during the day. She was understandably shocked at one of the cards now being distributed, the one declaring OPEN SEASON ON COONS. I agreed that the card was shocking, as others had been. But I knew, now, that the federal government was not trying to stop such propaganda and that the state government was in sympathy with it, if not actually behind it. Governor Faubus was being quoted in the press as remarking that he would call out the National Guard again next year if necessary to stop integration. Jess was getting considerable telephone harassment again.

Wednesday was another restless day at school. There was another fight at the bus stop on the drugstore corner between a white girl I had first met during the September disorders and a black junior high girl. The guards had stopped the fight, and the police had taken the black girl to her school. The white girl did not come on to school; but at noon, Prosecuting Attorney Frank Holt called me to say that she and nine witnesses for her were in his office. He read me their names, and I knew them all, as usual for truancies and racial disorders. Prosecutor Holt had given the white girl and her mother a chance to swear out a warrant against the black girl, who was the aggressor, all declared, but they had declined. I suggested that all the girls sign in to school for the afternoon.

Our returned expellee and several of her friends were absent, a situation that I had grown accustomed to thinking of as a signal for trouble. Probably they were busy on the telephone. I had one call from an unidentified parent who had been disturbed by rumors of fighting between black and white students in school and blocking of black students from their classrooms.

Captain Stumbaugh told me a story. A package had come to our science department, mailed from Chicago, but with no sender's name. The address had been determined to be fictitious; so demolition experts were given the package to open. It was harmless, and useless. Some crazy crank, he supposed. But crazy people can be dangerous.

Because of the tenseness of our situation, six civilian guards reported on Thursday, hired by the school board as extra protection during exam days. These six men, looking stiff and uncomfortable in their coats and ties, took stations about the building. The fact that they were there caused much talk among teachers and students, but there was no official explanation. One girl with a history of delinquency was convinced that the men had been placed at school to watch her. Most students seemed to think they were FBI agents, and that misconception among the students may have been useful.

I called in each of the Eight to talk about Friday and Monday. Those who had finished all their exams before Monday I advised to stay at home that day. Those who had to come to school for a required class or an exam either day, I advised to come only for those necessary hours, signing in with a note from home and out again, also with a note; and to arrange their transportation to and from school to suit these schedules. Ernest would have to come at the usual time on Monday, for seniors were to practice for graduation.

Captain Stumbaugh told me the general plans for graduation that had been made at a meeting of local police officers, the military, the superintendent, the principal, and the board. Local police were to handle the spectators. Federalized National Guardsmen would be in reserve—for emergencies. The FBI would be there. The *Arkansas Democrat* reported that both NBC and CBS were sending film crews to cover the event for TV news.

Jess told me of some fun he had had with a *Democrat* reporter who had called him to check on the blacks' grades. She was particularly interested, he knew, in whether Ernest would qualify for graduation. He told the reporter that of course he could not give out individual grades, but that at the last reporting time all had been passing. He asked the reporter whether she had not noticed the name of one of the Eight on the last honor roll published in her paper on Sunday, April 27. She hadn't; but she would find there the name of Carlotta Walls.

The extra guardsmen appeared at school on Friday morning, trailing the black students to their classroom doors as they had in the fall. Elizabeth Eckford did not come to school, for she had no exams scheduled. Gloria told me of the usual boys trying to block their entrance. The guard intervened. Eggs had been thrown, but they missed their targets. Yvonne Thompson, vice-president of the senior class, had been hit by one that missed. When I told Miss Carpenter of this incident, she said that she left school the afternoon before amid egg throwing, and one had splashed at her feet.

Melba got upset in English class and came into my office midway in the period. I could not understand from her report exactly what had disturbed her, but the general atmosphere around school was enough. Gloria took refuge in my office during her lunch period. She was scared of getting soup thrown on her, she said. The day was a noisy one. Both teachers and students were on edge, a normal condition during final exams, but made worse by rumors flying about. Carlotta, Gloria, and Jefferson signed out at 2:30 since they had no exams the last period. J. O. went to the exit to watch the remaining black students leave at 3:30.

Practice for the baccalaureate to be held on Sunday had been on Friday morning between eleven and twelve. For this occasion, senior boys and girls form separate lines, in alphabetical order, and march to their seats in the stands, boys and girls filing into alternate rows so that the dark blue of the boys' caps and gowns and the white of the girls' make horizontal stripes in the stands as the seniors sit or stand in their places. Students are not assigned partners for the march-in. As it works out, however, a boy and a girl walk down four or five steps opposite each other before they turn in to their respective rows. A few seniors each year do not appear for baccalaureate, since attendance at the religious service is optional.

But by counting down the list, we determined that the girl most likely to walk down those few steps opposite Ernest Green would probably be a girl whose last name began with E. Jess suggested that I call in those girls and tell them that they would not be required to walk opposite Ernest if they did not want to. They could leave a slight gap in the line if they preferred. Ann Emerson let me know at once that she would not hesitate to walk with Ernest if she happened to be opposite him. The others said nothing. Rehearsal went off without incident.

Seniors had been given three tickets each for use by their family or friends in case rain forced the service into the school auditorium, where only about two thousand could be seated. If the service could be held outside, tickets for the stadium would not be needed. Trouble, if there were to be any at graduation, would not come at a religious service but at the time of diploma giving. So the baccalaureate, weather permitting, was to be open to the public.

Late Sunday afternoon I had a call on the telephone from an old man who identified himself. He said he had known and thought highly of my husband years ago and wondered whether he was still alive. After this remarkable beginning, he proceeded to give me a lecture on the necessity for segregation in schools, based on all the usual reasons: the inferiority of one race, the necessity of maintaining racial purity, the horrible example of Washington, D.C., etc. I finally excused myself and hung up.

On Sunday evening I went by for Emma Scott, who wanted to attend the baccalaureate with me. The stadium was well surrounded with local police, we noticed as we drove by. We left our car in the teachers' parking lot at school and walked back to the stadium. The National Guardsmen were in the old shop area of the school, in reserve. We walked across the grassy practice field to the stadium. Seniors in white or navy caps and gowns were lining up in the stadium ramps. Emma and I took seats in the south end of the stands, where we found Velma Powell, J. O.'s wife. She was as nervous as I was, but she showed it more. Ernest Green's family came in and sat above us in the stands. Other parents coming in shunned that area for a while; but before long, others came in and pointedly chose it. The seniors marched in to the stands as the band played the processional. There was nothing unusual to observe. The invocation was given by the Reverend Maurice Webb, a Methodist, whose daughter, Marcia, was a member of the class. The Reverend W. Harold Hicks, a Baptist, whose son Bill was also in the class, preached the sermon. No mention was made of our unusual year by anyone. After the benediction and the recessional, we walked out with the crowd. It was a normal departing crowd, except for the small group of blacks waiting for each other, children, adults, grandparents—Ernest's friends.

We walked on with the departing guests out to Sixteenth Street. One cap-and-gowned senior boy was in conversation with the police, but there was no scuffling or loud talk, so we supposed the conversation friendly. We went home, feeling good about this first formal presentation of our integrated graduation class.

The *Gazette* on Monday morning mentioned the "minor incident" for which the senior boy was being detained by the police as we saw him Sunday night. This boy, standing on the low retaining wall beside the exit walk, had spat on a young black girl as she walked with her family. Police Chief Eugene Smith and Captain R. E. Brians were walking behind the blacks and arrested the boy. His mother came up and verbally attacked the police. Then with a No Parking sign she physically attacked a *Democrat* photographer. During this commotion, the boy walked away but was reapprehended. His family, joined now by Margaret Jackson, rode to the police station, where the boy's mother fainted and her two daughters, according to the account, kicked at police officers and screamed. I was glad I hadn't been in on this affair. The boy's mother was the one who had reported that I must know something about the bomb that time when she came to collect her son and daughter. I was too calm, she had said.

The mother was in the principal's office on Monday morning, fearful that her son was not going to be allowed to graduate because of the spitting incident. Jess was withholding his decision, he told her. He held a trump card, which he saw that he might use to prevent other incidents by the Mothers' Leaguers. The mother was apologetic, too, about the behavior at the police station of her two daughters, one a Central pupil. They were upset, she said, because they knew their mother had a heart condition.

Alberta Harris, the homeroom teacher for the girls whose last name began with E, told me that it turned out in rehearsal that Jane Emery was the one to walk opposite Ernest in the practice for baccalaureate. On Sunday, Jane and her mother had so many obscene calls that Mrs. Emery had been made ill. When Miss Harris learned of the harassment, she told Jane to drop back a couple of steps if her partner in the processional turned out again to be Ernest. Whatever the outcome, pictures of the processional showed Ernest walking alone.

Many students presented notes from home on Monday, asking for them to be excused as soon as their exams were over. There are always some requests, but this year I was more willing to grant those requests. I was glad to reduce our responsibilities at school by as many students as possible. By arrangement, the Eight, except for Ernest, were not present, not having exams scheduled for morning. At midday, one of the unsympathetic teachers came in to see me. "What have you done with your niggers today, Elizabeth?" she smirked. I was disgusted and showed it. I didn't even answer her.

Seniors practiced for graduation on Monday morning. The maneuvers necessary to get 602 boys and girls seated alphabetically in chairs on the playing field, the chairs in V-shaped rows facing the spectators in the stands, the speakers' platform at the apex of the V, is a logistical feat accomplished annually by Jeanne McDermott, office secretary, and carried out by homeroom teachers, who have been given diagrams and sets of directions. At rehearsal, the seniors find their chairs, boys and girls in alternating rows, each chair seat labeled with the name of a senior. Then the seniors practice the long walk to the platform to receive a diploma and shake the principal's hand and then back to their chairs. Class president Ronnie Hubbard made a few remarks at the rehearsal. His concluding statement: "I know everyone will do what is right tomorrow night. I don't think anyone wants to do anything to ruin our commencement" was understood perfectly by his hearers. They applauded. The practice went smoothly.

Black students with exams after noon Monday signed in just for those exams. Gloria was a little early, so she sat in my office and we visited for a while. With guards following each black student closely, there were no incidents reported.

As a security measure, Commencement, unlike Baccalaureate, was to be closed to the general public. Each senior had been given eight tickets for family or friends. Jess had announced that he would give a few extra tickets individually to any senior who needed more. Students (juniors and sophomores) singing in the choral groups or acting as ushers were given tickets for themselves and their escorts. Many of our regular harassers would be present through these tickets. And Jess reported that a disproportionate number of his requests for extra tickets were coming from the segregationist seniors. Faculty members would need tickets, too, since entrance to the stadium would be by ticket, only, and ticket takers would be members of the police force, who would not recognize the faculty. One staff member who asked for extra tickets was one we thought might have been the source of leaks to the *Democrat* about what was said in staff meetings.

Tuesday was test-grading and report card filling-out day. There were no classes, though a few students were there to help teachers and run errands. One of those present was a girl whom I had reprimanded once for stamping segregationist signs on bannisters. Since the school year was over, I called her in to talk with her. She had been an office helper and had occasionally worked at the switchboard; and I suspected that she was one of the sources of information to the Mothers' League about what went on in the office. Possibly she had telephoned reports to the *Democrat* as incidents occurred. I told this girl that Mr. Matthews and I had agreed that, if she wanted to work in the office next year, she would have to make up her mind about her loyalty. She could not work in Mr. Matthews' office again and report to Mrs. Jackson of the Mothers' League. She was angry, naturally, but she did not deny my implications.

A general tenseness about graduation was evident all day Tuesday. Ernest had passed all his subjects. He would graduate. The editorial in the *Gazette* that morning had pleaded, "Let This Night Be Marked by Dignity." And by safety, some of us added, mentally, knowing the violence of the opposition. I tried to work on the final report to the PTA on student aid, but I found it almost impossible to concentrate on books and lunches and clothing for indigents. Captain Stumbaugh, having no students to guard, came by for a visit.

Preparations for safety at graduation had been very carefully made, he assured me, even to the checking out by the FBI of the upper windows of houses overlooking the stadium for possible sniper positions. He was as nervous as the rest of us about the possibility of a catastrophe. The thought of even minor disruptions was repulsive. Captain Stumbaugh said that an adult group—Capital Citizens' Council? Mothers' League?—was distributing boxes, each holding two eggs, with directions about throwing them at the proper time. He even knew the address from which the containers were being distributed.

Jess, aided by his long experience and knowledge of the reactions of young people and of parents whose children were "on the program," had worked with senior class sponsors to arrange a Commencement program that directed itself to other foci than the first black graduate, and that used as many youngsters on the program as possible. That would mean that the smoothness and success of the program and the evening were very important to many of the people who were to be in the audience: parents of band members, choral groups, National Honor Society ushers, and readers of the long poem that was to take the place of the usual graduation student speakers. This choral reading group was to read "The Story of Arkansas," a free verse composition by students in Josephine Feiock's senior English class, the presentation directed by Kaye Taylor, also an English teacher. This poem traced Arkansas from prehistoric times, through Indian habitation, through Spanish and French explorations, through the settlement by pioneers from the east coast, and through the *War Between the States*, as the United Daughters of the Confederacy refers to the Civil War:

> Negroes, slaves to Old King Cotton
> Toiled beneath the broiling sun,
> While their masters lived in leisure,
> Heeding not impending doom.
> . . . .
> Then the gloom of war enveloped the nation,
> Brother gray 'gainst brother blue. . . .

There was no other reference to the beginnings of our present social revolution or its implications. There was a particularly unpoetic conclusion:

. . . tomorrow's Arkansas,
The true Wonder State, a real land of opportunity—
Opportunities for the artist, for the laborer,
For the housewife, for the businessman.
Opportunities for all of us—the citizens of tomorrow!

This epic was certainly no worse than the usual graduates' speeches; and it employed fifty-three readers rather than four speakers.

There was to be another among our 602 graduates who would attract some attention away from Ernest Green. Robert Shaw, who had attended Central via a two-way communication system provided for him by the Forum Class of the First Methodist Church, was also to receive his diploma. Robert, a polio victim in his early childhood, was almost incredibly handicapped, except for his mind. Through the years during which they knew him only from his voice, dozens of seniors got to know Robert. A few had visited him in his home, and the whole student body had met him one day during the winter when he was brought in his wheelchair to the March of Dimes assembly. Jess and Emily Penton, Robert's homeroom teacher, had arranged for him to attend his commencement and receive his hard-earned diploma with his class. A crippled child has great appeal for the public, and Robert's appearance might help us through the evening.

At the early afternoon faculty meeting, the conclusion of our grade-recording day, Jess reminded us that we would need tickets to attend commencement. He also asked for volunteers to help this afternoon in checking to see that each student's name was pasted on the correct chair on the field. I volunteered, with others.

There had been much talk about who was likely to sit next to Ernest on the field. It would be a boy in Ernest's homeroom. To some, the position seemed both socially undesirable and potentially dangerous. Jerry Goshien had no objection to sitting in the place he would normally be, alphabetically, next to Ernest. It was not known how others would feel; so the chair on the other side of Ernest was moved several inches farther away than it needed to be. As the other teachers and I worked with the chairs, a final conference was in progress on the field: the military; Police Chief Eugene Smith; Harry Carter, manager of the stadium; Mr. Blossom; and Jess Matthews. They were men I knew could be trusted to take all precautions possible and to meet any foreseeable emergency. The question in all of our minds was: were there any unforeseen ones? I suggested to Miss Carpenter that we attend commencement together. We would sit in chairs on the cinder track, our backs to the spectator stands, on the same level as the graduates and facing them.

At home, I had an early supper—a dish of cornflakes, all I felt I could swallow. I dressed in a summer cotton since it was a warm evening, picked up Emma Scott and her mother, Adgie Williams, and Miss Carpenter, and drove to the teachers' parking lot. The streets around the school were being patrolled by police cars. Army transport trucks were parked by the entrance to the old shops at Central. Inside the shops were soldiers. At the gate from the parking lot to the practice field was a soldier in battle dress, including helmet. I almost failed to recognize Sergeant Blackwood. I said, "This is it," and he nodded agreement.

At the stadium, uniformed police were everywhere. No doubt there were plainclothesmen, too, both local and FBI. Miss Carpenter and I left the Scotts and Mrs. Williams to find seats in the stands and went to our chairs on the field. Graduates were milling about in the half light of the entrances across the field on both Fourteenth and Sixteenth streets, where teachers were helping line them up alphabetically. Members of choral groups and the band who were undergraduates were taking their places on risers and chairs, band members in black uniforms with gold stripes down the outside of trouser legs; girls in the chorus in pastel dresses, boys in suit pants and white shirts with ties. Dignitaries, school board members and their wives, principals, and supervisors were being escorted to a special section of chairs on the field. On the central platform, in front of a painted backdrop of the state of Arkansas, the speaker's microphone was being tested, the stacks of diplomas double checked for accurate arrangement. From the ramps on either side of this central platform stretched the V-shaped rows of chairs for the graduates. Everything was just as it always is at commencement, except that this one was different. It would be the *first*, in one respect, not the 149th, as the program listed it under the picture of the façade of Central High School, a picture that was now world-famous.

A car drove up the cinder track from the south entrance to the field, and Robert Shaw in his wheelchair was lifted out. Miss Carpenter and I went to speak to him. He had been a telephone student in my English class two years before, and I had visited him in his grandmother's home. Miss Carpenter had met him the day he was at school. As we walked to greet Robert, I saw a group of black adults seated in the south section of the stands. I didn't recognize them, but I knew they were sitting in that spot because Ernest would be directly in front of them when he reached his place among the graduates.

Promptly at eight o'clock, the band began the processional. Lines of graduates, eight lines from each side, came in simultaneously, each row stopping in front of its designated chairs. They stood, alternate rows of navy and white, while a color guard presented the flags and the bugle sounded "To the Colors," after which we pledged allegiance to the flag, sang one stanza of "America the Beautiful," and heard the Reverend Kenneth Shamblin (his son a member of the class) invoke God's blessing. We all sat down. Ronnie Hubbard presented the gift of the class to the school, a check for the cost of a bronze tiger to adorn the school lobby. (Fortunately, the sculptor never completed it.) Then "The Story of Arkansas" was read by choral readers to a background of music by glee clubs and band. Read by young voices, with music to accompany it, it sounded much better than it read, cold, in the program. Mr. Blossom introduced the special guests. Jess Matthews announced winners of scholarships as each came to the platform to be recognized. And then it was time for the presentation of diplomas.

Jess presented the class, declaring that each had completed the requirements for graduation. Harold Engstrom, president of the board, declared that each was officially a graduate of Central High School. Preceded by the class officers, who received the first diplomas, the first line of girls approached the platform. As each graduate's name was called by Gene Hall, head football coach with a good voice, she walked up the ramp (a teacher was there to see that she didn't trip), Jess handed her the diploma with his left hand while he shook her hand with his right, and Bill Lincoln, photography teacher, took her picture (if she had paid for it in advance). Then, as the next name was called, the first student walked down the ramp on the other side of the platform, circled in front of the stand to the far end of her row, and inched across to her chair as others in the row made their long journey to and from the platform. Gail Blossom came with her row. Jess Matthews stepped aside so that her father, the superintendent, could give her her diploma. After the girls' row, there was a boys', then a girls', again—and then it was time for Ernest's row. Every person in the stands could follow the names of the graduates printed alphabetically in the program. So everyone knew when Ernest Green's name was the next and it was his time to take that solo walk across the platform, down the other side, back across in front of the stand, and back to his chair.

An expectant silence fell on the spectators and the graduates. The photographers for the *Gazette* and the *Democrat*, the only photographers allowed on the field except Mr. Lincoln (their pictures were to go into a pool for all the news services) became more active, seeking out the one dark face in the line and then moving in close for pictures. The moment arrived. It passed. A few derisive whistles from the stands. That was all. Ernest Green had become number 203 among the graduates given diplomas this evening, number 1 among the black graduates of Central High School.

Miss Carpenter and I had not watched Ernest's descent from the platform or his walk back to his place in his row. We were concentrating on watching the seniors sitting within range of him— egg range. We knew that we could identify any of them by row and seat assignment if we saw a throwing motion from any of them. We also knew that there was less likelihood of anyone's attempting to throw anything if our eyes were on them. No eggs were thrown. There were no incidents of any kind. The other 399 seniors got their diplomas, including the boy who spat on the black child after Baccalaureate on Sunday evening. The only demonstration was when Ronnie Hubbard wheeled Robert Shaw to the foot of the ramp and Jess walked down and handed him his diploma. The applause was prolonged.

After the singing of the school song—"Hail to the Old Gold, Hail to the Black"—and the benediction, the seniors erupted into the usual pandemonium, the boys throwing their stiff caps into the air, the girls hugging each other and crying and revealing a few secret marriages for which the school could no longer penalize them, and all rushing to the front of the stands where their parents were waving suit boxes at them in which the seniors had to turn in their rented gowns to the coaches' office under the spectator stands. We did not see Ernest leave.

Miss Carpenter and I were elated. So were the other school officials we met as we were walking out from the field. The *Gazette* on Wednesday morning gave some details of the evening that I hadn't known about. One man, prominent in the mobs in front of school last fall, had attended the graduation but had spent the entire evening below the spectator stands, his every movement followed by plainclothesmen. One of the black spectators I had seen in the stands was the Reverend Martin Luther King, Jr., of Montgomery, Alabama, bus boycott fame, who had been the Commencement speaker during the morning at all-black Arkansas A. M. & N. College in Pine Bluff. The *Gazette* reporter stated that Mr. King had left by taxi with Ernest after the program.

At school on Wednesday morning almost everyone was in a gay mood. We were delighted with the success of graduation, ebullient with the lifting of the tensions of the year. Most senior homeroom teachers had episodes to report, things that had been said or done in their lines of graduates. Bill Hicks's teacher said that Bill had spotted a boy with a package of eggs and had taken it away from him.

We who had worked with them for so many months said goodbye to Captain Stumbaugh and Sergeant Blackwood, who were as delighted as we were to be relieved of their responsibilities and to be shedding their National Guard uniforms for civilian clothes and occupations.

The *Arkansas Gazette* on Wednesday announced a dinner honoring the *Gazette* and its editor, Harry Ashmore, for the Pulitzer Prize awarded for editorials on the Little Rock integration crisis, the dinner to be held on Tuesday, June 3, at the Hotel Marion. The civic committee planning the dinner was headed by Mrs. D. D. Terry, whose brother, John Gould Fletcher, had been the only other resident of Little Rock ever to be awarded a Pulitzer Prize. Eleanor Cooke, a member of Mrs. Terry's committee called me on Wednesday evening to bubble a bit about the success of Commencement. After talking with her, I called my brother in New York to suggest that he plan to get here in time to attend the dinner, since he was coming to Little Rock anyway on his vacation. He was delighted, and said he would be in on Monday afternoon. I got tickets for the appreciation dinner for Glen and me, for Bill, and for our father. It would be the best way I could think of to celebrate the conclusion of what the *Gazette* had called an "unparalleled year"—a euphemism, if I ever heard one.

There was one more matter of unfinished business. The school board had petitioned the federal court to postpone desegregation at Central High School for three years because of the difficulties of this year. The case was to be heard on Tuesday, the day of the appreciation dinner for the *Gazette*. The school board was going to base its case on the contention that it had been next to impossible to run the school this past year; that teacher time had been used in keeping order rather than in teaching; that troops in the school had been disturbing to students and teachers and would still be needed if desegregation continued. I was not in sympathy with the abandonment of integration; but I realized that, if the complete burden of desegregation was placed on the school, without the cooperation—no, with the active opposition of the community and the state, and with only a sort of scolding and half-hearted federal backing such as we had had the past year—we could not run the school with safety for children of either race.

On Saturday morning Mr. Blossom asked me to come to the school administration office to meet with others who were to develop the school board case for the hearing on Tuesday. Archie House and Dick Butler, the lawyers, outlined what they had planned to ask me under direct questioning. Dick, who had known me for a long time (I had lived in his parents' home before I married, and our fathers were first cousins) said he knew better than to suggest any answers to me. Orlana Hensley, J. O. Powell, and Paul Magro were the other teachers at this briefing. Jess Matthews was not to be called as a witness, and was to be out of town and unavailable for subpoena. He didn't much like avoiding the issue, but he was willing to abide by the decisions of the lawyers and Mr. Blossom. (He went fishing Sunday and didn't get home till Tuesday evening.)

The final conference with the school board lawyers was to be at

3:00 on Monday, and Bill's plane was due at 2:17. I picked up Father at his apartment and we met Bill. One of the passengers who deplaned was Thurgood Marshall, the NAACP's lawyer, who would oppose the school board's request for delay of integration. He was met by a young black man who greeted him, "Hello, Chief." I left Bill with Father and Mother at their apartment and went on to the final conference with the lawyers. On Monday night, I went back to my practice of not sleeping well.

I dressed carefully for my court appearance: navy shantung suit and a small white hat with a feather stick-up. I must have looked my part, for out-of-town papers (friends were quick to send me clippings) described me variously and unflatteringly as either *prim* or *grim*. Both looks, unfortunately, are occupational hazards of girls' vice-principals. Glen let me out of the car at the Federal Building. I spoke to Mrs. Bates outside. Inside, by prearrangement, I met others who were to be called for testimony: Margaret Reiman, Zinta Hopkins, and Shirley Stancil. Most of the spectators seemed to be either Mothers' Leaguers (Margaret Jackson, *et al.*), who hovered around their school board member, Dr. Dale Alford; or blacks (no hovering around any school board member, here).

The opposing lawyers chatted amiably across the table at the front of the courtroom: Archie House and Dick Butler, with Mr. Blossom by their side; Thurgood Marshall, Wiley Branton, and U. Simpson Tate on the other side. Judge Lemley entered; and I was the first witness called.

The questioning led me through the fact that I had had to give up teaching my usual two English classes because of the desegregation troubles, which meant added expense for the district in hiring a substitute; then through the necessity of my devoting my full time to desegregation matters, to the neglect of the normal activities for girls, this, in spite of the fact that the enrollment at Central had been five to six hundred less than last year. The general breakdown of school decorum in the cafeteria (chili and soup), the problems of physical violence between pupils, the bomb threats, the upsetting of school routine by these and other problems were developed. And I further mentioned the hoodlumism and vandalism, approved and encouraged by out-of-school groups, and the printing and distribution of libelous literature intended to undermine the authority of school officials, which had not been curbed, in spite of the orders of the Supreme Court for us to proceed with integration.

Thurgood Marshall's cross-examination of me sought to develop the fact that we allowed students to stay in school who should have been expelled. He wanted me to name our girl segregationist leader, and this I did, but only after he had called her name, first. I did not want to put it into the record myself. His final question was whether I would not be glad to have the school segregated again. I told him no; but I hoped that, if we remained integrated, we could get the full cooperation of the court that ordered desegregation and not be left as school people to handle the problems alone.

J. O. Powell was next on the stand. He agreed with the NAACP lawyer that firmer discipline of the white pupils involved would have been a good policy. Margaret Reiman's and Alonzo Lape's testimony took us to lunchtime. Back to the court for the testimony of Shirley Stancil, Lawrence Mobley, and W. P. Ivy, and of O. W. Romine, school maintenance supervisor, who had had to deal, night and day, with school security and make searches for bombs and dynamite as calls were telephoned in. I left before members of the school board testified, to get ready for the Pulitzer Prize dinner.

Glen, Bill, Father, and I met Emma and Hilda Scott and their mother, and Helen Marshall in the lobby of the Hotel Marion, to sit together at the dinner. There was a huge crowd in the ballroom, all the stability of the community, it seemed to me. For the first time all year, I did not feel isolated. Winthrop Rockefeller presided graciously. His tributes to J. N. Heiskell, editor and president of the *Gazette*; Hugh B. Patterson, publisher; and Harry Ashmore, executive editor, were inspiring. Their responses were excellent. Ralph Magill of the Atlanta *Constitution*, the chief speaker of the evening, was as interesting and constructive in his remarks as I expected him to be. Everyone stayed till eleven. Then we went home to talk some more.

For the first time in ten months I felt really good. I could even believe that this year had been a commencement, not a conclusion, for Central High School.

Epilogue: 1980

In the governor's chair at Little Rock sits Bill Clinton, who was only eleven years old when Governor Faubus called out the National Guard to block the integration of Central High School. Orval Faubus now lives in Texas; and the young governor of Arkansas has none of his hang-ups. There are blacks in his cabinet, in the state police, in the legislature. In the city, there are blacks on the boards that govern the town and the schools. All public schools in Little Rock are integrated, "balance" being maintained by a fleet of eighty buses that crisscross the town. Daisy Bates, the mentor and inspiration of the Nine, still lives in Little Rock. Last year she was invited to sign her name in a cement block to be a part of the celebrity walk in the downtown Metrocenter Mall. The word in Little Rock now is not *segregation*. It is *progress*.

In 1977 Central High School marked the twentieth anniversary of its desegregation by an assembly at which its first black graduate, Ernest Green, was the principal speaker. The most widely known of the Nine, Ernest, Bachelor of Arts, Master of Arts, Michigan State University, is assistant Labor secretary for employment and training in President Carter's cabinet. Only two others of the Nine were graduated from Central; Jefferson Thomas and Carlotta Walls finished with their class in 1960. All Little Rock public high schools had been closed for 1958–1959, and students who should have been seniors that year had to find other places to earn their diplomas. All the blacks did, and most of them earned college degrees, too.

News stories, from time to time, bring word of the Nine. Minnijean graduated from Southern Illinois University. She, her husband, and their children live and work on their farm in Canada. Elizabeth joined the Women's Army Corps briefly, took some courses at University of Arkansas, Little Rock, and worked as a clerk in one of the state offices. She is a homemaker, with one son. Thelma, her heart problem corrected by surgery, has a five-year-old son. She is supervisor of counseling for several schools in the East St. Louis district. She is a graduate of Southern Illinois. Melba went to school in California. She works now as a free-lance writer and TV announcer and lives, with her teen-age daughter, in the San Francisco area. Gloria graduated from Illinois Institute of Technology, married a Swede, and lives in Sweden. Terrence earned a Ph.D. in psychology at Southern Illinois and is director of mental health services for a hospital in the San Francisco area, where he lives with his young family. Jefferson returned to Little Rock in 1966 to act as the central character in a film made by Charles Guggenheim for the United States Information Agency, "The Nine from Little Rock." Jefferson has served in the army, taken college work in accounting, and operated a family record shop in the Los Angeles area. Carlotta finished her college work in Denver, sold real estate there, and now lives in Atlanta. She has two children.

Jess Matthews remained as principal of Central High School until his retirement in 1965. Now he, Virgil Blossom, and many of the strong faculty members of 1957–1958 are sadly missed from this world. But Central High School remains, a great school. Half its student body and a third of its faculty are black. It has had two black principals in recent years. Its students still win more than their share of scholastic honors, including National Merit Scholarships. It prepares its graduates for colleges, for business and art and music and journalism and family living. It has a tremendously loyal group of graduates, as attested by the great ingathering of them at the celebration in 1977 of fifty years in its famous and beautiful building. It stands, a living memorial to those students and adults whose fortitude helped it to endure.